Democratization and Identity

GLOBAL ENCOUNTERS: STUDIES IN COMPARATIVE POLITICAL THEORY
Series Editor: Fred Dallmayr, University of Notre Dame

This series seeks to inaugurate a new field of inquiry and intellectual concern: that of comparative political theory as an inquiry proceeding not from the citadel of a global hegemony but through cross-cultural dialogue and critical interaction. By opening the discourse of political theory—today largely dominated by American and European intellectuals—to voices from across the global spectrum, we hope to contribute to a richer, multifaceted mode of theorizing as well as to a deeper, cross-cultural awareness of the requirements of global justice.

INTERNATIONAL ADVISORY BOARD

Border Crossings: Toward a Comparative Political Theory, edited by Fred Dallmayr

Beyond Nationalism? Sovereignty and Citizenship, edited by Fred Dallmayr and José M. Rosales

Gandhi, Freedom, and Self-Rule, edited by Anthony J. Parel

Race and Reconciliatiation in South Africa: A Multicultural Dialogue in Comparative Perspective, edited by William E. Van Vugt and G. Daan Cloete

Comparative Political Culture in the Age of Globalization: An Introductory Anthology, edited by Hwa Yol Jung

Conversations and Transformations: Toward a New Ethics of Self and Society, by Ananta Kumar Giri

Hinterlands and Horizons: Excursions in Search of Amity, by Margaret Chatterjee

New Approaches to Comparative Politics: Insights from Political Theory, edited by Jennifer S. Holmes

Comparative Political Philosophy: Studies under the Upas Tree, edited by Anthony J. Parel and Ronald C. Keith

Iran: Between Tradition and Modernity, edited by Ramin Jahanbegloo

Democratization and Identity: Regimes and Ethnicity in East and Southeast Asia, edited by Susan J. Henders

The Politics of Affective Relations: East Asia and Beyond, edited by Daniel Bell and Hahm Chaihark

From the Margins of Globalization: Critical Perspectives on Human Rights, edited by Neve Gordon

Imagining Brazil, edited by Jessé Souza and Valter Sinder

Islamic Democratic Discourse: Theory, Debates, and Philosophical Perspectives, edited by M. A. Muqtedar Khan

Democratization and Identity

Regimes and Ethnicity in East and Southeast Asia

Edited by
Susan J. Henders

LEXINGTON BOOKS

A division of
ROWMAN & LITTLEFIELD PUBLISHERS, INC.
Lanham • Boulder • New York • Toronto • Plymouth, UK

LEXINGTON BOOKS

A division of Rowman & Littlefield Publishers, Inc.
A wholly owned subsidiary of The Rowman & Littlefield Publishing Group, Inc.
4501 Forbes Boulevard, Suite 200
Lanham, MD 20706

Estover Road
Plymouth PL6 7PY
United Kingdom

British Library Cataloguing in Publication Information Available

The hardback edition of this book was previously cataloged by the Library of Congress as follows:

Democratization and identity : regimes and ethnicity in East and Southeast Asia / edited by Susan J. Henders.
     p. cm. — (Global encounters)
     Includes bibliographical references and index.
     1. Democratization—East Asia. 2. Group identity—East Asia. 3. Nationalism—East Asia. 4. Democratization—Asia, Southeastern. 5. Group identity—Asia, Southeastern. 6. Nationalism—Asia, Southeastern. I. Henders, Susan J., 1960– II. Series.

     JQ1499.A91D46 2004
     320.54'095—dc22
                                                                          2003018917

ISBN-13: 978-0-7391-0689-1 (cloth : alk. paper)
ISBN-10: 0-7391-0689-9 (cloth : alk. paper)
ISBN-13: 978-0-7391-0767-6 (pbk : alk. paper)
ISBN-10: 0-7391-0767-4 (pbk : alk. paper)

Printed in the United States of America

♾™ The paper used in this publication meets the minimum requirements of American National Standard for Information Sciences—Permanence of Paper for Printed Library Materials, ANSI/NISO Z39.48–1992.

Contents

Acknowledgments

I wish to express my gratitude to the contributors to this volume for their hard work, enthusiasm, and encouragement. B. Michael Frolic and Arthur Rubinoff warrant a special thank you for their support, without which the book, and the conference and workshop that began the project, would not have been possible. I am very grateful to the following institutions for their generous financial contributions: the Chiang Ching-kuo Foundation; the Canadian Centre for Foreign Policy Development; the Taipei Economic and Cultural Office, Toronto; the School of Graduate Studies, Department of Political Science, and Department of Geography and Planning at the University of Toronto; and the former University of Toronto–York University Joint Centre for Asia Pacific Studies. My thanks also to the York Centre for Asian Research at York University for its support. Lynne Russell deserves special credit for her administrative work in organizing the conference and workshop, her careful copyediting and indexing in later stages of the book, and her advice, patience, and enthusiasm. I also thank all of those who participated in the conference and workshop for their thoughtful contributions as paper presenters, their insights as discussants and members of the audience, and their administrative contributions. Finally, I am grateful to my family, to whom I dedicate this volume.

1

Political Regimes and Ethnic Identities in East and Southeast Asia: Beyond the "Asian Values" Debate

Susan J. Henders

The "great experiment in reconciling democratic governance and cultural pluralism" (Young 1993: 19) has seldom seemed so tenuous. This is not a new concern (see Horowitz 1986; Brass 1985; Young 1976; Enloe 1973). However, the ethnicized conflict that marked the end of the Cold War and, more recently, the events surrounding the September 11, 2001, attack on the World Trade Center have shaken the faith that liberal democracy, human rights, and economic liberalization—the supposed touchstones of the post–Cold War order—are mutually compatible in a world seemingly fractured on religious and other ethnic lines (see Snyder 2000; Linz and Stepan 1996; Diamond and Plattner 1994). The questioning even reached the pages of the World Bank *Human Development Report 2000*, which devoted much of a chapter to the difficulties of democratizing societies deeply trenched by ethnic differences.

The experiences of East and Southeast Asia have figured relatively little in the renewed debate about democratizing ethnically plural societies.[1] Three reasons stand out. For one, many states, especially in East Asia, are assumed to be highly ethnically homogenous and, therefore, undisturbed by the costly tensions plaguing other societies. The nondemocratic or less than fully democratic character of many governments in the region also suggests that these countries have little to teach us about the impact of democratization on interethnic relations. The "Asian values" debate of the 1990s has probably also stifled discussion. Renewing earlier plural society arguments, former Singaporean Prime Minister Lee Kuan Yew and others have claimed that ethnically divided societies cannot afford to democratize or expand liberal rights if they want to remain peaceful (see Bell 2000: 201–13). In the context of these claims, some scholars may be reluctant to explore the relationship

1

between democratization and ethnicized tensions, fearing that their work might be used to legitimate continuing authoritarian rule.

The present book shows that, despite these issues, and even because of them, East and Southeast Asian experiences can add much to our understanding of democratization in ethnically diverse societies. The book's regional coverage is not comprehensive—and even includes a brief comparative discussion of South Asian contexts in the chapter by Katharine Rankin and Kanishka Goonewardena. Nor are the book's regional specialist contributors primarily engaged in the standard political science literature on transitions from authoritarian rule. Rather, from their bases in various disciplines they offer provocative reconceptualizations of democratization and collective identities—and of the links between political regimes, collective identities, and ethnicized exclusion and conflict. In this way, the book's primary contribution is theoretical and conceptual, raising questions about conventional ways of thinking about democratization in ethnically diverse societies and identifying generalized hypotheses about what contributes to ethnically inclusive democracy. The chapters that are mainly theoretically and conceptually driven, though based on empirical examples from the region, are grouped together in Part I, while Parts II and III draw together theoretically and conceptually provocative case studies concerning East and Southeast Asia respectively.

Taken together, the contributions here challenge formal, procedural understandings of democratization as a linear process centered only on formal constitutional change and leading to a neat meshing of liberal and democratic institutions. The contributors also question whether democratizing and democratic regimes are entirely distinct from authoritarian rule and always beneficial to interethnic accommodation. Which is not to say that the book's contributors agree with Lee Kuan Yew that authoritarian government can be necessary for interethnic peace, of which I say more below. Rather, they reveal how political regimes and ethnic identities are co-constitutive. That is, the process of (re)producing political power—whether authoritarian, democratizing, or democratic—is simultaneously a process of (re)producing collective identities, including those of an ethnic nature, and vice versa. The book also identifies patrimonial, economic production, and colonial processes as additional factors shaping the co-constitution of collective ethnic identities and political regimes, elements easily left out when democratization is understood only in formal procedural terms. Finally, several chapters demonstrate that, because regimes and collective identities are co-constitutive, the ways in which ethnic identities are produced under authoritarian rule fundamentally affect how they are constituted later under democratizing or democratic regimes.

With these general findings in mind, the present chapter has two aims. Its first three sections offer elements of a conceptual framework for analyzing democratization in ethnically diverse societies, premised on the co-constitutive relationship between political regimes and ethnic identities, as well as on the interconnectedness of authoritarian and democratizing processes. Although the framework is drawn in large part from the insights of the contributors to this book, not all of them adopt, nor necessarily accept, all of its elements. The final section of the present chapter sets out the contributors' findings concerning the specific conditions that help explain the nature of interethnic relations during democratization processes.

DO AUTHORITARIAN REGIMES DO
IT BETTER? RETHINKING THE QUESTION

This book began as an exploration, in the East and Southeast Asian context, of the argument that ethnically divided societies cannot afford to democratize if they want interethnic peace. It is intended to examine the contentions that authoritarian regimes manage ethnic pluralism better than democracies and that the process of democratization is itself destructive of interethnic accommodation. While associated with Asian leaders such as Lee Kuan Yew, shades of these arguments are not exclusive to their side of the "Asian values" debate. The plural society approach argues that deeply divided multiethnic societies can only remain stable through the use of force, wielded by a colonial or other authoritarian government, or a dominating ethnic group (Ryan 1990).[2] Similarly, Rustow (1970) has argued that democratization can only work if the great majority of citizens accept the boundaries of the political community as legitimate (see also Dahl 1989). Where "stateness" itself is at issue, democracy cannot itself resolve contestation over the identity or borders of the *polis* or *demos* (Linz and Stepan 1996), as David Wurfel points out with respect to Mindanao in the Philippines and Jacques Bertrand with respect to Aceh and West Papua (Irian Jaya) in Indonesia.

Daniel Bell's chapter explores these themes, serving as a foil for most of the other contributors. He makes the relatively moderate assertion that East and Southeast Asia offer some of the strongest evidence that nondemocratic governments have some advantages over democratizing and democratic ones in dealing with ethnic differences in ways that avert ethnicized conflict. Bell contends that the governments of "less-than-democratic" states like Singapore, Indonesia under Suharto's *Pancasila*, Malaysia, and China have had some success protecting the legitimate interests of minority ethnic groups. In the absence of electoral competition, he says, they are less likely than their democratic or democratizing counterparts to resort to nation-building around the nationalist symbols, institutions, and discourses of a majority ethnic group. To Bell, the achievements of these countries, despite their failures and the costs of authoritarianism, should prompt questions about the assumed correlation between both democracy and democratization and minority rights. Thus, he is cautious about advocating democratization in multiethnic states, in at least some circumstances.

Other contributors question even Bell's moderate claims. They assert that, despite their freedom from electoral pressures, the governments of China, Indonesia in the Suharto era, the Philippines under Marcos, Malaysia, and Taiwan under authoritarian Kuomintang (KMT) rule, *have* engaged in ethnic majority nation-building at great cost to vulnerable ethnic groups and with potentially negative long-term consequences for ethnically inclusive, non-hierarchical democratization. For instance, Chang Maukuei notes that the KMT in its authoritarian phase did not resist using majority Han Chinese nationalism to legitimate its rule in Taiwan and its claims to mainland China. The failure of this policy in Taiwan helped foster a prodemocracy opposition movement centered on "Taiwaneseness," sometimes understood in ethnic terms. By the 1980s in Taiwan, "fighting for democracy was also fighting for equal participation and representation of 'our kind.'" This was because the KMT's exclusive Han nationalism could not encompass the transformative experiences of Taiwan people under the previous fifty years of Japanese colonial authoritarian rule, modernization, and industrialization. These unique experiences had fostered a sense of local identity and demands for autonomy and social justice that clashed with the KMT vision of a unified Chinese state. Thus, while it is tempting to see the relatively ethnically harmonious nature of Taiwan's democratization as overdetermined by the shared Chinese identity of native Taiwanese and those Taiwan people of more recent mainland descent, Chang suggests that this outcome was far from inevitable (see also André Laliberté, chapter 8 in this book).

Also challenging Bell, several authors suggest that, even where authoritarian governments do foster pan- or multiethnic identities, the needs of vulnerable minority communities are not always protected. David Brown, Rankin and Goonewardena, Judith Nagata, and Bertrand ask who benefits from the techniques used by less-than-democratic governments to (re)produce pan- and multiethnic identities. In Suharto's Indonesia, Singapore, and Malaysia, corporatist or patrimonial institutions, based on co-opted ethnic elites and a centrally enforced unitary identity, hold together the governments' multiethnic vision of the nation. In these situations, the government, in conjunction with selected ethnic elites, set the narrow parameters of acceptable minority group identities and entitlements, excluding alternative visions of group identity and multiethnicity more compatible with democratic values.

Dru Gladney paints a paradoxical picture of the potential and limits of the Chinese government's attempts to consolidate an ethnically inclusive nation and protect vulnerable minorities. Consistent with Bell, he grants limited success to China's multiethnic policies, especially in the post-Mao period.

Ethnic minorities have generally welcomed concessions such as exclusion from the one-child policy, ethnic quotas for education and political representation, and limited administrative and decision-making autonomy in designated territories, despite the restricted and non–liberal democratic nature of these policies. Yet, these measures have neither satisfied all groups nor averted violent ethnicized conflict, especially in Tibet and borderland Muslim areas. This is partly because the Chinese government still resorts to Han Chinese ethnonationalism to legitimize its rule, especially in the face of rising ethnicized economic inequalities amongst the Han since the post-Mao economic reforms. Gladney suggests that, in this way, the reproduction of authoritarian rule and ethnic identities as China liberalizes economically shapes future possibilities for both interethnic accommodation and democratization.

Despite their disagreements, the findings of Bell and the other contributors converge in an important way. They suggest that the key question is not *which type of regime*—democratizing, democratic, or authoritarian—best fosters interethnic accommodation. Rather, it is *under what conditions* authoritarian, democratizing, or democratic regimes are associated with ethnicized conflict and exclusive, hierarchical ethnic identities—and why. Some of their hypotheses are set out later in this chapter. Meanwhile, note that recasting the question in this way makes particular sense in a region where polities do not always neatly fit the authoritarian, democratizing, or democratic ideal types (Bell, Brown, Jayasuriya, and Jones 1995). Moreover, the new question also suggests a need to rethink two problematic assumptions generally made by both sides of the "Asian values" debate: the assumption that authoritarian, democratizing, and democratic polities are entirely distinct and that collectivities such as ethnic groups are ontologically prior to political regimes. A critical examination of these assumptions in the next section destabilizes the simplistic dyads of "East" and "West" and "democratic" (or "democratizing") and "authoritarian," opening the way for rethinking both democratization and ethnic identities—and the relationship between them.

POLITICAL REGIMES AND ETHNIC IDENTITIES

Ethnic groups can be understood as collectivities centered on contested, shifting claims to a shared cultural identity, broadly defined, whether based on language, religion or other beliefs and customs, lineage, history, territory, or way of life.[4] Most of the contributors understand ethnic groups to be socially constructed, rather than primordial.[5] Their work suggests that both ethnic groups and nations are not fixed solidarities, but ongoing constitutive processes. Understood this way, the boundaries between ethnic groups are fluid and porous, their "content" is heterogeneous and internally and externally contested (see

Barth 1969). Their political salience also varies. As Brown notes, the identity markers of "nation" and "ethnicity" sustain differing interpretations with the same "facts." The unexplained problem is the existence of the collectivity itself and under what historical and social conditions ethnic identities and nations are constructed in ways that contribute either to ethnicized conflict or to the exclusion of vulnerable groups and individuals from meaningful political and economic participation in the life of the country.[6] The contributors by and large find that these undesirable outcomes are more likely when ethnic identities are constituted as exclusive, hegemonic, and/or hierarchical. This reduces the possibilities for inclusive and nonhierarchical pan- or multiethnic identities that can "buffer" exclusive ethnic or ethnonationalist appeals (to borrow Brown's term). It is in the human capacity to maintain multiple and overlapping collective identities—what Saul Newman calls "political schizophrenia" (1996: 20)—that we locate the potential for ethnically inclusive and nonhierarchical democratization and democracy in ethnically diverse societies.[7]

Underlying the sometimes problematic attributes of democracy and democratization in multiethnic societies—though often unacknowledged and undertheorized—is the co-constitutive relationship between political regimes and collective (including ethnic) identities. By co-constitutive I mean that the content, boundaries, and political salience of collective identities such as ethnicity are in significant ways reproduced by processes of creating, maintaining, and transforming political regimes, and vice versa.[8] We can in part trace the conceptualization of ethnicity as a political process to Max Weber (1968: 389), who wrote that "it is primarily the political community, no matter how artificially organized, that inspires the belief in common ethnicity."[9] The constitution of collective identities is necessary for regime legitimacy and for the mobilization of populations for collective action. In this light Chang criticizes Benedict Anderson and Ernest Gellner for failing fully to address the politics of regime reproduction and change in their theories of the origins and transformation of "nation": "Whether we agree with Anderson that nation is conceived in the mode of consciousness of the ordinary people, or with Gellner that nation is a useful cultural construct for both the state and the elite to pursue industrialization and other objectives, then the 'uses' of nation in real politics and regime transformation processes must be normal and prevalent." The constitution of collective identities is also a condition of a regime's very possibility.

This book's contributors understand the co-constitutive nature of regimes and identities in multiple ways: in terms of the instrumental acts of political and/or ethnic actors who evoke ethnic identities for political purposes, as the more or less unconscious effects of discourse, and as a consequence of broad structures and processes, such as imperial or colonial expansion and governance, decolonization, industrialization, modernization, and global laissez-faire capitalism.[10] In each case, collective identities are created, maintained, and transformed partly through processes of making, maintaining, and transforming political regimes. These identities, in turn, partly constitute those same regimes.

The literature has identified some institutional features of democratization as potentially problematic in light of the political bases of ethnic and other identities. Linz and Stepan (1996) note that ethnic identities can become politically salient during democratization because the very processes that determine the symbols and norms to be entrenched in new democratic constitutions and laws also constitute identities, which not all citizens necessarily share. The negotiation of laws establishing electoral systems; representative institutions; and the boundaries, rights, and duties of citizens, for instance, require decisions about the boundaries, membership, and values of the *polis* and *demos*. These have important effects on the constitution of ethnically inclusive identities (see also Snyder 2000). Gladney (1998) points out that the maintenance of democratic political power also requires the making and reproduction of majorities for such purposes as (re)creating electoral coalitions, redistricting electoral boundaries, and (re)producing interest groups. If these collectivities are defined on narrow ethnic grounds, ethnic identities may become a focus of political mobilization both for the "majority" and those excluded from it.

As several chapters in this volume remind us, the economic processes associated with political regimes also have implications for the inclusiveness of the collective identities that sustain and are sustained by political power. Partly echoing Gellner, John Lie and Chang note that industrialization was central to forging collective identities in late Imperial Japan and in Taiwan under Japanese imperial rule. Drawing from socialist and feminist approaches, Rankin and Goonewardena assert that the neoliberal economic practices and ideologies associated with post–Cold War democratization imply a notion of individual identity and marketized social relations that challenges preexisting collective identities. Some ethnic minorities are disproportionately disadvantaged as a consequence.[11] They note that the civic norms of citizenship equality and individual rights associated with liberal democracy increase the potential for ethnicized conflict and oppression: given the primacy it grants to the autonomy of the individual as equal citizen, unfettered liberal democracy ignores or suppresses the rootedness of individual identities in intersubjective processes within communities, rendering difficult the institutional recognition of these identities (see also Kymlicka 1990, 1989; Taylor 1993). However, as Gladney's chapter makes clear, neoliberal economic processes in nondemocratic contexts such as contemporary China can also increase the ethnicization of identities and inequalities. To Rankin and Goonewardena, in both formally democratic and nondemocratic contexts, it is the reduced inability of governments enmeshed in neoliberal economic regimes to claim legitimacy on social grounds that encourages them to mobilize ethnonationalist identities. Meanwhile citizens under late capitalism resort to ethnic identities because they cannot rely on the formal political system for their socioeconomic well-being.

Thus, reconceptualizing political (including economic) regimes and ethnic identities as co-constitutive processes departs from the dominant academic and political discourses about the region in several ways, especially with respect to East Asia. For one, these discourses constitute states in the region, such as Korea, Japan, and even China, as highly ethnically homogeneous.[12] Elsewhere, Gladney has attributed this to "uncritically accepted ideas of purity, numerical superiority, and social consensus" (1998: 1), which naturalize ethnic identities and nations as fixed, easily discernible, and uncontested entities *predating* and, therefore, *unrelated* to, processes of constituting political regimes. By contrast, scholarship on the region influenced by constructivist and post-structuralist perspectives asserts that "nations," including the supposedly homogeneous Han Chinese and the Japanese, are recently "imagined" or "constructed" collectivities inherent in processes of constituting political regimes (see Lie, Gladney, and Chang in this volume; see also Brook and Schmid 2000; Gladney 1998; Anderson 1991; Fujitani, White, and Yoneyama 2001).

The constructed nature of ethnic identities—and the centrality of their political constitution—does not necessarily negate the findings that suggest that minorities are better off in democratic polities. However, casting regimes and ethnic identities as co-constitutive, especially if we also problematize what is meant by democracy (a point addressed later), raises questions about what is assumed and what is left out when a correlation between democracy and ethnic peace is asserted. For instance, Gurr (1993: 184–5) argues that communal rebellion occurs more often in nondemocratic polities than in democratic ones. He also says that, for those societies that consolidated democracy in the 1990s, minority rights improved and ethnicized conflicts seldom happened (Gurr 2000). However, Gurr narrowly defines democracy, conflict, and the meaningful inclusion of minorities. He assumes that minority rights improve under democratic rule because fewer overt protests or conflicts occur. However, as Rankin and Goonewardena's chapter suggests, this approach ignores structural violence, such as ethnicized economic inequalities. Moreover, Gurr's approach appears to naturalize ethnic identities and assume their ontological priorness to political regimes. When ethnic identities and regimes are understood instead as co-constitutive, a different picture emerges.

Lie's analysis of ethnic identity and regime change in Japan is illustrative. Lie argues that postwar democratization constituted the country as a mono-ethnic nation. Okinawans, *Burakumin*, *Ainu*, and Korean Japanese could become part of the nation as individuals, but only through losing or hiding their ethnic identities. Thus, these groups were neglected, discriminated against, and silenced. However, from the late 1960s, they began openly re-sisting their exclusion. Notably, this resistance does not appear on Gurr's sta-tistical radar screen prior to the 1990s (Gurr 1990: 74). Even then, the as-sumption seems to be that that relatively low levels of ethnic protest indicate meaningful inclusion, when it could as easily indicate particularly effective silencing under democratic institutions and monoethnic ideology. This brings us to the next pillar of the book's conceptual contribution—the reconceptualization of democratization itself.

RECONCEPTUALIZING DEMOCRATIZATION

I have already argued that the process of democratization includes, but is much more than simply establishing free and fair competitive elections re-sulting in a government with binding authority. It also involves the constitu-tion and reproduction of collective, including ethnic, identities. The contrib-utors make several other significant conceptual departures from formal, procedural approaches to democratization, which I outline here.

Firstly, definitions of democratization that assume a linear process from authoritarian rule to liberal democracy mean that most of East and Southeast Asia should be excluded from the analysis of the impact of democratization on ethnic relations.[13] Such an analysis could not include "illiberal" weak democracies such as Malaysia and Singapore (some would argue Japan), weakly liberal nondemocracies such as Hong Kong and Macau, or enduring authoritarian but economically liberalizing regimes such as China. However, reconceptualizing democratization in broader, less linear terms allows us to explore the impact on ethnic identities of the democratic and liberal features of these states, however imperfect they might be. Here it is useful to employ Nagata's reconceptualization of democratization as "a process of continual adjustments over rights and relationships in a political system, rather than an essentialized state of being (a 'democracy')." This definition encompasses the particularistic historical trajectories of democratic institutions and processes across the region and recognizes that key concepts from global human rights discourse, such as democracy, take on new meanings and resonate differ-ently in diverse political cultures. As Nagata notes, this discourse can be used to claim ethnic and other privileges even while simultaneously serving as a justification for challenging such claims. Thus, she suggests that, if democra-tization in multiethnic polities is to be ethnically inclusive, it must involve *continuous processes of creating and maintaining* a pluralist citizenship co-existent with a common civic identity. While broadly consistent with ele-ments of liberal democratic theory, Nagata's conceptualization challenges as simplistic the analytical distinction amongst authoritarian, democratizing, and democratic politics made in much of the transitions literature.[14]

The book's second challenge to formal, procedural approaches to democratization comes from Rankin and Goonewardena's notion of "deep" democratization and democracy. By this, they mean the establishment and maintenance of public involvement in policy processes at all levels, both within *and between* states, so that economic institutions are held accountable for the social and recognition needs of ethnic minorities and other vulnerable communities (see also Rankin 2001). "Deep" democratization—rather than the formal procedural version centered on elections, individual rights, and (neo)liberal marketization—requires more inclusive, less hierarchical ethnic identities and understandings of the nation, as well as constitutionally guaranteed secularism and the democratization of the economy.

A third reconceptualization comes from Brown, who argues that democratization not only involves the reconstitution of political institutions and collective identities, but also significant shifts in the patrimonial relations constructed under authoritarian rule, with implications for interethnic relations. He states that patrimonial institutions potentially facilitate inclusive ethnic identities if two conditions hold: patron–client relationships make new elites, in search of electoral support, responsive to ethnocultural and multicultural visions of the nation generated from below by community leaders seeking resources, autonomy, and recognition for their communities; and liberal civic nationalism mutes the disintegrative potential of majority and minority ethnonationalism. The problem, Brown says with his eye on post-Suharto Indonesia, is that the unequal social statuses perpetuated by patrimonialism weaken the egalitarian ethic of liberal civic nationalism, potentially undermining democratization itself, an issue I return to later.

Together, these reconceptualizations understand democratization as a multifaceted process involving the co-constitution of collective (including ethnic) identities and regimes, as well as both formal political as well as informal patrimonial and economic processes. The challenge is to identify the conditions in which this complex dynamic results in exclusive and/or hierarchical ethnicized identities, the question to which I now turn.

SOME TENTATIVE HYPOTHESES

In light of the theoretical and conceptual framework outlined above, this book identifies several hypotheses concerning the conditions that contribute to unbuffered appeals to exclusive and/or hierarchical ethnicized identities during democratization. These are summarized below as generalized hypotheses. As anticipated by the above framework, many of the factors identified have little directly to do with democratization itself and often predate this transformation. Rather than identifying which type of regime is better for ethnic minorities, the hypotheses identify how ethnic identities constituted through processes of reproducing authoritarian rule affect the ethnicization of identities during democratization. The hypotheses also address the nature of democratization itself (although also in terms of authoritarian legacies); the institutionalization of identities; economic liberalization; the nature of pan-ethnic identities; and demographic factors.

The Nature of Authoritarian Rule

Most generally, this book's findings suggest that *the risk of ethnicized conflict, exclusion, or hierarchy during democratization is higher if authoritarian processes constituted ethnic identities as exclusive and/or hierarchical.* This is consistent with the literature on transitions from authoritarian rule in the former Soviet Union and in Western Europe that ties ethnicized conflict to the constitution of ethnic identities by authoritarian institutions (e.g., Leff 1999; Brubaker 1996). In chapter 6, Lie traces ethnic tensions and exclusion during democratizing and democratic processes in Japan to the constitution of ethnic and national identities in imperial times. As Japan's empire grew, the discourse increasingly constituted the political community as *hierarchical*, but *multiethnic* befitting its growing diversity: if the Japanese nation was the offspring of the emperor as "divine patriarch," Lie writes, Koreans and Taiwanese were part of the extended family, and Japanese "racial ideology asserted racial isomorphism, or at least kinship, among the conquered peoples throughout East and Southeast Asia." However, Lie argues that, with postwar social and political transformations—including the shift from constitutional monarchy to democratic government—the nation was reconstituted as a collectivity of equal citizens that was, however, mono-ethnic and, paradoxically, less tolerant of ethnic diversity than the authoritarian imperial nation. As already noted, Okinawans, *Ainu, Burakumin*, and Korean Japanese—the remnants of multiethnic empire—were excluded from the nation as groups though individual members could "pass" as Japanese. In the latter two cases, Japan's Cold War alliances also encouraged marginalization, as most *Barakumin* and Korean Japanese were left leaning (see Lie 2001).

Lie's picture of comparatively benign, if hierarchical, multiethnicity in imperial Japan—like Bell's assertion that authoritarian regimes can sometimes better sustain multiethnicity—is not uncontested. Chang's chapter suggests that the imperial regime's recognition of ethnic diversity was or became superficial even prior to democratization and especially under the demands of total mobilization for war: in Taiwan under Japanese rule, individual advancement effectively required Japanization, and expressions of Chinese ethnicity were increasingly suppressed. The suppression of ethnic differences continued in Chinese nationalist-ruled Taiwan until the latter years of the KMT government, but now aimed at silencing Taiwaneseness. However,

KMT reformers beginning with Chiang Ching-kuo became aware that the failure to incorporate Taiwan people into the KMT's pan-Chinese nationalism threatened the regime's legitimacy both locally and abroad. Even prior to democratization, they began adopting "Taiwan" as the shared political community of everyone on the island. Laliberté suggests that the increasing ethnic inclusivity of Taiwan's soft authoritarian regime was a key reason why Taiwan people came to see themselves as "citizens by virtue of their shared destiny rather than ethnicity" as democratization progressed. When elections were introduced, the electoral success of the KMT in evoking a civic "Taiwan" identity created incentives for the opposition Democratic Progressive Party (DPP) to adopt a more inclusive understanding of Taiwaneseness, partly abandoning its Taiwanese ethnonationalism. Electoral competition continues to push the DPP in this direction now that it is the ruling party, though some factions resist. This leaves the question of why the KMT in crisis chose a more inclusive rather than exclusive notion of Taiwan identity, a point I return to later.

Bertrand also points to the crucial impact of military identity under authoritarianism on the probability of ethnicized conflict during democratization. He argues that *the constitution of exclusive or hierarchical ethnicized identities under authoritarian processes are especially dangerous if, during the transition, they cause the military to identify itself with a particular ethnic group rather than a pan-ethnic collective identity.* The problem in Indonesia, Bertrand notes, began with Suharto's turn to Islam prior to democratization. The shift shook the traditionally secular orientation of the Muslim-dominated military, making it difficult for military personnel to act in support of a pan-ethnic Indonesian identity. After the fall of Suharto, then, people could appeal to exclusive ethnicized identities centered on Islam without fear of military sanctions.

The Nature of Democratization and the Authoritarian Legacy

A second factor conditioning Taiwan's relatively ethnically harmonious democratization was the gradual and significantly "top down" nature of the regime change and the fact that it did not coincide with severe economic dislocation. By contrast, democratization was bottom up and abrupt in Indonesia, triggered in part by the tremendous economic hardships brought on by the 1997 Asian financial crisis. In this light, Bertrand argues that, *when democratization is sudden, ethnicized conflict is more likely if "prior tensions in relations between two ethnic groups were fostered by policies adopted during the authoritarian phase and were also contained through authoritarian means."* In Maluku, Muslim–Christian conflicts in the post-Suharto period were the result of conditions that predated democratization. Specifically, they stemmed from the resentment some Muslims harbored due to the crony ties between ethnic Chinese business people and the Suharto regime, particularly after Suharto began defining the nation in narrower Islamic terms in the 1990s in an attempt to maintain legitimacy. By this time, tensions in Maluku had been augmenting for years due to Muslim migration into predominantly Christian areas. Thus, Maluku was ripe for explosion once the fall of Suharto brought an abrupt end to the "balance" maintained between the groups by authoritarian processes.

The Institutionalization of Identities

New institutionalist theory contends that institutions not only shape, but also constitute identities. Institutionalized ethnic identities help constitute ethnicized political leaders with ethnicized political resources (Brubaker 1996). In this light, Nagata's chapter suggests that, because of both the incentive and constitutive effects of institutions, *exclusive and/or hierarchical ethnic identities are more intractable when they are institutionalized, including in electoral and party systems.* In Malaysia, pan-ethnic alliances do emerge but are fragile because exclusively defined ethnic identities have been institutionalized in recent decades as the most important markers of interaction in all social realms. To Nagata, this accounts for the failure of the consciously multiethnic Party Keadilan to form a viable opposition to Prime Minister Mahathir Mohamad in the late 1990s. What Nagata calls the iron cage of institutionalized ethnicities constitutes individual identities and makes the appeal of ethnicized voter mobilization at the local level irresistible for political parties. The chapters by Laliberté and Wurfel both also stress the roles of institutions in shaping and constituting nonhierarchical pan-ethnic identities, the former looking at the role of Buddhism in Taiwan, the latter the role of electoral systems and economic and civil society institutions in East Timor and the Philippines.

Economic Liberalization

Several chapters suggest that *ethnicized conflict, hierarchy, or exclusion is associated with the social or economic tensions that come with economic liberalization under authoritarian, democratizing, and democratic regimes. These cause weakened or threatened governments and elites to appeal to exclusive and/or hierarchical ethnic identities to seek legitimacy and mobilize supporters.* Further work is required to identify the specific contexts in which this is the case. For Bertrand, socioeconomic dislocations and inequalities due to economic liberalization in the later Suharto years and during democratization fueled extremist state-led and popular religious and ethnolinguistic mobilization. Lie (2000: 151) has elsewhere noted the coincidence from the late 1960s of the popularity of *Nihonjinron* writings (which assert an "Occidentalist" theory of Japaneseness) and the rise of ethnic minority demands for recognition and inclusion. Notably, these developments followed a period of rapid economic growth and coincided with the increasing internationalization of Japan and the expanding global reach of its trade and investment links. As noted earlier, Gladney describes how the growing income disparities associated with China's integration into the international market economy has shaken the Communist legitimacy of the post-Mao party-state. The regime has sought new legitimacy in Han Chinese ethnonationalism and concessions to ethnic minorities. Meanwhile, Gladney says, claims of linguistic, religious, and other ethnic differences are growing in political and economic salience, including *amongst* the Han, as ethnolinguistic communities seek economic and political advantage and as economic inequalities are ethnicized (see also Pei 1995: 77–8). Under such conditions, an expansion of political rights and freedoms, let alone the introduction of democratic elections, could reinforce exclusionary ethnicity and contribute to ethnicized conflict (see also Friedman 1993).

The Nature of Pan-Ethnic Identities

This book explores pan-ethnic identities based on shared religion, on coalitions formed through anticolonial or antiauthoritarian struggles, on shared threats, and on interethnic patrimonial relations. Each presents particular problems for the goal of ethnically inclusive and nonhierarchical democratization. Each has implications for whether the nation will have clearly defined terms of inclusion for all ethnic minorities, the absence of which, Bertrand notes, increases the likelihood of conflict involving the excluded groups.

Pan-Ethnic Religious Identities

Several contributors found that pan-ethnic religious identities constituted under authoritarian rule—and sometimes in opposition to it—contribute to harmonious ethnolinguistic relations in their countries of study. Laliberté argues that Buddhist identities forged in the KMT years have helped moderate the exclusive impulses of both Taiwanese and Chinese ethnonationalism in Taiwan. Wurfel points to the role of Catholicism in cementing a pan-linguistic, pan-tribal East Timorese identity and in uniting the majority of the otherwise ethnolinguistically diverse peoples of the Philippines.

However, as the Philippine case suggests, *pan-ethnic identities centered on religion can unite across linguistic and tribal lines, but tend to exclude minority ethnic groups constituted around a common religious identity.* As Wurfel notes, the same Catholicism that facilitates a pan-ethnolinguistic Philippine identity also excludes Muslims. This is particularly so in Mindanao, where the Philippine Catholic identity is especially threatening in the context of Christian migration to the region and, more recently, of the U.S. war on terrorism, cast as an anti-Islam crusade. Other sources of pan-ethnic identity in the Philippines, particularly antiauthoritarian struggles and patrimonial relations, have only partly mitigated the conflict. Although Muslim ethnonationalists and anti-Marcos groups cooperated to unseat the dictator in the 1980s, the pan-ethnic alliance has since largely crumbled. The reasons partly lie in the failure of the autonomy concessions granted by the Acquino and Ramos governments, to satisfy both Mindanao Muslims and Christians (Bertrand 2000). I will say more later about the durability of pan-ethnic anti-colonial and antiauthoritarian coalitions.

Meanwhile, it is important to note that religious identity is not always a pan-ethnic bridge even *within* a supposed community of faith, because of "internal" differences over the meaning and political role of religious values. The struggles between moderate and more radical understandings of political Islam in Indonesia and Malaysia demonstrate the problem. Bertrand suggests that the turn to a less moderate political Islam in the late Suharto and post-Suharto years threatened many Christians in Maluku and caused Papuans to fear that inclusion in the nation increasingly meant a denial of the distinctness of West Papua. By contrast, many Achenese felt that the turn to Islam did not sufficiently Islamicize the state. In each case, a resort to an exclusive interpretation of religious identity to shore up authoritarian rule contributed to ethnicized tensions and mobilization during democratization. This helps explains why Rankin and Goonewardena assert that "deep" democratization requires constitutionally guaranteed secularism.

The chapters on Taiwan, the Philippines, and Indonesia suggest that several factors help determine whether religious identities encourage ethnically inclusive, nonhierarchical democratization, or undermine it. Laliberté writes that the dominant Buddhist organizations in Taiwan adopted an inclusive pan-ethnic position for reasons at once instrumental, normative, personal, and institutional and that reveal the interconnected roles of state and civil society in fostering inclusive citizenship. Cut off from their mainland Chinese roots because of hostilities between the governments of Taiwan and mainland China, the Buddhist groups were forced to seek converts and new clergy amongst the "native Taiwanese" majority. Buddhist leaders also had incentives to interpret Buddhist teachings on love, forgiveness, and compassion in ethnically inclusive ways. Encouraged by the KMT government in its search for international allies, Buddhist groups built links with overseas organizations that espoused inclusive civic norms. The need of Buddhist groups for state support also encouraged them to reflect the KMT's increasingly inclusive civic understanding of the nation; Buddhist followers, who were also voters, reinforced the government's inclusive stance as the use of democratic elections expanded.

Pan-Ethnic Threats

The geopolitical context also seems critical. On one level, perceptions of a mainland Chinese security threat shared by all ethnic groups have been a key force constructing Taiwan identity in more inclusive, nonhierarchical pan-ethnic terms centered on democratic civic values. This suggests that *the perception by key ethnic groups of a common threat to cherished values increases the likelihood that pan-ethnic identities will emerge.* The hypothesis, applied in a colonial context, helps explain Wurfel's contention that a pan-ethnic identity emerged in East Timor and somewhat in the Philippines as a result of common experiences of and struggles against colonial rule. Nagata also identifies widespread public opposition to the Malaysian government's arbitrary treatment of former Finance Minister Anwar Ibrahim in the late 1990s as the force galvanizing Keadilan, arguably the most significant cross-ethnic coalition in Malaysian history. Still, not all actors perceive threats in the same way, suggesting that pan-ethnic identities built on shared fears are fragile. While the People's Republic of China's (PRC) military threat helps maintain a sense of shared destiny amongst Taiwan people of different ethnic backgrounds, the PRC government's nationalist appeals and the mainland's huge economy have the potential to undermine Taiwan's emergent civic identity. Chang also suggests that Taiwan's best defense against ethnicized conflict may be the complexity of its postindustrial society, where national and ethnic identities are politically salient, but do not encompass all dimensions of life nor coincide neatly with religious, gender, class, and status group identities.

Pan-Ethnic Antiauthoritarian and Anticolonial Coalitions

As Bell points out, however, civic identities and majority rule sometimes hide the dominance of one ethnic group. *Pan-ethnic coalitions built on shared commitments to end authoritarian rule will be weakened if subsequent democratization is experienced as majoritarian or exclusionary by vulnerable minorities, whether in the political or economic realms.*[15] In prodemocratization movements, the demands of ethnic minorities for political self-rule and/or inclusion can initially harmonize with broader societal demands for political decentralization and civil society participation in government. However, as the Philippine Mindanao case illustrates (Romero 1999; Bertrand 2000), over time, tensions can emerge between egalitarian liberal democratic and laissez-faire economic norms, and minority demands for meaningful autonomy and economic inclusion.[16] For instance, Wurfel notes that the failure of post-Marcos democratic governments to address land distribution issues has meant the continued Christian encroachment on Moro lands, a root cause of the Moro rebellion. The hard-won anticolonial pan-ethnic identity of the East Timorese could crumble if, despite independence and democratization, poverty is not alleviated and becomes ethnicized.

Pan-Ethnic Patrimonial Relations

Finally, several authors identify patrimonial relationships as a key pan-ethnic force in the region. However, the authors take conflicting positions on whether cross-ethnic patrimonialism ultimately reduces the exclusiveness and hierarchical nature of ethnic identities during democratization. Brown notes that new patrimonial links between moderate Acehnese factions and post-Suharto governments could help bring about a negotiated settlement to this prolonged conflict. Wurfel suggests that patrimonialism across ethnic lines could help cement a pan-ethnic East Timor nation, while a failure fully to integrate Muslim elites into wider Philippine patronage networks remains a feature of the Mindanao conflict. Brown also reminds us of the extent to which the consociational and other practices said to foster interethnic accommodation within ethnically diverse older democracies like India and Canada are analogous to patrimonialism—and may similarly contradict egalitarian democratic values. Moreover, as Bertrand and Nagata point out for Indonesia and Malaysia, interethnic patrimonialism has fueled the resentments that feed ethnicized tensions as much as it has been a cross-ethnic bridge.

Demographic Factors

A final hypothesis arising from this book centers on how the number, relative strength, and geographical distribution of ethnic groups influence prospects for pan-ethnic identities and ethnically inclusive, nonhierarchical democratization. With respect to the Philippines, Wurfel argues that the multiplicity and relative equality of "size" of ethnolinguistic groups, and the fact that no large ethnolinguistic group dominates the capital region, has contributed to strong pan-ethnic identities, at least in non-Muslim areas. This demographic situation, along with Catholicism and historically homogenous elite socialization, has helped build long-standing pan-ethnolinguistic elite patronage networks. Thus, Wurfel suggests that "balanced diversity" may be more beneficial for democracy than cultural homogeneity because it encourages the practice of interethnic, and then intergroup, bargaining. Consistent with this, Bertrand suggests that the fact that the proportion of Christians and Muslims in Maluku was almost equal, and unbuffered by the presence of other major ethnic groups, contributed to the propensity to conflict in that part of Indonesia. Therefore, the general hypothesis is that the *likelihood of ethnicized exclusion, hierarchy, and conflict during democratization is lessened if there is balanced diversity, that is, if there is a multiplicity of ethnic groups of similar size, none of which defines the nation or dominates the country's most politically or economically significant region(s).*

CONCLUSION

In summary, the experiences of the East and Southeast Asian societies studied here suggest that categorizing multiethnic polities as "good" and "bad" based on their regime type alone ignores the political nature of ethnic and other collective identities. The alternative conceptual framework offered here understands political regimes—authoritarian, democratizing, democratic, or somewhere in the middle—and ethnic identities as co-constitutive processes shaped by patrimonial and economic production processes. Moreover, it suggests that the constitution of ethnic identities by authoritarian political processes significantly influences how they will be understood during democratization, though democratizing regimes also raise their own characteristic challenges for the creation and maintenance of ethnically inclusive and nonhierarchical political communities. Fundamentally, the politics of ethnic and other collective identities are not peripheral or incidental to democratization, but rather integral to it, just as they are central to the creation and maintenance of authoritarian or democratic rule. With the "naturalness," "pureness," and "discreteness" of the region's ethnic and national identities challenged by constructivist and poststructuralist perspectives, the study of past and potential regime changes across East and Southeast Asia is ripe for analyses that illuminate this complex relationship. The present book furthers our understanding of the role of ethnicity in the constitution of political, including economic, regimes: the conceptual and theoretical tools and tentative general hypotheses it identifies suggest directions for future research on prospects for peaceful, ethnically inclusive, and nonhierarchical democratization and democracy throughout the region and beyond.

NOTES

My thanks to Daniel Bell, David Brown, Lynne Russell, and the anonymous reviewers for their insightful comments on earlier versions of this chapter. I remain responsible for the remaining weaknesses and errors.

1. Exceptions are Singh (2001); Friedman (1993); Snyder (2000).
2. This is similar to Lustick's (1979) notion of "hegemonic control," discussed in McGarry and O'Leary (1993).
3. On the origin of and contradictions in these policies under Mao, see Connor (1984).
4. While ethnic groups are distinct from social classes, shared economic circumstances are sometimes central to claims of cultural difference, as with *Barakumin* in Japan and Subei people in the PRC.
5. For a discussion of these contending approaches, see Young (1993) and Hutchinson and Smith (1996, esp. Part II).
6. On *ethnicized* as opposed to *ethnic* conflict, see Campbell (1998) and Fearon and Laitin (2000).

7. Tully (1995) makes a similar point with his notion of "interculturality," that is, the assertion that cultural difference is *internal* to rather than *between* cultures and individuals.

8. On the political and cultural processes by which majorities are constituted in East Asia, see Gladney (1998). For poststructural and feminist formulations of the links between ethnic identities and political communities, see Campbell (1998) and Anthias and Yuval Davis (1989), respectively.

9. However, as Hutchinson and Smith note (1996), elsewhere Weber emphasized historical memory and cultural and biological differences, rather than political bases, in determining ethnic identities.

10. These are akin to the instrumental, discursive, and structural strands of constructivism identified by Fearon and Laitin (2000).

11. On the complex ethnic dimensions of flexible accumulation in late capitalism, see Ong (1999).

12. For example, see Connor (1994: 22, 139) on Japan.

13. Although this book does not include a chapter on the Koreas, I have no reason to believe that they are different from the rest of the region in this regard (see, for instance, Cho 1998).

14. On the distinction, see Snyder (2000).

15. On the fragility of pan-ethnic alliances as democratization progresses, see Henders (1997, 1999).

16. On the politics of autonomy and identity in Mindanao since September 11, 2001, see Geoffrey York, "Former Philippine revel fears fresh violence," *The Globe and Mail*, 9 November 2002.

REFERENCES

Anderson, Benedict O. 1991. *Imagined Communities: Reflections on the Origin and Spread of Nationalism*. London: Verso.

Anthias, F., and N. Yuval Davis, eds. 1989. *Woman—Nation—State*. London: Macmillan.

Bauer, Joanne R., and Daniel A. Bell, eds. 1999. *The East Asian Challenge for Human Rights*. Cambridge: Cambridge University Press.

Barth, Frederick, ed. 1969. *Ethnic Groups and Boundaries: The Social Organization of Cultural Difference*. Boston: Little Brown.

Bell, Daniel A. 2000. *East Meets West: Human Rights and Democracy in East Asia*. Princeton, N.J.: Princeton University Press.

———, David Brown, Kanishka Jayasuriya, and David Martin Jones. 1995. *Towards Illiberal Democracy in Pacific Asia*. Houndmills: Macmillan/St. Antony's College.

Bertrand, Jacques. 2000. "Peace and Conflict in the Southern Philippines: Why the 1996 Peace Agreement is Fragile." *Pacific Affairs* 73, no. 1 (Spring): 37–54.

Brass, Paul, ed. 1985. *Ethnic Groups and the State*. Totowa, N.J.: Barnes and Noble.

Brook, Tim, and André Schmid, eds. 2000. *Nation Work: Asian Elites and National Identities*. Ann Arbor: University of Michigan.

Brown, David. 2000. *Contemporary Nationalism: Civic, Ethnocultural, and Multicultural Politics*. London: Routledge.

Brown, Michael E., and Sumit Ganguly, eds. 1997. *Government Policies and Ethnic Relations in Asia and the Pacific*. Cambridge, Mass.: MIT Press.

Brubaker, Rogers. 1996. *Nationalism Reframed: Nationhood and the National Question in the New Europe*. Cambridge: Cambridge University Press.

Campbell, David. 1998. *National Deconstruction: Violence, Identity, and Justice in Bosnia*. Minneapolis: University of Minnesota Press.

Cho, Hae-joang. 1998. "Constructing and Deconstructing 'Koreanness.'" In *Making Majorities: Constituting the Nation in Japan, Korea, China, Malaysia, Fiji, Turkey, and the United States*, ed. Dru Gladney. Stanford: Stanford University Press.

Connor, Walker. 1984. *The National Question in Marxist-Leninist Theory and Practice*. Princeton, N.J.: Princeton University Press.

———. 1994. *Ethnonationalism: The Quest for Understanding*. Princeton, N.J.: Princeton University Press.

Dahl, Robert. 1989. *Democracy and its Critics*. New Haven, Conn.: Yale University Press.

Diamond, Larry, and Marc F. Plattner, eds. 1994. *Nationalism, Ethnic Conflict, and Democracy*. Baltimore, Md.: Johns Hopkins University Press.

———. 1998. *Democracy in East Asia*. Baltimore, Md.: Johns Hopkins University Press.

Enloe, Cynthia H. 1973. *Ethnic Conflict and Political Development*. Boston: Little Brown.

Fearon, James D., and David D. Laitin. 2000. "Violence and the Social Construction of Ethnic Identity." *International Organization* 54, no. 4: 845–77.

Friedman, Edward. 1993. "Ethnic Identity and the De-Nationalization and Democratization of Leninist States." In *The Rising Tide of Cultural Pluralism: The Nation-State at Bay?*, ed. Crawford Young. Madison: University of Wisconsin Press.

———, ed. 1994. *The Politics of Democratization: Generalizing East Asian Experiences*. Boulder, Colo.: Westview.

Fujitani, T., Geoffrey M. White, and Lisa Yoneyama, eds. 2001. *Perilous Memories: The Asia-Pacific War(s)*. Durham, N.C.: Duke University Press.

Gladney, Dru, ed. 1998. *Making Majorities: Constituting the Nation in Japan, Korea, China, Malaysia, Fiji, Turkey, and the United States*. Stanford: Stanford University Press.

Gurr, Ted. 1993. "Why Minorities Rebel: A Global Analysis of Communal Mobilization and Conflict since 1945." *International Political Science Review* 14, no. 2: 161–201.

———. 2000. *Minorities at Risk in the New Century*. Washington, D.C.: United States Institute of Peace.

He, Baogang, and Guo Yingjie. 2000. *Nationalism, National Identity, and Democratization in China*. Aldershot: Ashgate.

Henders, Susan. 1997. "Cantonisation: Historical Paths to Territorial Autonomy for Regional Cultural Communities." *Nations and Nationalism* 3, no. 4: 521–40.

———. 1999. Special Status Regions: The Territorial Accommodation of Cultural Difference. D.Phil. Thesis, University of Oxford.

Horowitz, Donald L. 1986. *Ethnic Groups in Conflict*. Berkeley: University of California Press.

Hutchinson, John, and Anthony D. Smith, eds. 1996. *Ethnicity*. Oxford: Oxford University Press.

Kymlicka, Will. 1989. *Liberalism, Community, and Culture*. Oxford: Oxford University Press.

———. 1990. *Contemporary Political Philosophy: An Introduction*. Oxford: Oxford University Press.

Leff, Carol Skalnik. 1999. "Democratization and Disintegration in Multinational States: The Breakup of the Communist Federations." *World Politics* 51, no. 2: 205–35.

Lie, John. 2001. *Multiethnic Japan*. Cambridge, Mass.: Harvard University Press.

Linz, Juan J., and Alfred Stepan. 1996. *Problems of Democratic Transition and Consolidation*. Baltimore, Md.: Johns Hopkins University Press.

Luskick, Ian. 1979. "Stability in Deeply Divided Societies: Consociationalism versus Control." *World Politics* 31: 325–44.

McGarry, John, and Brendan O'Leary. 1993. "Introduction: The Macro-political Regulation of Ethnic Conflict." In *The Politics of Ethnic Conflict Regulation*, eds. John McGarry and Brendan O'Leary. London: Routledge.

Newman, Saul. 1996. *Ethnoregional Conflict in Democracies: Mostly Ballots, Rarely Bullets*. Westport, Conn.: Greenwood.

Ong, Aihwa. 1999. *Flexible Citizenship: The Cultural Logics of Transnationality*. Durham, N.C.: Duke University Press.

Pei, Minxin. 1995. "Creeping Democracy in China." *Journal of Democracy* 6, no. 4 (October): 65–79.

Rankin, Katharine N. 2001. "Planning and the Politics of Markets: Some Lessons from Financial Regulation in Nepal." *International Planning Studies* 6, no. 1 (February): 89–102.

Romero, Segundo E. 1999. "Changing Filipino Values and the Redemocratization of Governance." In *Changing Values in Asia: Their Impact on Government and Development*, ed. Han Sung-Joo. Tokyo: Japan Centre for International Exchange.

Rustow, Dankwart A. 1970. "Transitions to Democracy: Toward a Dynamic Model." *Comparative Politics* 2: 337–63.

Ryan, Stephen. 1990. *Ethnic Conflict and International Relations*. Aldershot: Dartmouth.

Singh, Anita Inder. 2001. *Democracy, Ethnic Diversity, and Security in Post-Communist Europe*. Westport, Conn.: Praeger.

Snyder, Jack. 2000. *From Voting to Violence: Democratization and Nationalist Conflict*. New York: Norton.

Taylor, Charles. 1993. *Reconciling the Solitudes: Essays on Canadian Federalism and Nationalism*. Montreal and Kingston: McGill-Queen's University Press.

Tully, James. 1995. *Strange Multiplicity: Constitutionalism in an Age of Diversity*. Cambridge: Cambridge University Press, 1995.

Weber, Max. 1968. "The Origins of Ethnic Groups." In *Economy and Society: An Outline of Interpretive Sociology*, vol. 1, eds. Guenther Roth and Claus Wittich. Berkeley: University of California Press.

World Bank, 2000. *Human Development Report 2000: Human Rights and Human Development*. Oxford: Oxford University Press.

Young, Crawford. 1976. *The Politics of Cultural Pluralism*. Madison: University of Wisconsin Press.

———. 1993. "The Dialectics of Cultural Pluralism: Concept and Reality." In *The Rising Tide of Cultural Pluralism: The Nation-State at Bay?*, ed. Crawford Young. Madison: University of Wisconsin Press.

I

DEBATING THEORIES
AND CONCEPTS

2

Is Democracy the "Least Bad" System for Minority Groups?

Daniel A. Bell

Following the collapse of communism in the Soviet bloc, there was a brief moment of euphoria when democracy seemed to be the cure for all the world's political ills. Today, however, it is widely recognized that democratic political arrangements per se cannot resolve crippling poverty, environmental degradation, and pervasive corruption, to name some of the more obvious troubles afflicting the "developing" world.

Even more worrisome, it seems that democracy can actually conflict with some political goods—minority rights in particular. Brutal ethnic warfare in the postcommunist states has led many observers to conclude that there is a profound tension between democracy and minority rights (Gurr 1995: 213). In ethnically plural societies, the majority group can decide to oppress minority groups democratically (Zakaria 1997). Yugoslavia's treatment of the Kosovo Albanians is an obvious example. It is also dismaying to note that the typical mechanisms for dealing with group conflict in Western democracies—such as federalism and consociationalism—may not be workable in the absence of a deeply rooted culture of mutual respect and tolerance between groups. In societies with intense levels of hatred and mutual mistrust, dominant groups may not be willing to subordinate their interests under the framework of a constitutional system designed to protect minority groups. In the worst cases, only military intervention by third parties can keep the peace and (hopefully) protect the interests of minority groups.

One typical response to the failings of democracy is to invoke Winston Churchill's (apocryphal?) quip that democracy is the worst possible system, except for all the others. But is democracy really the "least bad" system for protecting minority groups? Should we rule out of court the possibility that non-democratic forms of government can better protect the legitimate interests of

minority groups in various ways? The recent experience of several countries in East Asia suggests otherwise. While the debate on "Asian values"
has largely focused on the alleged benefits of East Asian–style authoritarianism for rapid economic development, some less-than-democratic political systems in the region can also be defended on the grounds that they
help to secure the interests of minority groups—and that democratization
can be detrimental to those interests. In this chapter, I will discuss one
specific way that democracy can harm minority interests, namely, that it
tends to promote a form of nation-building centered on the culture of the
majority group. I will also try to argue, pointing to actual examples from
the East Asian region, that these problems need not arise to the same extent in less-than-democratic political settings. My argument will be directed specifically at Will Kymlicka's argument that less-than-democratic
states do not have any comparative advantages for minority groups in the
East Asian context.

This chapter should not be read as a critique of democracy. Democracy is
better than alternative political systems, other things being equal. But other
things are rarely equal, especially for minority groups. Any judgment regarding the benefits of democracy needs to be balanced against the actual
and potential costs for minority groups.

SOME DEFINITIONS

First, however, let me begin by defining the relevant terms. Democracy will
be defined in the "minimal" sense as free and fair competitive elections under universal franchise for occupants of those posts where actual policy decisions are made (Nathan 1993: 3). Democracy thus understood is a proce-
dure for the filling of political offices through periodic free and fair elections.
Such elections are only possible if there is some measure of freedom of
speech, assembly, and press, and if opposition candidates and parties can
criticize incumbents without fear of retaliation (Huntington 1993: 28). This
definition is provided in most international rights documents,[1] and it is the
least controversial definition available. More importantly (for our purposes),
this definition of democracy is helpful for identifying the tension between
democracy and minority rights.[2] The standard definitions of minority groups
in multiethnic societies are more problematic, however.[3] Political thinkers
tend to define ethnocultural groups in terms of language, race, or religion.
Vernon Van Dyke, for example, defines an ethnic community as "a group of
persons, predominantly of common descent, who think of themselves as collectively possessing a separate identity based on race or on shared characteristics, usually language and religion" (Van Dyke 1995: 32). If the aim is to
identify vulnerable minority groups, however, definitions in terms of shared

language, race, or religion may have the effect of unjustifiably rewarding some groups and denying the legitimate aspirations of others.

It is instructive to look at some examples from China. According to the Chinese government, there are fifty-six ethnic minorities in the country, amounting to more than 8 percent of the population. These officially recognized minorities are labeled as such by virtue of being "non-Han," meaning they do not use the Chinese script or bear all the physical characteristics of the Han Chinese. Leading experts on the subject such as June Teufel Dreyer and Colin Mackerras also operate with the government's definition of a minority group (Dreyer 1976; Mackerras 1994).

Contrary to popular belief, the Chinese government does recognize in principle that minority groups are entitled to special status in the Chinese political system. For example, the National People's Congress in 1984 passed "The Law on Regional Autonomy for Minority Nationalities" that allows for self-administration in Tibet and other "minority regions." Self-administration in practice, needless to say, does not amount to much. But some tangible benefits are in fact granted to officially recognized minority groups. For example, they are exempted from most stringent applications of the regulations on birth control, and members of minority nationalities can be admitted to universities with lower marks.

The problem, however, is that, under the current system, benefits may accrue to individuals and groups not in need of special protection. Not surprisingly, the children of mixed marriages between Han and minority members usually choose minority rather than Han status. Whole countries and districts have applied for autonomous minority status on the basis of extremely slender evidence, such as the discovery of non-Han names in genealogies of several generations' depth.

At the same time, restricting the definition of minority groups to shared language or ethnicity can conceal minority groups from political view—and so play into the hands of conservative majorities intent on denying legitimate aspirations for self-administration. As Emily Honig explains (1992: 2–3), the prejudice against Subei people is comparable to that experienced by African Americans in the United States. Unlike (most) African Americans, however, the Subei people are not physically distinct from the rest of the Shanghainese population, almost all of whom are Han Chinese. Rather, they are defined as Subei by virtue of being individuals whose families were originally poverty-stricken refugees from Jiangsu province. The political result is that Subei people do not benefit from the official Chinese policy of positive discrimination and special political representation for minority groups.

Consider as well the case of the *Burakumin* (literally, the people of the hamlets) in Japan. The *Burakumin*—numbering almost three million—speak Japanese and are ethnically indistinguishable from other Japanese. While they enjoy the same legal rights as their fellow citizens, they are the victims of various social practices that still serve to keep them sexually and socially apart from Japanese society. There is a commonly shared social myth that they are descendants of a less human "race" than the stock that fathered the Japanese nation as a whole. They are regarded as hereditary outcasts (de Vos and Wagatsuma 1967: xx). The majority live in impoverished ghettos known as *buraku*. Other Japanese shun contact with them as much as possible and carefully check the pedigrees of prospective sons-in-law or daughters-in-law to make sure they do not carry the taint of *Burakumin* "blood" (Christopher 1983: 50). Yet the usual definition of minority groups in terms of shared language or race allows the Japanese government to declare to the United Nations (in 1980) that there are no discriminated minorities in Japan (McLauchlan 1993: 3).[4]

Similar problems arise if we consider the development of a distinctive Taiwanese identity defined primarily by a common experience with free market institutions and (more recently) a relatively democratic form of government, rather than by shared language or ethnicity. Any prospect for a fair and workable political arrangement with the People's Republic of China cannot ignore the fact that many Taiwanese now think of themselves as sufficiently distinct to seek some form of self-administration, if not complete independence. But this is a nonissue if one accepts the official Chinese view that the Taiwanese are not a distinct cultural grouping. And defining minority groups in terms of language or ethnicity leads one to endorse the official view.[5]

In the same vein, it is difficult to make sense of the political conflicts within Taiwan itself by relying on the standard definition of what constitutes a cultural group. The sharpest and most politically influential conflict is that between the Taiwanese and the "mainlanders" who came to Taiwan with the Kuomintang (KMT) government in the late 1940s. More than one million mainlanders came to Taiwan. They proceeded to establish political dominance over the native Taiwanese (approximately 80 percent of the population). In 1947, the KMT brutally put down an uprising by native Taiwanese, and it did not permit political opposition for the next four decades. The KMT denied that it officially discriminated against the native Taiwanese, but provincial origins were, in practice, often used by the KMT as a criterion for decisions on political inclusion or exclusion.[6]

Not surprisingly, this generated resentment among the native Taiwanese, and provincial origin was made into a political cause following political liberalization in the late 1980s. The opposition movement identified the Taiwanese as the oppressed and the mainlanders as the oppressors, and this became the main source of political conflict. The KMT responded by opening itself up to native Taiwanese, particularly under the leadership of the native Taiwanese President Lee Teng-hui. Nonetheless, the opposition Democratic Progressive Party, supported almost exclusively by native Taiwanese, made steady inroads into the corridors of power, culminating in Chen Shui-bian's election to the presidency in mid-2000.[7] Today, it is the mainlanders who complain about limited political opportunities (Chang 1994: 98). While there is a linguistic dimension to this conflict (many mainlanders are unable to converse in dialects commonly used by native Taiwanese), provincial origin is the main line of demarcation between the two groups.

Once again, this suggests the need for defining group identity in terms not restricted to language or race. The standard definition of ethnocultural groups cannot adequately shed light on the nature of group conflicts in some East Asian societies. Nor can it identify all the vulnerable groups in need of special political protection. Thus, ethnocultural groups in multiethnic societies will be defined as groups of persons who think of themselves (and/or who are defined by others) as possessing a separate identity based primarily on shared noneconomic characteristics. This definition is broad enough to allow for common characteristics other than race, language, or religion, yet narrow enough to exclude class identification as the key variable. The "details" will have to be filled in by particular accounts of political conflict that are sensitive to the actual history and self-understanding of minority groups.

DEMOCRACY AND NATION-BUILDING

Let us now turn to the main source of tension between democracy and minority rights[8]—the need for democratic states to promote nation-building centered on the majority culture. The nineteenth-century political thinker John Stuart Mill laid the intellectual foundations for this view. According to Mill, democracy is "next to impossible in a country made up of different nationalities. Among a people without fellow-feeling, especially if they read and speak different languages, the united public opinion, necessary to the working of representative government, cannot exist" (Mill 1975: 382). In other words, democratic deliberation requires mutual trust and understanding, and this can only be provided by a shared language and a common national identity. Mill recognized, however, that the boundaries of governments do not always coincide with those of cultural groups: "There are parts even of Europe, in which different nationalities are so locally intermingled, that it is not practicable for them to be under separate government" (Mill 1975: 384). In such cases, Mill argued that minority groups can and should be absorbed into the culture of the relatively "civilized" group:

> Experience proves, that it is possible and desirable for one nationality to merge and be absorbed into another: and when it was originally an inferior and more backward portion of the human race, the absorption is greatly to its advantage. Nobody can suppose that it is not more beneficial to a Breton, or a Basque of French Navarre, to be brought into the current of the ideas and feelings of a

highly civilized and cultivated people—to be a member of the French nationality, admitted on equal terms to all the privileges of French citizenship, sharing
the advantages of French protection, and the dignity and prestige of French
power—than to sulk on his own rocks, the half-savage relic of past times, revolving in his own little mental orbit, without participation or interest in the general movement of the world (Mill 1975: 385).

The experience of the twentieth century, needless to say, points to different lessons. Far from being content with "being brought into the current of
ideas and feelings of a highly civilized and cultivated people," minority
groups have typically sought to assert their distinctive identities in various
ways. Some contemporary liberals have responded by recognizing the need
to protect minority rights against the tendencies of absorption into the dominant national culture.

Will Kymlicka is the most prominent contemporary liberal defender of minority rights. He argues that justice requires equality between ethnocultural
groups in a state. But because minority groups may be particularly vulnerable
to the economic, political, or military power of the majority, this can justify special political protections for minority groups. In a series of lectures delivered in
Japan in 1998, Kymlicka argues for the universal applicability of his theory.[9]

Minorities in non-Western states, he claims, need the same sorts of protections against majority power that minorities in Western states need (Kymlicka 1998: 6). Kymlicka's key argument for this claim is that modern nation-
states must engage in "nation-building" programs centered on the majority
culture, and these programs pose grave threats to minority interests and
identities. He notes that

> historically, virtually all liberal democracies have, at one point or another, at-
> tempted to diffuse a single societal culture throughout all of their territory. They
> have all engaged in this process of "nation-building"—that is, a process of pro-
> moting a common language, and a sense of common membership in, and equal
> access to, the social institutions based on that language. Decisions regarding of-
> ficial languages, core curricula in education, and the requirements for acquiring
> citizenship, all were made with the express intention of diffusing a particular
> culture throughout society, and of promoting a particular national identity based
> on participation in that societal culture (Kymlicka 1998: 11).

Nation-building of this sort is essential because only the existence of a national identity centered on a common language can motivate and mobilize
citizens to act for common political goals. But these goals need not be liberal, thus explaining why nation-building has been so ubiquitous. Nationalism can be used to promote liberal goals such as democratization and equality of opportunity, but it can also be used to promote illiberal goals such as
chauvinism and unjust conquest. Thus, it is not surprising

that the model of the "nation-state" has been adopted by many non-Western countries as well, which have embarked on their own nation-building programs. In Asia, as in the West, nation-building has appealed to both democratic reformers and authoritarian conservatives, since it can be used to mobilize people behind a wide range of political projects. And Asian governments have often used the same tools of nation-building as Western governments: regulating the language and content of education and public services; establishing a national media; controlling immigration and naturalization (Kymlicka 1998: 12).

Nation-building poses a distinctive threat to minority interests because it tends to be centered on the majority culture, with special emphasis on the language of the majority. In a democratic system, political leaders must be sensitive to majority preferences and, thus, the language and culture of the majority group tend to be the only feasible basis of nation-building. Given the danger that majority nation-building poses for minority interests, Kymlicka suggests a variety of measures such as language rights to protect vulnerable minorities.

But why should we expect the same dynamic of politically, economically, and culturally favored majority groups versus oppressed minorities in East Asia's less-than-democratic states? In such states, it may be easier for political elites to suppress majority nationalism. Although political leaders may have to construct a common national identity to promote goals such as political stability and economic development, they are not as constrained by the majority culture (in comparison with democratic states) if political leaders decide that the majority's culture conflicts with the state's goals.

Consider the case of Singapore. In 1965, Singapore was expelled from the Malaysian federation and forced to be independent. At the time, nation-building was perhaps Singapore's greatest challenge. As founding father Lee Kuan Yew put it, "[We had] to build a nation from scratch" (Lee 1994: 9). This was not made easy by the fact that Singapore was, and is, an ethnically plural society—77 percent Chinese, 14 percent Malay, and 8 percent Indian—and that the various groups were literally at war with each other in the early 1960s. The Malay minority in particular posed a challenge to the creation of national unity in Singapore, because its members were more inclined to side with Malays in the surrounding states than with the majority Chinese. Thus, the ruling People's Action Party (PAP) felt it could not create a new identity by appealing to Chinese culture. Instead, it attempted to combat all forms of ethnic parochialism by fostering the growth of a new Singaporean identity that would underpin security and prosperity. For example, the government broke up ethnic enclaves by moving people into ethnically mixed public housing blocks. It also promoted the use of English, which involved overriding the wishes of all groups, including the majority Chinese. Lee is quite explicit that Singapore's nation-building exercise was incompatible with democracy:

> Supposing we had chosen Chinese or tried to sponsor Chinese, how would we make a living? How would we fit ourselves into the region and into the world? We could not have made a living. But the Chinese then would have wanted it. And if we had taken a vote, we would have had to follow that policy. So when people say, "Oh, ask the people!," it's childish rubbish. We are leaders. We know the consequences. . . . They say people can think for themselves? Do you honestly believe that the chap who can't pass primary six knows the consequences of his choice when he answers a question viscerally, on language, culture and religion? But we knew the consequences. We would starve, we would have race riots. We would disintegrate.[10]

In the same vein, other less-than-democratic states in Southeast Asia suppressed manifestations of majority culture in the interests of promoting a form of nation-building relatively conducive to political stability and economic development. Indonesia has approximately 180 million Muslims—more than any other country—yet President Suharto managed to suppress political manifestations of Islam during his thirty-four-year reign (1965–1998). Suharto proclaimed a vague philosophy termed *Pancasila* that was originally formulated by his predecessor Sukarno. *Pancasila* was defended "as a moderate, middle-of-the-road ideology, somewhere between Communist ideology on the Left and Islamic theocracy on the Right,"[11] and all religious and political groups were required to pledge adherence to it. Whatever the drawbacks of this approach, it succeeded in suppressing ethnic and religious conflict and allowed for political stability and economic development.

Malaysia has been relatively democratic,[12] and it cannot suppress political manifestations of Islam to the same extent. Still, Prime Minister Mahathir Mohamad, the ruler of Malaysia since 1981, has placed some restrictions on public religious activity that would have been impossible to justify in more democratic states.[13] The freedom of the press is severely restricted on the grounds that this is necessary to preserve social stability in a communally divided society (Neher and Marlay 1995: 80). Moreover, Prime Minister Mahathir often uses the bully pulpit to criticize manifestations of Islam deemed to be incompatible with economic modernization. In 1994, the Malaysian government made explicit the limits of religious expression that threaten his political program by banning *Al Arqam*, a relatively "fundamentalist" Islamic group, and arresting its leader Ashaari Mohammed. This arrest was carried out in accordance with a ruling from the "National Fatwa Council" and justified on religious grounds,[14] though the government was probably more concerned by the political threat posed by *Al Arqam*'s growing popularity[15] and its multimillion dollar business empire.

From the standpoint of the minority group, another "advantage" of a less-than-democratic political system is that it might be easier for members of minority groups to strike bargains with political elites that suit the interests of both parties—and to subsequently suppress protests by the majority group. The Chinese minority in Suharto's Indonesia is a case in point. President Suharto acquired power in murky circumstances that included a race pogrom against those of Chinese ancestry in the mid-1960s. For the next three decades, the Chinese minority—roughly 3 percent of the population—was constrained from expressing its cultural identity. Public manifestations of Chinese festivals were banned, the Chinese language could not be taught in schools, and Chinese language newspapers (with the exception of one small publication issued by the army) were forbidden. However, the Chinese were among the main beneficiaries of state-led economic development (Freedman 2000: 186). Suharto built his own family's wealth through connections with wealthy Chinese business leaders, and Chinese tycoons were granted substantial economic benefits in return. Indonesia's nontycoon Chinese minority, described as "a small prosperous class socially situated between traditional nobles and common peasants" (Neher and Marlay 1995: 87), also reaped economic benefits from Suharto's regime. By the late 1990s, the Chinese minority controlled more than half of the country's wealth (some estimates range as high as 70 percent).

Elections in Malaysia have been more vigorously contested,[16] but the political process has been tightened of late. The ruling National Front's (BN) electoral advantage has been guaranteed by its control of the press and its deep pockets. After the 1986 elections, Mahathir purged his political party of dissidents and invoked the Internal Security Act to arrest critics of the government (Neher and Marlay 1995: 105). More recently, Mahathir's deputy prime minister Anwar Ibrahim, was sacked and jailed on dubious charges.

The Chinese minority—roughly 29 percent of the population—has also been marginalized from the political process. Prior to the 1969 race riots, Malay politicians needed to rely on Chinese political support to help thwart the Communist insurgency and to consolidate financial strength. Since then, however, there has been less of a need to reach out to the Chinese community. The BN has imposed several constraints on political participation by the Chinese minority, most notably by using its power to create new electoral districts in rural areas where Malays are the majority. As Amy Freedman notes,

> This marginalizes the Chinese in two ways: first, it violates the principle of one person one vote, or the notion that all votes have equal weight. Second, it serves to keep the number of Chinese elected officials to a minimum because it is not likely that the BN would run a Chinese candidate in a rural Malay district (Freedman 2000: 188).

Notwithstanding the less-than-democratic political system, however, the Chinese business community has continued to prosper by becoming closely tied with state development goals. Chinese businesses, which were once family and community centered, rely increasingly on state or public financing. As a result, Malay political elites have become increasingly involved in Chinese business enterprises,[17] though the Chinese still control the largest share of Malaysia's capital. This mutually beneficial arrangement has been in place for over two decades.

In short, the experience of the Chinese minority groups in the less-than-democratic states of Indonesia and Malaysia shows that members of minority groups can rely on personal networking (what Brown and others in this volume refer to as patrimonialism or clientelism) for economic benefits. So long as political elites find it to their advantage to maintain mutually beneficial arrangements with members of minority groups, the latter can benefit from less-than-democratic arrangements. Of course, the economic dominance of minority groups often leads to resentment among the majority culture. But the political elites of less-than-democratic states need not be as responsive to majority preferences, and they can rely on coercion and control of the media to suppress threats to political stability.

To be fair, Kymlicka does recognize the possibility that less-than-democratic states are less prone to nation-building centered on the majority culture, along with the implication that minority groups are not as vulnerable to injustice in less-than-democratic states. But he develops three responses to this kind of objection.

Firstly, he says that countries like Singapore are "the exception, rather than the rule. Most authoritarian regimes in Asia, like most authoritarian regimes in the West, have engaged in majority nation-building: consider Burma/Myanmar, China, or the Philippines under Marcos" (Kymlicka 1998: 13). If the focus is Southeast Asia, however, the "exceptions" include Indonesia, Malaysia, and Singapore, which together constitute the majority of the population in the region.[18] The presence of several "exceptions" is sufficient reason to cast doubt on efforts to democratize countries in the region. The possibility that democratization can worsen the situation of vulnerable minorities in Southeast Asia—even if "most authoritarian regimes" do not fall in this category—should be a reason for caution. At the very least, foreign governments, international agencies, and nongovernmental organizations need to be well acquainted with local circumstances to assess the likely impact of democratization on particular minority groups and to consider what political processes, institutional arrangements, and norms would best promote minority rights.[19]

Kymlicka's second response is to call into question the assumption that nation-building occurred in response to populist pressures in democratic countries:

It may be true that authoritarian regimes can, in principle, ignore populist pressures more readily than democracies. But it is a mistake, I think, to suppose that nation-building policies in the West were adopted in response to populist pressure. Even in Western democracies, nation-building has almost always began as an elite-initiated project, which only later became a matter of passion for the masses. Far from being the result of majoritarian preferences, nation-building policies were initially adopted by elites precisely in order to create a cohesive sense of "nationhood" amongst the masses, which could then be mobilized in pursuit of various public objectives. And, as I've noted, this need to mobilize citizens applies to all modern states—it applies as much to authoritarian regimes as to democracies, and as much to Asian countries as to Western countries (Kymlicka 1998: 13).

Kymlicka, however, is referring primarily to the experience of nineteenth-century Europe. John Stuart Mill and other nineteenth-century liberals viewed nation-building primarily as a civilizing mission, as a way of uniting various groups by the language and culture "of a highly civilized and cultivated" people. Liberals worried about "half-savage relic[s] of past times" that impeded the spread of Enlightenment values, and the task was to unify peoples in a state dominated by one of the "civilized" languages (English, French, German, or Italian). Thus, Kymlicka is correct to note that nation-building was not the result of "majoritarian preferences"—in the *nineteenth* century. But elites could initiate these projects precisely (or at least partly) because European countries were not fully democratic. In nineteenth-century England, women and non-property-holders did not have the right to vote, and even liberals such as Mill argued for qualifications to the one-person, one-vote principle (such as granting extra votes to the educated) (Mill 1975: Ch. 8).

In contemporary democracies, however, it would be relatively difficult to initiate and maintain nation-building projects that run counter to the majority culture. Even if nation-building projects do not result directly from majoritarian preferences, those preferences would serve as an important constraint upon feasible nation-building projects. Less-than-democratic Asian states, in contrast, do not face these constraints to the same extent.

This hypothesis can be supported with the experience of nation-building following "twentieth-century style" democratization. In the postcommunist states of Eastern Europe, perhaps the most obvious political development was a resurgence of nation-building that explicitly drew on the language and culture of the majority group. Majority-centered nation-building may not have been the direct result of majority preferences, but political leaders did find that invoking the majority culture was the most effective way of mobilizing "the masses." It is difficult to imagine that, say, a democratically elected leader inspired by Lee Kuan Yew could have successfully suppressed the Serbian language in Yugoslavia's schools in favor of an external "common" language such as English.

As Bertrand explains later, recent democratization in East Asia has also led to nation-building centered on the language and culture of the majority. In Indonesia, the collapse of Suharto's rule has been followed by a resurgence of Islam in politics and society. Abdurrahman Wahid, leader of the country's largest Islamic group (Nahdlatul Ulama), was elected president in 1999. Wahid's group had played an important social and educational role in Suharto's Indonesia, but it had eschewed competitive politics (Neher and Marlay 1995: 84). Relatively "fundamentalist" Islamic groups have been at the forefront of the proindependence movement in Aceh, and open conflict between Muslims and Christians has broken out in the Molucca islands, leading to thousands of deaths.

Even in Taiwan, which, as noted earlier, has avoided such violence, political liberalization in the late 1980s has led to the growth of an independence movement almost entirely supported by the native Taiwanese (approximately 80 percent of the population). The Taiwanese dialect has been promoted in schools, and the educational curriculum has been revised to place more emphasis on Taiwan's distinctive culture and history (as opposed to the history of mainland China).

In short, democratization in contemporary societies has typically been accompanied by nation-building policies centered on the culture of the majority group. While political leaders may not have been directly responding to majority preferences, they realized that appealing to the majority culture was the most effective way of promoting various nation-building projects (not to mention cementing their own grip on power). Given that nation-building is more likely to be centered on majority culture in democratic states, minority groups may be particularly vulnerable during democratization and advocates of democracy need to take this factor in account.

Kymlicka's third response to the claim that less-than-democratic Asian states can better protect minority groups is to (briefly) question the assumption that these states can resolve—as opposed to postpone—ethnic conflict. But the experience of at least some Asian states suggests otherwise. In Singapore, since the ethnic wars of the early to mid 1960s, various nation-building measures centered on the promotion of the English language seem to have reduced tensions between ethnic groups.[20] No doubt economic development has also played a role, but development occurred at least partly because the PAP succeeded in promoting the use of the English language and checking ethnic conflict.

In Hong Kong, the British colonial authorities also suppressed majority culture by encouraging the use of English in primary and secondary schools (and suppressing the Cantonese language, spoken by 97 percent of Hong Kongers). Whatever the advantages of this approach, it is now widely recognized that Cantonese-language education would be a more effective medium of instruction for most Hong Kong students.[21] In response, the government has been trying to limit the number of English-language schools and promote the use of Cantonese in local schools, but many parents object because they want their children to be educated in English.[22] In this sense, the British colonial authorities were too successful in promoting the use of English in schools.

Still, it must be conceded that measures to limit ethnic conflict in less-than-democratic societies do not always succeed. In the worst cases, they can exacerbate conflict, because tensions are allowed to build up and they can explode when the political system opens up. But this is yet another reason to be cautious about democratization! In Taiwan, as noted above, the roles have been reversed and now the mainland Chinese minority feels victimized by discriminatory practices. From the perspective of the local Taiwanese, the special benefits granted to this minority group could not be justified. But arguably the pendulum has swung too far the other way. In public demonstrations, for example, local Taiwanese oppose the use of Mandarin, insisting that speakers articulate their demands exclusively in the local Taiwanese dialect (Chang 1997: 52).

More worrisome, the explosion of ethnic conflict in Indonesia since political liberalization has exposed deep fault lines. In the spring of 1998, long bottled-up antagonism against the relatively wealthy Chinese minority finally resurfaced. Riots destroyed Sino–Indonesian property throughout Indonesia, hundreds were killed in Jakarta's Chinatown, and an unknown number of Chinese women were raped and abused by roving bands of thugs (Freedman 2000: xii).[23] From the perspective of minority groups, this illustrates the risk of depending on personal relationships with unpopular leaders for protection. But it also suggests the need to consider the likely impact of democratization on minority groups.[24] If harsh measures to suppress ethnic conflict in less-than-democratic societies have not reduced tensions, this is yet another reason to worry about the potential impact of democratization.

In sum, nation-building centered on the majority culture in democratic states may pose distinctive threats to vulnerable minority groups.[25] This should not be too controversial; on reflection, I suspect that most persons will accept the weak prodemocracy thesis that democracy is generally advantageous for majorities and sometimes for minorities, but that it may also hinder legitimate minority rights, depending on the context. It only challenges the strong thesis that democracy guarantees minority rights (with a few minor exceptions that should not affect public policy). To the extent that only academics defend the strong thesis, it may not be worth worrying about. However, it remains possible that outside prodemocracy forces act on the strong prodemocracy thesis, perhaps causing real harm to minority groups, so let me say something about the policy implications of the weak prodemocracy thesis.

IMPLICATIONS FOR OUTSIDE PRODEMOCRACY FORCES

Democracy as it is usually understood tends to benefit most members of a political community. Sometimes, it also benefits minority groups who can mobilize and voice their interests in the political system. In some contexts, however, democracy can be detrimental to the interests of minority groups. I have tried to show, by pointing to the experience of several East Asian countries, that democracy may pose special dangers to vulnerable ethnocultural minority groups because nation-building projects centered on the majority culture can marginalize or eliminate expressions of minority traditions and languages.

I have also tried to show that some minority groups in less-than-democratic states of East Asia may benefit from constraints on democracy. The state can promote a form of nation-building that does not privilege the culture of the majority group, and minority groups can strike deals with political elites in a way that might not be possible in relatively democratic states. Also, political elites in less-than-democratic states may find it easier to resist pressure from the local population to enact policies detrimental to the interests of vulnerable minority groups.

In other words, democratization in East Asian states may worsen the situation of minority groups. This would not really undermine the practical case for democracy in those states where military dictators rely on systematic terror to govern most people. But the less-than-democratic states of East Asia often do well at providing political goods like economic growth, political stability, and personal freedom[26]—goods that benefit "the many"—and the fact that minority groups can also benefit from "Asian-style" constraints on democracy is an extra reason for caution.

Once again, this is not to suggest that democratization in an Asian context necessarily harms minority groups. In some cases, minority groups will benefit from the goods traditionally associated with democracy—more opportunities for political participation, greater respect for civil liberties, a better environment for business, and so forth. Still, the real possibility that democratization may harm minority groups means that outside prodemocracy forces (Western governments, international human rights NGOs, etc.) need to investigate the local reality to determine the likely effects of democratization. If it turns out that democracy is likely to be detrimental to minority groups, then outside prodemocracy forces should also pay special attention to measures designed to protect the legitimate interests of minority groups (e.g., giving extra funds to local NGOs that struggle for minority rights).[27] The aim, in other words, would be to minimize, if not eliminate, the negative effects of democratization on minority groups. In the worst cases, however, it could be that democratization would result in serious harm to minority groups, no matter what is done from the outside. This might require outside prodemocracy forces to admit that democracy may not be appropriate in that particular context. In such cases, they should pack up their bags and return in more propitious times.

NOTES

I would like to thank Susan Henders for helpful comments and Jenny Lam for outstanding research assistance. My work on this chapter was supported by a grant from the Research Grants Council of the Hong Kong Special Administrative Region, China, on *The Theory and Practice of Human Rights in Mainland China, Hong Kong, and Taiwan: A Comparative Study.*

1. See, e.g., Article 25 of the United Nations International Covenant on Civil and Political Rights (1966).

2. It is possible to define democracy in such a way that it secures minority rights in its very definition, but such terminological sleights of hand will not help us to shed light on and/or resolve conflicts between the majoritarian tendencies of democracy and minority rights in the real world.

3. This section expands my earlier discussion in Bell (1996).

4. In other ways, however, the Japanese government does recognize the *Buraku* problem—the Law on Special Measures for *Buraku* Improvement Projects, intended to improve the housing, health, and education of the *Burukumin*, was passed in 1969 and remained in force until 1997. Much remains to be done, however. The Fundamental Law for *Buraku* Liberation (first drafted in 1985) "has still not come to pass, yet it is this law which, perhaps more than any of the others, would set the platform for what could become a practical implementation of government assurances over the last decade that *Buraku* problems must be addressed and solved" (McLauchlan 1993: 6).

5. It is worth noting, however, that in a different context even the Chinese government concedes that minority groups with legitimate aspirations for autonomy need not be defined in terms of language or ethnicity. In the case of Hong Kong, the Chinese government has officially implemented a "one country, two systems" political proposal for postcolonial rule. What defines group particularity in this case is shared attachment to the rule of law and experience with a capitalist economic system and other legacies of colonialism, not shared language or ethnicity. The case of Macau is similar.

6. The KMT did, however, reserve certain political posts for native Taiwanese. The mayorships of Taipei and Kaohsiung, for example, were traditionally reserved for native Taiwanese (Ge 1991: 173).

7. As Laliberté discusses later, Taiwan has avoided violent ethnonationalism and other particularly serious forms of intergroup conflict.

8. There are other tensions not discussed in this chapter. For example, democracy can fail to protect (and may actually harm) the interests of foreign resident minority groups. I discuss this tension, with reference to the case of Filipina domestic helpers in Hong Kong and Singapore, in Bell (2001).

9. More precisely, Kymlicka argues that his account of justice *between* ethnocultural groups (requiring equality between groups, which can justify special protection for vulnerable minority groups) is applicable in the East Asian context. He recognizes that the part of his theory dealing with justice *within* groups—individual members of minority groups should have the freedom to question and revise group traditions and practices—may presume a conception of the importance of freedom and autonomy that is not shared in East Asia (Kymlicka 1998: 3).

10. Quoted in Han, Fernandez, and Tan (1998: 134). It is worth noting, however, that native tongues (including Chinese) were not entirely suppressed, as they could still be taught as second languages: "We needed a common language. We solved this by encouraging everyone to learn two languages, English and the mother tongue as a second language. English is not any group's mother tongue, so no one gained any advantage" (Lee 2000: 5).

11. Neher and Marlay (1995: 80).

12. Compared to Suharto's Indonesia, not the present regime in that country.

13. A reminder that the term "democracy" here refers to free and fair competitive elections along with the associated freedoms of the press and association.

14. According to Abdullahi An-Na'im (1999), however, the Malaysian government's decision to ban the group was not in accordance with the essence of Islam.

15. It could be argued that *Al-Arqam* was a minority group in conflict with the majority of Muslims, but part of the problem (from the government's viewpoint) was precisely that this group was gaining in popularity and could conceivably have become the majority had it not been banned.

16. Once again, the comparison is with Suharto's Indonesia.

17. The increasing participation of the Malays is also the product of the New Economic Policy (implemented in 1971) that granted special privileges to Malays in business ownership, investment incentives, and employment quotas. From 1971 to 1991, Malay ownership of Malaysia's capital increased from 3 to 20 percent (Neher and Marlay 1995: 100).

18. One might also ask how Kymlicka distinguishes between "the exception" and "the rule."

19. Even a single "exception" should lead to caution in that particular country and (less obviously) in other countries with similar characteristics.

20. In fact, the PAP may have been too successful for its own good. The main justification for less-than-democratic rule has been the need to preserve political stability in an ethnically volatile social and political context. But the PAP's strong-arm measures are less justified now that the various groups are less likely (compared to the 1960s) to engage in communal violence. A cynical view is that the PAP is deliberately refanning the flames of ethnic conflict (e.g., by proposing ethnic-based welfare schemes and filling the pages of local newspapers with horror stories of ethnic conflict from around the world) in order to further justify constraints on democracy.

21. Lin Fengmei, "Zhongwen zuoda kaosheng chengji jiao jia" ("Answering exam questions in Chinese leads to better grades"), *Ming Pao*, 4 November 2000.

22. Parents object because they believe that English language skills increase the likelihood of landing high-paying jobs, but Ruth Hayhoe, former Head of Hong Kong's Institute of Education, argues that even English language skills can be improved if courses other than English are carried out in Cantonese because English-

language education tends to demoralize students and negatively affects their performance in school, including English classes (conversation with Ruth Hayhoe).

23. Subsequent democratization, however, does seem to have benefited the Chinese minority to a certain extent, as cultural symbols such as dragon dances and open celebration of the Lunar New Year are allowed for the first time in years. However, "the window of political opportunity has offered little. . . . Campaign promises have not been fulfilled. After more than a year, parliament has done almost nothing to address a stack of antidiscriminatory bills and abolish 62 laws seen as racist" (Dini Djalal, "Empty Party Promises," *Far Eastern Economic Review*, 30 November 2000).

24. It is worth keeping in mind the broad definition of an ethnocultural group noted above. If the definition of an ethnocultural group is restricted to language and/or race, the Indonesian Chinese may not count as a minority. The harsh measures to curb the expression of Chinese identity under Suharto's rule did "succeed" (to a substantial extent) in assimilating the Chinese into the Indonesian language and culture. But in the minds of many Indonesians, they were still "Chinese" and, rich or poor, they were targeted by ethnic programs in 1998.

25. Note that my critique has been directed at Kymlicka's argument to the contrary, but I have not specifically questioned Kymlicka's view that justice requires equality between ethnocultural groups in the state. I challenge such views in Bell (2001, esp. 27–28), where it is argued that inequality between groups may be justified if this benefits the least well-off minority groups and/or inequality creates opportunities for relatively deprived groups in other societies to improve their lives. For an interesting discussion of "Confucian" critiques of Kymlicka's argument for equality between ethnocultural groups, see He (n.d.).

26. With a few exceptions, like Burma and North Korea, that I did not deal with here.

27. It is important, needless to say, to weigh the advantages of such policy proposals against their disadvantages. If promoting minority group rights would only marginally benefit the relevant group(s), but have the effect of unnecessarily politicizing ethnicity and undermining the establishment of cross-cutting ties between members of different groups in the political community, then such proposals may not be desirable.

REFERENCES

An-Na'im, Abdullahi. 1999. "The Cultural Mediation of Human Rights: The Al-Arqam Case in Malaysia." In *The East Asian Challenge for Human Rights*, eds. Joanne Bauer and Daniel Bell. New York: Cambridge University Press.

Bell, Daniel A. 1996. "Minority Rights: On the Importance of Local Knowledge." *Dissent* (Summer): 36–41.

———. 2001. "Equal Rights for Foreign Resident Workers: The Case of Filipina Domestic Workers in Hong Kong and Singapore." *Dissent* (Fall): 26–34.

———. 2002. *The Theory and Practice of Human Rights in Mainland China, Hong Kong, and Taiwan: A Comparative Study*. Research Grants Council of the Hong Kong Special Administrative Region, China (HKU/7129/98H).

Chang, Maukuei. 1994. "Toward an Understanding of the Sheng-chi Wen-ti in Taiwan." In *Ethnicity in Taiwan*, eds. Chen Chung-min, Chuang Ying-chang, and Huang Shu-min. Taipei: Institute of Ethnology, Academia Sinica.

———. 1997. "Taiwan de zhengzhi zhuanxin yu zhengshi de 'zuqunhua' guocheng" ("The political transformation of Taiwan and the emergence of politically significant ethnic identity"). *Jiaoshou Luntan Zhuankan* 4.

Christopher, Robert C. 1983. *The Japanese Mind*. Tokyo: Charles E. Tuttle Company.

de Vos, George, and Hiroshi Wagatsuma. 1967. "Introduction." In *Japan's Invisible Race: Caste in Culture and Personality*, eds. George de Vos and Hiroshi Wagatsuma. Berkeley: University of California Press.

Dreyer, June Teufel. 1976. *China's Forty Millions: Minority Nationalities and National Integration in the People's Republic of China*. Cambridge, Mass.: Harvard University Press.

Freedman, Amy. 2000. *Political Participation and Ethnic Minorities: Chinese Overseas in Malaysia, Indonesia, and the United States*. New York: Routledge.

Ge, Yong Guang. 1991. *Wenhua duoyuan zhuyi yu guojia zhenghe (Cultural pluralism and national integration)*. Zhengzhong Shuyu. Taipei.

Gurr, Ted. 1995. "Communal Conflicts and Global Security." *Current History* 94, no. 592 (May): 212–17.

Han, Fook Kwang, Warren Fernandez, and Sumiko Tan. 1998. *Lee Kuan Yew: The Man and His Ideas*. Singapore: Times Editions.

He, Baogang. n.d. "A Confucian Response to Kymlicka's Theory of Minority Rights: A Dialogue between Confucianism and Liberalism over the Question of Non-Assimilation." Unpublished manuscript.

Honig, Emily. 1992. *Creating Chinese Ethnicity: Subei People in Shanghai, 1850–1980*. New Haven, Conn.: Yale University Press.

Huntington, Samuel. 1993. "American Democracy in Relation to Asia." In *Democracy and Capitalism: Asian and American Perspectives*, eds. Robert Bartley et al. Singapore: Institute of Southeast Asian Studies.

Kymlicka, Will. 1998. "The Future of the Nation-State." *Fifth Kobe Lectures*. December.

Lee, Kuan Yew. 1994. *The Singapore Story*. Singapore: Prentice Hall.

———. 2000. "For Third World Leaders: Hope or Despair?" *Collins International Fellowship Lecture*. John F. Kennedy School of Government, Harvard University (17 October).

Mackerras, Colin. 1994. *China's Minorities: Integration and Modernization in the Twentieth Century*. Hong Kong: Oxford University Press.

McLauchlan, Alastair. 1993. "Introduction." In *An Introduction to the Buraku Issue: Questions and Answers*, ed. Suehiro Kitaguchi. trans. Alastair McLauchlan. Richmond, Surrey: Japan Library.

Mill, John Stuart. 1975. "Representative Government." In *Three Essays*. Oxford: Oxford University Press.

Nathan, Andrew. 1993. "Chinese Democracy: The Lessons of Failure." *Journal of Contemporary China* 4: 3–13.

Neher, Clark, and Ross Marlay. 1995. *Democracy and Development in Southeast Asia*. Boulder, Colo.: Westview Press.

Van Dyke, Vernon. 1995. "The Individual, the State, and Ethnic Communities in Political Theory." In *The Rights of Minority Cultures*, ed. Will Kymlicka. Oxford: Oxford University Press.

Zakaria, Fareed. 1997. "The Rise of Illiberal Democracy." *Foreign Affairs* 76, no. 6 (November/December): 22–43.

3

The Democratization of National Identity

David Brown

Attempted transitions to democracy, and outbursts of ethnic conflict, seem to coincide sufficiently frequently to raise the question as to whether ethnic tensions promote or inhibit democratization, and whether democratization promotes or inhibits ethnic tensions. The answer, as always, is "It depends . . ." but on what does it depend?

The purpose here is to examine some aspects of this issue in the Asian context. The case of Indonesia will be used for purposes of illustration, but the intention is to develop a framework argument of wider relevance. This argument suggests that democratization should be understood as a transition in the character of national identity, and that the stability or otherwise of this transition depends crucially on the impact of democratization upon personalist (patrimonial and patron–client) political networks. Rather than following Daniel Bell's suggestion (in chapter 2) that democratization implies a nation-building centered on the prioritization of the majority ethnoculture, it is argued here that democratization involves the uneven spread of potentially incompatible ideas of individual rights, majority rights, and minority rights. These ideas are embodied, respectively, in visions of civic nationalism, ethnocultural nationalism, and multicultural nationalism. Political stability and national unity, thus, depend crucially on the capacity both of restructured patrimonial alliances and of nascent civic institutions, to contain the resultant tensions between the three types of nationalist vision.

The discussion is prompted by recent events in Indonesia, including both Acehnese and West Papuan demands for secession,[1] and also ethnic rioting in the Moluccas, Kalimantan, and Sulawesi. As Jacques Bertrand's careful examination of these issues shows later, the relaxation of authoritarian rule unleashed ethnic tensions, which had been suppressed under the Suharto

43

regime. Moreover, the resultant crisis of Indonesian national identity seems quite capable of destabilizing and undermining the process of transition to democracy. However, there is some uncertainty as to why this might be so. Sometimes it is suggested, from a primordialist perspective, that "atavistic" ethnic identities are inevitably stronger than are ties to an intrinsically weak sense of Indonesian nationhood. At other times, as with Bertrand's contribution, a more instrumentalist analysis focuses on the options for the advancement of ethnic minority interests, which are opened by the new uncertainties accompanying the removal of authoritarian state controls. The suggestion here, however, is that it is neither the politics of primordial instinct nor of rational instrumentalism that explains the relationship between ethnic tensions and democratization. Rather, the relationship is explainable in constructivist terms, as the politics of contending ideological visions of community.

A four-stage argument can be initially summarized as follows. First, theories of democratization differ in the explanation of its causes, but they concur in depicting it as a transition toward the institutionalized rule of law (Merkel 1998). It is certainly the case that the building of strong, effective administrative, electoral, party, judicial, and other institutions of government constitutes the aim and end point of the transition to democracy. But the process of transition itself is characterized by the existence of government institutions that necessarily have not (at least not yet) attained sufficient capacity to ensure the effective implementation of government policies responsive to civil society demands, or sufficient legitimacy to mobilize civil society support for those policies. In cases such as Indonesia, where democratization begins with the fracturing of a personalist, patrimonial elite under pressure from below, the process of transition involves the ousting of the most corrupt elements of the old patrimonial elite and their replacement by those individuals who appear less corrupt, and who have hitherto been on the fringes of the ruling elite.[2] The change of patrons at the top serves to fracture preexisting patron–client linkages, but this does not signal the abandonment of such patron–client politics, which permeate the institutions of government. Rather, corrupt patrons associated with the old, unresponsive regime are replaced by new, more responsive patrons. Thus the first argument of this chapter is that the democratization process might involve, not the replacement of patrimonial rule by institutional rule, but rather the restructuring of patrimonialism.

Second, this restructuring of patrimonialism involves more than just the replacement of authoritarian patrons by responsive patrons. It also involves a fundamental shift in the way in which patronage is legitimated. Authoritarian patrimonialism seeks legitimacy by depicting the patrimonial ruler as the embodiment of a collectivist national will, as defined by the regime.[3] Democratization involves the emergence of new visions of national community, which are articulated in various civil society sites and depict the nation less as a unified collectivity and more as an arena for the exercise of individual, majority, and minority rights and freedoms. Thus, the second argument of the chapter is that the democratization process can be understood as the restructuring of national identity away from the authoritarian and collectivist nationalist visions articulated by the previous state elites and toward more democratic and pluralist visions of the nation.

The shift from authoritarian to democratic forms of national identity is, however, complicated by the fact that there will exist competing visions of the nation. The civic nationalist vision is of a community of equal citizens; the ethnocultural nationalist vision portrays the community as built around a high-status ethnocultural core; and the multicultural nationalist vision is of a community able to protect the integrity of its various ethnic and ethnoregional minorities. Each of these nationalist visions may be articulated either in an authoritarian-collectivist form or in a democratic-pluralist form. In some countries these three different visions have never been clearly distinguished and disentwined, whereas in others they seem to come directly in confrontation with each other in ways that are politically destabilizing.[4] This is significant because it indicates that, for democratization to succeed, the articulation of new pluralist nationalist visions (civic, ethnocultural, and multicultural) must proceed in such a way as to avoid a clash of visions. The fragility of the democratization process is thus explainable in terms of the potential for democratization to disentwine these divergent visions, engendering their confrontation.

The question thus arises as to the relationship between these two facets of the democratization process (i.e., the restructuring of patrimonialism and the restructuring of national identity), the focus of the third argument made here. It is frequently suggested that democratization undermines national unity in that it involves "lifting the lid" on preexisting ethnic tensions that authoritarian rule had suppressed. But it is also recognized that democratization can facilitate the negotiation and bargaining that might resolve preexisting confrontations between ethnic minorities and the state. It will be argued here that the patrimonial politics of the transition from authoritarian rule can facilitate the emergence of new pluralist ethnocultural and multicultural visions of the nation, with the tensions between the two potentially ameliorated by the growth of a new liberal version of civic nationalism. It is, however, the inhibitory impact of patrimonialism upon this emergent liberal civic nationalism that poses the main threat to the democratization process. If the articulation of a liberal civic nationalism is inhibited by the weakness of the civic institutions of the state and civil society and if, at the same time, liberal civic nationalism is not espoused by the influential individual patrons who dominate the politics of transition, then it will fail to act as a buffer between majority-focused ethnocultural nationalism and minority-focused multicultural nationalism. The interweaving of the three will fail. The result, in such a case, would be that ethnic minorities that had initially embraced democratization as promising them autonomy within a multicultural nation would confront an ethnic majority that had seen democratization as promising them enhanced status within an ethnocultural nation. As ethnic minorities come to perceive that the nation was being captured by its ethnic majority, they would begin to seek an escape. The result would be ethnic confrontation characterized by a clash between the incompatible nationalist ideologies adhered to by the ethnic majority and the ethnic minority.

Fourthly and finally, although patrimonialism might help to engender such ethnic tensions, it might also function in other ways to mitigate (or at least complicate) the resultant conflict. One of the key characteristics of patrimonial politics is the proliferation of factional rivalries. Such factionalism occurs when patrons compete amongst themselves for resources and power; when patrons employ "divide and rule" strategies to exert control over potential clients; and when clients become rivals in their search for patronage. This feature of patrimonial politics means that the tendency toward confrontation between ethnic majority and ethnic minorities outlined above is likely to be cross-cut, and, therefore, potentially diffused and ameliorated, by the impact of patrimonial politics at the center on the factionalization of ethnic minority nationalist movements. While the resultant factional disunity of such movements may inhibit attempts at central control in the short term, it may nevertheless serve to split the more radical secessionists from their more moderate multiculturalist allies and supporters, so as to promote the longer-term de-escalation of ethnic conflict.

The purpose of outlining such a theoretical model of democratization is not to provide a procrustean bed into which the politics of any one country or region can be pushed, but rather to offer a conceptual language that can help explain one aspect of political diversity. In order to develop and specify how the politics of transition might be examined in terms of tensions between changes in patrimonial politics and changes in national identity, the chapter will briefly refer to the case of contemporary Indonesia (and within Indonesia, the case of Aceh). Nevertheless, the focus here is more on the conceptual framework than on the Indonesian fabric. In various Asian countries, elements of democracy coexist with elements of patrimonial politics. Contentions between differing visions of national identity remain unresolved. Variations in the behavior of patrons and in the bases for national identity generate different political outcomes in each country. An examination of the structural features of the relationship between patrimonialism and nationalism might begin to elucidate such differences.

DEMOCRATIZATION AND
THE RESTRUCTURING OF PATRIMONIALISM

In the case of Indonesia, the democratization process began with student protests against the corruption and nepotism associated with the personalist patrimonial rule of Suharto. The fall of Suharto in May 1998 was then the signal for grassroots protests throughout the country demanding the removal of local government and village officials for having acted, like Suharto, as patrimonial rulers. From the outset the demands of the protesters were for fundamental reforms that would replace such patrimonial rule with new, open democratic and constitutional government. In such circumstances it is not surprising that democratization should be portrayed, by observers as well as participants, as the removal of patrimonial rule and its replacement by government based on strong, transparent, democratic institutions. From this perspective, the survival or revival of patrimonial politics would appear to be the key evidence that the democratization process had failed.

But there are two important doubts about this characterization of the democratization process. First, even if it is the case that democracy should be understood as the replacement of personalist rule by institutionalist rule, this would mean only that the formation of strong, effective, and legitimate democratic institutions was the consequential outcome of the democratization process. The actual process of transition toward this end-goal might well involve—not the removal of patrimonialism—but rather the replacement of one set of patrimonial rulers by another set, the shift from authoritarian patrons to more responsive patrons, and a change in the type of institutional framework within which patrimonialism functioned. In the Indonesian case, the fall of Suharto was precipitated by the fracturing of his patrimonial elite, the subsequent rivalries between individuals for the succession, the personalist deals that produced first the handover to Habibie, then after the elections the accession of Wahid, and finally the ousting of Wahid and his replacement by Megawati.[5]

Second, it is not even certain that a successfully completed transition to democracy would be characterized by the removal, or even the significant reduction, of patrimonial politics. This is implying more than merely the observation that patron–client relationships function within democratic institutions in all established democracies despite the constraints on favoritism, bribery, and nepotism. It is suggesting that there might be some versions of democracy that rely precisely on patrimonial practices for the building of party alliances, for the vibrancy of political competition, and for the resolution of leadership and succession problems. This has been suggested, for example, as regards democratic politics in South Korea (Jacobs 1985). The implication is that patrimonialism may take differing forms in that the transaction in which individual leaders promise to promote the interests of client communities in return for their political support is one with the capacity to generate both authoritarian rule and democratic politics, depending in part on the balance of power between patrons and clients.

The proposition is that, in the absence of the legitimate institutions of established democracy, patron–client networks remain the only means (other than mass action) through which the powerless can seek access to power. They are, thus, the only means through which the democratization process can be promoted. Even though the institutions of democracy (the rule of law, elections, political parties, etc.) may be introduced in the early stages of transition, it seems likely that the effective functioning of these institutions will depend in part upon whether they can build upon the nondemocratic clientelist structures already deeply embedded in the society. Democratization might begin with the removal of some of the authoritarian patrimonial elite. However, its further development might depend partly on attempts by other members of that elite to retain influence as more responsive patrons and partly on attempts by the hitherto excluded masses to gain access to new patrons. In both cases, patron–client politics occur within the nascent institutions of democracy, rather than being replaced by those institutions.

For analytical purposes, we can distinguish between three types of patrimonialism: (1) *exclusionary patrimonialism* in which a patrimonial leader appoints subordinate patrons who owe their positions to him or her and who are, in turn, unresponsive to mass demands and indeed seek to ensure the removal of the masses from political participation and from resource benefits; (2) *petitionary patrimonialism* in which patrons rely for their position partly on the patrimonial leader, but also partly upon the support of a mass clientele. They thus promote a petitionary political culture, whereby dependent clienteles who display political support for their patrons are rewarded with resource benefits; and (3) *mobilizational patrimonialism*, in which politics takes the form of rival patrons competing for mass support. In this protodemocratic form of patrimonial politics, the power balance shifts so that communal clienteles have some choice as to their patronage linkage with central government and can choose the patron most responsive to their claims.

If patrimonialism does have the capacity to shift from the authoritarian exclusion of the masses to their political mobilization, this does not imply that such a restructuring will be either inevitable or smooth. The restructuring of patrimonialism does not evolve; it has to be deliberately constructed. The removal of authoritarian patrons necessarily involves the fracturing of existing chains of patron–client linkages, thus disrupting the mutual ties of personal obligation upon which effective governmental–societal linkages depend. It is, thus, intrinsic to the patrimonial politics of transition that there will be areas where old patron–client linkages have been fractured, but new patron–client linkages have not yet been formed. To the extent that effective democratic and administrative institutions remain weak, and patron–client linkages become disrupted, central government control over the activities of local-level administrators, and its ability to respond to the concerns of local-level community leaders, will tend to be reduced. It is only when the new governing elites manage to build new patron–client linkages with mass clienteles, that responsive, more democratic government can develop. Moreover, this is contingent upon the success of the alliance strategies both of clients seeking patrons and of patrons seeking clients. In the Indonesian case, the impact of the fracturing of patron–client linkages has been most politically significant in the institutions of the armed forces and was manifested, for example, in the problems faced by the Wahid government in its attempts to control or replace military officers with administrative positions in the regions.

Of course, by their very nature, patrimonial structures based on personal loyalty and favoritism transgress the democratic norms of institutionalized universalism. This is one of the reasons why transitional democracies so frequently attract allegations of corruption from Western observers. But the extent to which patrimonialism and democratization are in tension with each other does vary. Their relationship depends in part upon the character of the political community within which the restructuring of patrimonialism is attempted. Democratization implies a change in the understanding of political community. To examine this, we need to turn to the idea of national identity.

DEMOCRATIZATION AND THE
RESTRUCTURING OF NATIONAL IDENTITY

The idea that a group of people might constitute a "nation" with some right to political autonomy sometimes rests mainly on the claim that they have common ethnic ancestry and similar ethnocultural attributes, and sometimes mainly on the claim that they occupy a particular territory and have a common pride in the public institutions and public way of life associated with that territory. These two bases for national identity are usually referred to, respectively, as cultural (or ethnocultural) nationalism and civic nationalism. Ethnocultural nationalism depicts the nation as a community of (ethno)cultural sameness, while civic nationalism depicts the nation as a community of equal citizens. Until recently, it had been assumed that all claims to nationhood would employ one or both of these ideas. However, in the last few decades, the tensioned relationship between the two has generated a new basis for national identity, that of multiculturalism. Multicultural nationalism depicts the nation as a community made up of diverse ethnic segments, all united by their common commitment to the public institutions of the state, which guarantee their equal status. These three different visions of community refer to the objective facts of territory, race, language, religion, and the like in each country. However, they are not in any direct sense derived from or determined by such facts. Rather, it is the ambiguities and complexities of the diverse potential identity markers in each country that sustain the development of the differing ideological interpretations of nationhood.

Countries, nevertheless, vary as to which of the three forms of national identity (civic, ethnocultural, and multicultural) is dominant, as well as in the degree of political tension that exists between proponents of the three. The important point is that countries also vary as to whether their national identity is articulated primarily by state elites seeking to inhibit or close popular debate or primarily within a civil society seeking to promote such debate. This is significant because the character of national identity depends upon the purpose for which it is being articulated.

The defining feature of authoritarian regimes is not their reliance on coercion so much as their concern to justify coercion by the claim that they constitute the sole legitimate articulator and defender of the common interest or will of the people as a whole.[6] They vary markedly in the way they define that will: to restore order, to promote religious virtue, to pursue economic development, and so on. However, in each case they depict themselves as the experts who can deliver what the singular entity, "the people," want or need. They thereby identify the interests of the whole community with the interests of themselves as the elite.

Nationalism is, thus, particularly useful as a legitimating ideology for authoritarian regimes because it allows them to depict the diverse individuals and groups within their society as comprising one community with one will. The use of coercion against oppositionist individuals or minority groups within the society is thus legitimated by the Rousseauian argument that the pursuit of partial vested interests threatens to subvert the sovereignty of the collective national will.

This can be illustrated in the Indonesian case. The disunity that accompanied Indonesian agitation against Dutch and Japanese colonialism meant that those political leaders who sought to lead the emergent nation were unable to portray themselves as merely reflecting an established consensual national will arising from the common Islamic culture of the overwhelming majority.[7] They, therefore, promoted a version of Indonesian national identity that did not depict it is as cohering around a majority core. Instead they stressed its fragmentation. They emphasized that Indonesia consisted of diverse Islamic, Hindu, Buddhist, Catholic, and Protestant communities and hundreds of different language communities. Once the nation had been defined as fragmented in this way, it followed that it could only be unified from above by an authoritarian regime that could reconcile the conflicting demands and interests by rising above them. Power was depicted in Javanese terms as the ability to transform disunity into oneness (Anderson 1972; Jones 1995). The nationalist leaders therefore asserted a *Pancasila* vision of national identity that superimposed an ideological unity on the social and political diversity and that marginalized Islam.[8] This policy of stressing the centrifugal fragmentation of the country, rather than pointing to its centripetal core, was undoubtedly successful in legitimating an increasingly authoritarian Sukarno regime and, subsequently, the Suharto regime too, both of them lacking close ties to their mass constituencies. *Pancasila* was interpreted and employed by these regimes to reinvent Indonesia so that the ethnically fragmented society could be depicted in monistic terms. Indonesia's authoritarian regimes portrayed this collectivism in three overlapping ways: firstly, as a unitary civic nation whose common good demanded limitations on individual citizenship rights; secondly, as an ethnocultural nation built historically around its status core, the secular, *priyayi* (aristocratic), Javanese elites; and, thirdly, as a multicultural nation whose very diversity demanded corporatist management. "Unity in diversity" (*Bhinneka Tunggal Ika*) thereby became the ideological slogan, which justified administrative centralization.

But nationalism is not inherently collectivist in this way. Indeed, as Liah Greenfeld has argued, nationalism began as a doctrine that rejected the idea that there was a mass of people within the society who deserved lesser status and rights than those accorded to an elite (Greenfeld 1992). In her examination of civic nationalism, she shows how it developed as the novel idea that each and every individual member of the community deserved the superior status that had hitherto been granted only to the elite. The nation was defined as the community of equal individuals, each having the same status, liberties, rights, and duties of citizenship by virtue of his or her membership in the nation. Thus, rather than legitimating authoritarian rule, this individualist civic nationalism provides the basis for liberal democracy. Moreover, the distinction applies equally to ethnocultural nationalism and to multicultural nationalism, in that they can each be articulated in either an authoritarian-collectivist or a democratic-pluralistic form. It is thus possible to denote the democratization process as a shift of national identity along each of the three axes.

Ethnocultural nationalism indicates that full status and membership in the national community be given only to those possessing the required ethnic attributes. In its authoritarian form, this is interpreted to mean that the state treats the other residents of its territory as second-class citizens, either excluding them from the full rights and status of citizenship, or employing the state machinery to enforce assimilation. In the Indonesian case, authoritarian ethnocultural nationalism employed mythologizations of history to depict the Javanese as the ethnic core, while recruitment into elite positions came, to some degree, to be conditional on "Javanisation."[9] In the democratic version of ethnocultural nationalism, the nation is still defined in terms of the

culture of its ethnic core, but that culture is itself now defined in such a way
as to make assimilation voluntary, attractive, and feasible. Thus racial definitions of the ethnic core tend to give way to linguistic, religious, and cultural
definitions, which are more open to assimilation; and minority definitions of
the ethnic core begin to give way to majority definitions. Moreover, instead
of relying on the state machinery to force the pace of assimilation, the state
relies more on the self-interests of ethnic minorities to acquire the high-status
values of the ethnic majority, or on the assimilationist implications of intermarriage. In the Indonesian case, the democratic form of ethnocultural
nationalism involves the depiction of the nation as identified by an Islamic
majority, which is portrayed as a diverse religio-cultural core able to accommodate the heterogeneity of Islam and to respect the rights of non-Muslims.[10]
However, the pluralism of the majority-based ethnoculture means that democratization involves the articulation of both tolerant and intolerant strands
of Islam, and there is no inevitability that democratic pluralistic tolerance will
be victorious. The only inevitability is that contentions develop between the
tolerant and intolerant strands of Islam: "all of Indonesian politics is in flux
now . . . and Islamic factions are shifting and rolling as they seek a new place
in a political order."[11] The contentions arise because democratization generates the rising expectations of members of the Islamic majority that the government will at last give full recognition and status to Islamic values and interests as the core ingredient of the country's national identity.

In the case of *multicultural nationalism*, the authoritarian version is that
in which the state creates institutions that legitimate each of the diverse ethnic identities within the country, but does so in order to facilitate their centralized corporatist control and to emasculate and co-opt ethnic minority
elites.[12] In its democratic version, by contrast, multicultural nationalism involves the state seeking to reflect the ethnic diversity of the society in its own
institutional structures, precisely so that the distribution of power and resources can be on a decentralized and fair "ethnic arithmetic" basis. In post-
Suharto Indonesia, this was reflected in Wahid's devolutions to the
provinces; in the reopening of debate concerning the possibility of federalism and of further forms of autonomy for West Papua and Aceh; and in the
reassuring of Christian minorities that their rights will be respected under the
new regime. The appeal of such a multicultural nationalist vision is also evident in Burma, where ethnic minorities seek ethnically fair membership,
rather than asserting the goal of ethnocultural secession.

Finally, the *civic nationalist* vision stresses that all citizens are granted
equal status irrespective of ethnic attributes, on the sole condition that they
grant loyalty to the public institutions of the territorial community. Civic nationalism is sometimes depicted as being merely a camouflage for the promotion of the interests and values of ethnocultural majorities. But this seems
to be mistaken in that it takes for granted that the majority mobilized in de-

mocracy is necessarily mobilized on an ethnic basis, or that the language adopted for public affairs necessarily promotes ethnic domination. It is certainly true that the civic ideal of ethnic neutrality may be as rarely achieved as is the ethnocultural ideal of ethnic exclusivity. However, that does not prevent it from offering a powerful and distinct vision and from engendering public policies that, in various countries, inhibit ethnic discrimination and enhance transethnic civic integration.

In authoritarian civic nationalism, state elites claim that they themselves are the objects of patriotic loyalty, and that it is they who articulate the true will of the collective nation.[13] In its democratic version, civic nationalism celebrates the autonomy of the pluralistic civil society and calls for the equal rights of each citizen to be protected by the state through universalistic, ethnically color-blind laws and institutions. It was indeed the call by students for such civic rights that triggered the Indonesian transition.[14] Nevertheless, as will be noted, it is the promotion of this liberal civic nationalist vision of individual citizenship rights that constitutes the most problematic aspect of the democratization process.

Once the democratization process is mapped in this way (as the change of national identity, in its civic, ethnocultural, and multicultural types, from authoritarian to democratic forms), it becomes clearer why the democratization process is so politically fragile. Even if an authoritarian regime had been able to articulate and promote a national ideology that interwove civic, ethnocultural, and multicultural threads together (as was attempted in the *Pancasila* ideology in Indonesia), the process of democratization is liable to see the unraveling of those threads as different political actors begin articulating differing conceptualizations of the democratic nation. While proponents of civic nationalism advocate a politics that disregards ethnic difference, those of ethnocultural nationalism stress the need to give higher priority to the cultural values of the majority ethnic community, while those of multicultural nationalism advocate the rights of ethnic minorities. Nevertheless, the tensions between these different visions of a democratized national identity might be contained within the emergent democratic contention. In order to examine why this is sometimes the case, but not always, we need to examine the political forms of democratization.

NATIONAL IDENTITY AND PATRIMONIALISM: EXPLAINING ETHNIC CONFLICT

This begins with consideration of the impact of patrimonial politics upon the various visions of national identity, and thence upon the incidence of ethnic conflict. In general terms, ethnic conflict occurs when linguistic, religious, or racial minority groups are politically mobilized by ideologies of community identity that counterpose "their" vision of ethnic nationalism with the vision of state nationalism identified with an ethnic majority. The development of such community consciousness on the part of both ethnic minorities and ethnic majorities may proceed in two ways. First, it may occur when ordinary citizens adopt for themselves the "categories of identity" employed by political elites seeking to mobilize support. The clients follow the lead of their ethnic entrepreneurial patrons and adopt the patrons' categories of identity as their own, along with the patrons' ideological diagnoses and prescriptions. Alternatively, communal identities may arise initially from grassroots perceptions of economic power or status disparities between those belonging to differing cultural groups. Political elites who wish to gain authority and support amongst such groups may then have little alternative but to articulate, reflect, and promote these preexisting or nascent identities. In the first case, the clients respond to the ethnic ideologies of their patrons; in the second, the patrons respond to the ethnic consciousness of their clients. The distinction simply indicates that democratization, understood as involving a shift in the balance of power between patrons and clients, also implies some shift from an elite-initiated politicization of ethnicity to a client-initiated ethnicity. This has immediate implications for changes in the character of ethnocultural nationalism and multicultural nationalism. The argument here is that patrimonialism has the potential flexibility to facilitate the shift toward more democratic forms of both.

Patrimonialism and Ethnocultural Nationalism

The state-initiated *Pancasila* portrayal of Indonesia's national identity, which seemed to have achieved widespread currency, was immediately brought into question by the fall of Suharto. The rise of democratic expectations accompanying his fall, and the jockeying for power by various previously marginalized Islamic elites, combined to generate the grassroots demand that the dominance of Islam in Indonesian society should at last be reflected in its politics and state. Habibie, Amien Rais, and Wahid tried at various times to ride this wave. The assumption was that any leaders who replaced Suharto would need to show their responsiveness to the values of the Muslim majority that had felt marginalized by the previous regime's portrayals of national identity.[15] The implication was that a democratic Indonesia would need to be one whose national identity was able to reflect, rather than marginalize, its Islamic core, instead of political elites influencing and shaping the national consciousness of their clienteles so as to promote the high status of one ethnic segment, the Javanese (45 percent) ethnolinguistic community. It further meant that the success of a democratic Indonesia would depend upon the patrimonial skills of individual Islamic leaders, acting as political patrons, in building alliances between the various Islamic constituencies.

This offers a basis for national unity in that it provides the language of morality for almost all the population (90 percent). It also provides a potential basis for pluralistic democracy in that it contains diverse groups and, in its *Nahdlatul Ulama*[16] manifestation, seemed to offer a promise of tolerant and open government. Thus, if the politics of transition has a patrimonial character, the concern of new patrons to mobilize majority support can promote the widespread articulation of visions of more democratic and pluralistic forms of ethnocultural national identity.

Patrimonialism and Multicultural Nationalism

In its authoritarian form, patrimonial elite recruitment promotes a centralization of power that is then camouflaged by the legitimating claim that the co-opting of minority elites "proves" the multicultural "unity in diversity" basis for national identity. With democratization, patrimonial politics shift from co-optation to accommodation. Such accommodation was evident in Indonesia's electoral politics of the mid-1950s, when the parties that competed with each other for power at the center did so by competing for support from local-level communities, promising concessions to local brokers. This meant that ethnic minority communities began to pursue their interests by seeking alliances with the center, promising the political support of their communities in return for promises of increases in resources or autonomy for those communities (Liddle 1970). It was this kind of patrimonial accommodation that led, for example, to the alliance between Acehnese leaders and the *Masjumi* party between 1946 and 1953, with Aceh promising electoral support for *Masjumi* in return for promises of enhanced Acehnese autonomy. This patron–client relationship only broke down in 1953, when *Masjumi* was excluded from Sukarno's cabinet and, thus, was unable to deliver on its autonomy promise. As democracy subsequently weakened in Indonesia, from the late 1950s onward alliances between the governing elites and ethnic minority elites began in most cases to reflect the extension of central controls, rather than responsiveness to ethnic minority grievances.

Indonesia's recent transition from authoritarianism is thus perceived by some as offering a reversal of this centralizing trend and the promise of a new accommodation of ethnic minority claims to enhanced status and autonomy. Proponents of multicultural nationalism, perceiving democratization as offering enhanced minority rights, began to expect evidence of increased status for religious (non-Muslim), ethnic (non-Javanese), and regional (outer islands) communities. In some cases, there was even talk of the possibility of federalism. Initial signals of multicultural decentralization were given by President Habibie's enactment of two regional autonomy laws in 1999 and their implementation in 2001;[17] further moves in this direction were indicated in President Wahid's variously phrased offers of special autonomy for West Papua and Aceh,[18] enacted in Law 21/2001 and Law 18/2001. President Megawati continued the implementation of decentralization, but her decisions to divide West Papua into three provinces and to impose martial law in Aceh reflect her ambivalence on decentralization. The effectiveness and impact of such moves seemed to depend to a significant extent upon the ability of central political elites in search of political support to do deals with minority community leaders seeking resources and autonomy for their communities.

Patrimonialism and Civic Nationalism

It thus seems that the patrimonial politics of transition is at least potentially conducive to the articulation of a new more open and pluralistic ethnocultural vision of the nation, built around the ethnoculture of a largely tolerant majority core. It is also potentially conducive to the expression of a new more decentralized multicultural vision where the nation protects and respects its various ethnic minorities. If democratization is to succeed, then, these two distinct visions of the nation must not become directly counterposed, but be perceived as ambiguously overlapping and potentially compatible. In established democratic countries, the tensions between ethnic majority expectations embodied in ethnocultural nationalism, and ethnic minority expectations embodied in multicultural nationalism, can be somewhat buffered by the strength of civic nationalism. In other words, where state institutions are built primarily on civic norms of citizen equality and individual rights, then the ethnocultural claims to enhanced ethnic majority status, and the multicultural claims to enhanced ethnic minority status, can both be directed toward seeking reforms in those civic institutions, rather than being aimed directly at each other.

However, if the civic nationalist vision is weak, then there is little to prevent the trend toward confrontation between majority and minority rights expectations. Each nationalist vision can appeal to a different strand of the democratic idea. Ethnocultural nationalism appeals to the idea that democracy is government by the majority that embodies the will of the whole community. Multicultural nationalism appeals to the idea that democracy is government based on pluralistic bargaining, which promotes and protects ethnic minority rights. The articulation of these two competing ideas generates the potential for conflict between ethnic majority and ethnic minorities, each side having raised expectations of enhanced status in relation to the other. In the Indonesian case, Muslim communities expecting a more Islamic basis for Indonesian nationalism begin to come into conflict with non-Islamic minorities expecting an Indonesian nationalism that offers greater protection to ethnic minority rights. In the process, the prospects for democratic accommodation begin to fade. The intolerant face of Islam begins to assert itself against the tolerant face; the ethnic minority supporters of federal autonomy begin to be challenged by the proponents of secession.

The Problem of Civic Nationalism

The problem facing transitional countries is that the civic vision of equal individual citizenship rights, which provides a key initial impetus for the transition process, is nevertheless likely to become progressively weaker, so that it fails to provide a buffer. The reason is that the patrimonial element in the politics of transition is fundamentally incompatible with civic norms. While patrimonialism is (potentially) sufficiently flexible to accommodate and promote a shift from closed to open ethnocultural nationalism, and from a co-optive to an accommodative multicultural nationalism, it is not similarly able to promote the norms of citizenship equality associated with civic nationalism.

Patrimonialism is inhospitable to civic nationalism in various ways. First, the universalistic norms of civic nationalism are unlikely to be articulated by patrons seeking the personal loyalty of clients, or by clients seeking access to benefits through personal obligations to patrons. Inequalities of status are inherent in any form of patron–client relationship: all parties to such relationships have an interest in avoiding norms of status equality, which might erode access to beneficial patronage. Thus, even though ideas of equal individual citizenship rights might well be one of the sparks that initiated the democratization process, such ideas are less likely to be taken up by the various new patrons who dominate politics and government because these patrons are themselves embedded in the particularisms and status inequalities of patrimonialism. In the Indonesian case, the students who have been most articulate in espousing liberal civic visions pride themselves on being a moral force "above the self-interest and infighting of politics" (Schwarz 1999: 375). But it might be precisely this refusal to involve themselves with political networks that inhibits mass support for *reformasi* and "blunts their effectiveness and threatens the prospects for popular, sweeping reforms."[19] Those who most strongly articulate civic norms are precisely those who lack access to political influence.

Second, the new democratic civil society and constitutional institutions, which might be expected to embody civic norms, are themselves seen, increasingly, to function in patrimonial ways. The capacity of these institutions to symbolize civic ideals becomes eroded. This tendency was symbolized in the case of Indonesia by Wahid's apparent nepotism in appointing his brother to head the new bank restructuring agency.[20]

Third, the resilience of patrimonialism derives from the fact that it has become a core feature of the social structure and culture: individuals see themselves as members of communal clienteles of various types, seeking responsive patrons who can provide the resources they need. Ideas of minority or majority rights can thus easily resonate as individuals seek status and resource benefits by identifying with majority or minority clientele communities of various types. By contrast, ideas of the nation as a community of equal individuals with individual access to civic rights are less likely to resonate and be widely adopted. It is primarily in situations of rapid economic growth, where ordinary citizens believe in a future of upward socio-economic mobility, that visions of progress toward a community of equal-status individual citizens can gain widespread credence. In situations of economic decline, as with contemporary Indonesia, visions of equal individual civic rights are liable to carry less weight than visions of new access to a more responsive patron.

Fourth, the restructuring of patrimonialism of the transitional period, involves, as has been noted, the fracturing of authoritarian patrimonial linkages as new patrons seek new alliances. Consequently, central elites can lose effective control over subordinate officials. Faith in the possibility of progress toward civic rights is thus eroded, either because the errant behavior of subordinate officials is blamed on new governmental elites, or because the efficiency of state institutions is seen to decline.

If it is indeed the case that the persistence of patrimonial politics inhibits the development of a civic nationalist vision of democratization, then there is little to ameliorate the tensions between ethnic majority and ethnic minorities. Once ethnic minorities lose faith that the state can promote civic nationalism, they come to perceive the state as the agency of the ethnic majority and, therefore, cease to believe in its multiculturalist promises of status or autonomy to ethnic minorities. The weakening of civic nationalism leads to the erosion of multicultural nationalism. Calls for ethnic autonomy become radicalized and shift to becoming calls for full independence. What was ethnic minority support for a multicultural nationalist vision can easily become ethnic minority support for a separatist ethnocultural nationalism.

The discussion so far is but a partial framework within which to examine such issues as the West Papuan and Ambonese conflicts in Indonesia, which have a significant Christian versus Muslim dimension. The framework needs refining in that it seems wrong to imply that both the identity of ethnic minorities and their unity can be taken for granted, as the case of Aceh will illustrate.

It is not always self-evident who will align with the ethnic majority and who with the ethnic minority. In the Indonesian case, while there are proponents of all three nationalist visions, it nevertheless seems likely that many Indonesians subscribe to the vision of post-Suharto Indonesia as an ethnocultural nation built around a tolerant Islam. This vision of the nation was briefly personified by Wahid, who was initially seen as capable of accommodating sectarian differences.

While an ethnocultural vision of Indonesia as built on a tolerant Islamic core could potentially accommodate the more devout *santri* Islam practiced in Aceh, it is clear that many Acehnese do not define themselves as members of an Islamic Indonesian majority. Aceh's history of rebellion over much of the last fifty years is legitimated by myths of Acehnese resistance to more powerful external threats, with the result that Acehnese consciousness has been constructed reactively, counterposing Acehnese and Indonesian identities. This Acehnese sense of identity has been strong because it interweaves civic ideas of a regional–territorial minority community, with ethnocultural ideas of a linguistic and religious minority community. Once such an ideological identity has been constructed, it acts as a filter selectively to interpret new developments.[21] To a significant extent, therefore, many Acehnese are trapped within definitions of themselves as a beleaguered minority, which are focused on "a widespread sense of lost greatness" (Aspinall 2000). The result has been mutual incomprehension and suspicion, with most Indonesians unable to understand Acehnese intransigence and most Acehnese unable to understand Indonesian expectations of an end to conflict.

There is no strong civic nationalist buffer to ameliorate such majority–minority tensions. For the Acehnese, the civic vision of an Indonesian community of equal individual citizenship rights is both weak and fraudulent because of continuing if not escalating human rights abuses by the Indonesian police and army in Aceh since the fall of Suharto.[22] These abuses partly resulted from the fracturing of the old patron-client linkages between Jakarta and field commands within the armed forces, which left rogue officers or troops free of effective central control. Such behavior reinforced Acehnese ideological preconceptions of an unjust Indonesian state.[23]

The weakening of faith in civic nationalist promises means that ethnic minority support for the goal of multicultural autonomy necessarily begins to shift toward, or become ambiguously intertwined with, separatism. This is the situation with Aceh. Throughout the 1950s and 1960s, the main demand of the Acehnese rebellion was for effective provincial autonomy within Indonesia. There are indications that some Acehnese activists still seek autonomy within a multicultural and federal Indonesia. Certainly, as Ed Aspinall notes, "In those first few months [after Suharto's resignation] many Acehnese were genuinely optimistic that action would be taken [to resolve the 'Aceh problem']" (Aspinall 2000a). But some potential autonomy supporters lack the necessary trust in Indonesia's civic institutions and move toward separatism. There remains some ambiguity, however, between these two positions, which is reflected in the mass Acehnese support for "self-determination," as displayed most visibly in the Banda Aceh parades of November 1999. A "self-determination" referendum can be supported both by those who hope that the vote will be for multicultural autonomy within a looser Indonesia, and by those who hope the outcome will be ethnocultural independence outside Indonesia. To the extent that such ambiguity can be sustained, then the Acehnese rebellion can remain reasonably united. But there are signs that the politics of transition in Indonesia has increased disunity among the Acehnese.

PATRIMONIALISM, ETHNIC CONFLICT, AND FACTIONALISM

The argument so far is that patrimonialism, by inhibiting the development of a civic nationalist buffer, promotes tensions between the ethnocultural and multicultural nationalist visions. But the confrontation between nationalist visions does not of itself imply a straightforward clash between ethnic majorities and ethnic minorities, since such majorities and minorities might themselves be driven by internal disputes as to which nationalist visions to espouse. It is just as feasible for some members of ethnic majority communities to support multicultural visions of the nation-state, as for some within the ethnic minorities to support assimilationist ethnocultural visions. The patrimonial aspect of politics serves to make such intraethnic divisions more likely because it tends to engender factional rivalries between political activists. When patrimonial politics generate such rivalries amongst the elites of ethnic minority nationalist movements, they are likely to become the basis for splits in those movements as rival leaders seek to mobilize support by employing differing nationalist legitimations. The outcome is the tendency toward the splitting of ethnic rebellions into rival nationalist factions pursuing differing nationalist goals.

In the Indonesian case, the Aceh rebellion typifies the fictionalizing impact of patrimonial democracy on ethnic minorities.[24] The main Acehnese rivals for influence with Indonesian central government in the 1950s had been the Islamic *ulama* and the secular and civic-oriented elites, "the new *uleebalang*." These factional rivalries revived in the 1970s when the New Order government sought to co-opt "the new *uleebalang*" into the ruling party, Golkar. The rebellion renewed in the late 1970s when the marginalized Acehnese *ulama* allied with those "new *uleebalang*" who had been excluded from access to state patronage. While the Islamic *ulama* legitimated their opposition in ethnocultural terms, as arising from the betrayal of the promise of Aceh's Islamic autonomy, the secular *uleebalang* legitimated their opposition (in civic terms) by pointing to the class or "internal colonialist" exploitation of Acehnese citizens by a Javanese-centric government. The GAM (Free Aceh Movement) rebellion then sought to interweave these ethnocultural and civic visions of Aceh to mobilize popular support for Acehnese separatist nationalism.

However, once the post-Suharto Indonesian government began trying to make patrimonial linkages with influential Acehnese, rivalries amongst

Acehnese leaders, and uncertainties as to tactics, strategies, and goals, were highlighted. Wahid's initiatives in promoting Acehnese officials, offering a referendum, promising autonomy, and negotiating with various Acehnese elites all exacerbated factional disunity and uncertainty amongst student groups, *ulama*, village leaders, business and administrative elites, women's groups, and others. "Clearly, the aim [was] to split the Islamic leadership away from the students, GAM and other pro-independence groups" (Aspinall 2000a).[25]

This Acehnese disunity does not merely reflect personal rivalries amongst the elites, but, more fundamentally, the disentwining of an Acehnese civic nationalist vision from an Acehnese ethnocultural nationalist vision.[26] The divisions within the Acehnese rebellion have been partially reflected in rivalries between GAM, led at least nominally by Hasan di Tiro (based in Sweden), and a student group, SIRA (Central Bureau for an Acehnese Referendum). SIRA activists have frequently used the language of civic nationalism to call for a referendum. Hasan di Tiro's arm of GAM has primarily used the language of Acehnese ethnocultural nationalism to demand independence, but GAM is itself beset by further factional rivalries. The MP-GAM (Free Aceh Movement Government Council) faction, led by Daud Peneuek, Zulfahari, and others, appeared to be open to the multicultural nationalist vision of Acehnese autonomy within Indonesia (van Klinken 1999).

If the central government does manage to reach a negotiated settlement with the more moderate faction of the Aceh rebellion, then this is likely to further escalate Acehnese disunity. A more optimistic scenario is the progressive marginalization of the radical nationalists employing violence and the gradual reconstruction of an Acehnese identity compatible with, rather than antithetical to, an Indonesian identity. This might be illuminated by analogy with the Basques in Spain.[27] There, the period of transition between the weakening of authoritarian rule and the establishment of institutionalized democracy saw the intensification of radical nationalism on the part of the Basque minority and the escalation of political violence (notably by ETA—Freedom for the Basque Country). It also saw the factionalization and fracturing of the Basque nationalist movement as leaders and followers began to disagree about tactics, strategies, goals, and ideological visions. This factionalism added to a sense of instability and confrontation at the time, but can, in retrospect, be seen as the first step toward a modification of Basque identity constructions of self and other, with Basque identity clearly becoming more internally rather than reactively generated. Basque distrust of Spain thus began to weaken. In other words, democratization seems to have initially precipitated both the intensification and the factionalization of the ethnic rebellion, but has in the longer term generated a more accommodative and moderate ethnoregional nationalism. The proponents of violence remain active, but with declining popular support.

TENTATIVE CONCLUSIONS

The construction of national and ethnic identity relies on simplistic formulas being adopted by otherwise confused individuals to enable them to deal with complex social problems and acquire a sense of emotional security (Brown 1994: 5–24, 2000: 23–28). Nationalist and ethnic contention thus involves the construction of incompatible identity myths. These provide the resilient interpretative frameworks that transform potentially negotiable rivalries of interests and power into ideological confrontations structured on the basis of mutual incomprehension and exclusion, with the resultant distrust inhibiting the search for compromise solutions. Ethnic majorities construct histories, myths, and symbols of "their" nation-state so as to legitimate the authenticity of its cultural core and its territorial boundaries. Meanwhile, ethnic minorities construct their own myths of ancestry and homeland to legitimate their claims for autonomy. It is no surprise that each side comes to regard its own nationalism as powerful and authentic, and that of its opponents as weak and fraudulent.

However, such a depiction of ethnic conflict as the structural clash between incompatible ideologies might detract attention from the contingencies of politics. The above brief references to Aceh indicate the variable impact of democratization on ethnic conflict. In some respects conflict has escalated; in other respects prospects for negotiation have been enhanced. Acehnese communal unity has in some respects been enhanced, but its political disunity has increased. These complexities mean that the final impact of democratization on national unity cannot be predicted for one country, let alone generalized in respect to several countries. The purpose of this chapter has, therefore, merely been to indicate some of the political tensions that structure this unpredictability. The focus has been on the problems associated with the democratization of national identity in the context of patrimonial politics.

The democratization of national identity is problematic in various respects. It is not easy to contain the tension among emergent civic, ethnocultural, and multicultural visions of national identity; it is not easy to prevent the three visions from disentwining and coming to be seen as mutually exclusive. But these tensions do not make ethnic conflict inevitable. The problem is, rather, that democratization, which promises to deliver a strengthened civic nationalism, is sometimes dependent upon a patrimonial politics, which threatens to weaken it. The result is the tendency both to ethnic confrontation and to factional disunity. The uncertainties of patrimonial politics provide some explanation not only for the instabilities of democratic transitions, but also for the political deals that can inhibit national disintegration.

NOTES

I wish to acknowledge the help of Natalia Norris and Kathleen Turner for their research assistance. I also wish to thank Ed Aspinall for his valuable comments on an earlier draft.

1. "West Papua" is the name Papuan nationalists use for their territory. On the evolution of the name of the province, see Bertrand (chapter 9 in this book) at n. 23.

2. The term "patrimonial" refers to a political leader whose power rests to a significant extent upon his or her links with personal retainers, who owe their office to him or her. In a patrimonial system such patron–client ties, functioning both within and outside administrative institutions, provide the main linkage between central government and grassroots society. Thus the terms "patrimonial," "patronage," and "patron–client," are interconnected. For a discussion of the nature of patrimonialism in the Indonesian context, see Brown (1994).

3. It should be noted at the outset that the use of collectivist nationalist legitimation does not preclude authoritarian regimes from pursuing policies that promote the interests of ethnic minorities. It merely precludes their doing so on the basis of liberal conceptualizations of individual or minority rights.

4. The concepts of civic, ethnocultural, and multicultural nationalisms, and the model of a tensioned relationship between the three, are examined in Brown (2000).

5. The fact that patrimonial practices had survived the removal of Suharto was symbolized by Wahid's September 2000 cabinet reshuffle, which was widely interpreted as displaying personalist favoritism (Aspinall 1998; *Time*, 15 September 2000).

6. This means, as Leah Greenfeld (1992: 11) has argued, that collectivist nationalism necessarily implies authoritarian rule because "someone is bound to be its interpreter."

7. About 90 percent of Indonesia's population is Muslim. There are indeed several distinctions within this category, most notably between the *santri* (devout) and the *banyan* (nominal) Muslims. But the political and social salience of such distinctions is variable.

8. The *Pancasila* are the five principles of Indonesia's national ideology, namely belief in one God, nationalism, humanism, democracy, and social justice. Since at least 1953, state elites have employed the *Pancasila* principles to counterpose the idea of national unity to that of an Islamic state.

9. The depiction of the Javanese Majapahit empire as the precolonial basis for modern Indonesia has been crucial in this ethnocultural construction of the nation. The status dominance of Javanese is reflected in the fact that in the 1980s, "well over 70 percent" of armed forces officers were Javanese, whereas they formed only about 45 percent of the population (Anderson 1988). The policy of *transmigrasi*, which encouraged Javanese to migrate to the outer islands, was also widely interpreted as a policy of "Javanisation."

10. There is some debate as to whether a religious community (in this case Muslim) should be regarded as an ethnic community. If ethnicity refers to communities held together by myths of common kinship and ancestry, then it is clear that ideas of racial, linguistic, religious, and homeland homogeneity can all play a role. Where

religion does play such a role, the designation of the ethnic community in religious terms may be warranted.

11. S. Mydans, "Can She Run Indonesia: It's About Islam or Is It?," *New York Times*, 20 June 1999. The corollary of this rise in Islamic expectations was the intensification of rivalries for political influence between the differing Islamic groups, as Islamic factions in search of influential patrons sought patrons in search of support bases (ibid.).

12. In New Order Indonesia, such corporatist management was facilitated by ethnic minority recruitment into the three sanctioned political parties, the Islamic intellectual's group ICMI (Indonesian Muslim Intellectuals' Association), and the centralized institutions of provincial and district administration.

13. In the Indonesian case, this relationship was sometimes depicted overtly in patron–client terms, with Suharto portrayed as the father (*bapak*) to the Indonesian children-clients (*anak buah*).

14. Among their demands were: (1) reform of the political, legal, economic, and educational systems; (2) repeal of laws restricting political freedoms; (3) abolition of the army's "dual function"; (4) elimination of corruption, collusion, and nepotism; and (5) an end to the kidnapping of activists (Stanley 1998).

15. This was evident in the 1998 election campaign, especially in the attempts by Megawati and Golkar to make strategic alliances with various Islamic leaders, including Wahid.

16. The Revival of Islamic Scholars, one of the main political parties in the 1950s, but a target for Suharto's "departy-ization" in 1971, has remained the largest Islamic association in Indonesia and is headed by Wahid.

17. Law 22/1999 provides for some independent powers at district and city levels and for the election of provincial governors and district heads. Law 25/1999 provides for 80 percent of revenues produced in the regions (i.e., provinces, districts, and cities) to be retained by the regions. Implementation of these laws began in early 2001 (Lloyd 1999–2000).

18. His initial statement that he would allow a referendum on Acehnese independence was subsequently modified to an offer of a referendum on the implementation of *shari'ah* law in Aceh.

19. M. Cohen, "Unguided Missiles," *Far Eastern Economic Review*, 26 November 1998.

20. *The Economist*, 20 May 2000.

21. Instead of welcoming the accession of Wahid as indicating a new pro-Islamic Indonesia, the Acehnese self-identity led to a focus on the extent to which the New Order remained intact and interpreted Wahid's promises towards Aceh in the light of the previous betrayed promises by Sukarno. The sense of distance between Acehnese Islam and Indonesian Islam is symbolized in the Acehnese students' use of the self-designation *thaliban* rather than the Indonesian term *santri*.

22. While some soldiers and civilians were prosecuted for such abuses in Aceh, Acehnese distrust of these prosecutions focused on the fact that they held the lower ranks responsible (rather than senior officers), they were conducted under military rather than civilian law, and they imposed sentences widely seen as lenient or nominal.

23. "The powerlessness of the law enforcement institutions to provide justice" and the "mistrust of Indonesia's men in uniform" are thus probably the major reasons for

widespread Acehnese support for independence ("Asia: Ready to talk in Aceh?," *The Economist*, 15 April 2000).

24. On the impact of Indonesian patrimonial politics on factional structures of the Acehnese rebellion, see Brown (1994: Ch.4); Kell (1995); Morris (1983). On the contemporary situation see Aspinall (2000b). With the overthrow of the more secular, old administrative elite, the *uleebalang*, in 1946, the reformist Islamic *ulama* who comprised the main patron-elites of Aceh sought provincial status for an Islamic Aceh through a patrimonial alliance with the democratic government of the new Indonesian Republic. In 1953 Aceh's patrimonial linkages with the Indonesian center were broken. The Acehnese *ulama* shifted to the strategy of regionalist rebellion, which produced new patrimonial alliance linkages with the Indonesian military commander, General Nasution, and government concessions, including the granting of provincial status in 1956, the recognition of Aceh as a "special region" and an "Islamic Republic" in 1960, and the recognition of its right to implement "elements of Islamic Law" in 1962. Rebellion resumed as the New Order government eroded these concessions.

25. Wahid promoted several Acehnese, including Hasballah M. Saad as Indonesia's first Minister for Human Rights and Lt. Gen. Fachrul Razi as second in command of the armed forces. On his visit to Aceh in early 2000, Wahid met with village dignitaries to offer economic benefits and increased autonomy, but avoided meeting the leaders of the separatist movements. Instead he met with Zulfahari, a leader of the MP-GAM splinter group, who has indicated some willingness to opt for autonomy rather than full independence ("President on a Limp Mission," *The Economist*, 29 January 2000; M. Cohen, "Alarms in Aceh," *Far Eastern Economic Review*, 18 November 1999).

26. The "heterogeneity of political forces in Aceh" is summarized in Aspinall (2000).

27. Despite the obvious differences, there are some relevant parallels between the two cases. Firstly, the ethnic minority in both constructed their identity reactively against a state perceived as seeking to dominate them. The Basques depicted themselves as marginalized and exploited by a Castilian-dominated Spain; the Acehnese depicted themselves as marginalized and exploited by a Javanese-dominated Indonesia. Secondly, in both cases an ethnocultural vision of the minority community coexisted with a civic vision of that community to generate ambiguous calls for self-determination. The Basques employed both a racial-linguistic construction of Basque ethnic identity and a territorial autonomy construction; the Acehnese constructed their identity in religio-linguistic and also provincial-territorial terms. Thirdly, in both cases also, the removal of the authoritarian ruler—the death of Franco in Spain and the resignation of Suharto in Indonesia—opened up the prospect for a more democratic and more federal nation-state. On the Basque case, see Brown (2000: Ch. 4).

REFERENCES

Anderson, Benedict R. O'G. 1972. "The Idea of Power in Javanese Culture." In *Culture and Politics in Indonesia*, ed. Claire Holt. Ithaca, N.Y.: Cornell University Press.

———. 1988. "Current Data on the Indonesian Military Elite." *Indonesia* 45: 138.

Aspinall, Edward. 1998. "Opposition and Elite Conflict in the Fall of Soeharto." In *The Fall of Suharto*, eds. Geoff Forrester and R. J. May. Crawford House, London: Bathurst/ Hurst.

——. 2000a. "Whither Aceh?: An Update of Events in 1999." *Inside Indonesia* 62: 6–7.

——. 2000b. "National and Local Identities after the New Order: Reflections from Aceh." Paper presented to the Indonesia: Old Selves, New Selves conference. University of Tasmania, Launceston (December).

Brown, David. 1994. *The State and Ethnic Politics in Southeast Asia*. London: Routledge.

——. 1995. "Democratization and the Renegotiation of Ethnicity." In *Towards Illiberal Democracy in Pacific Asia*, eds. Daniel A. Bell, David Brown, Kanishka Jayasuriya, and David Martin Jones. London: Macmillan and New York: St. Martin's.

——. 2000. *Contemporary Nationalism: Civic, Ethnocultural and Multicultural Politics*. London: Routledge.

Connor, Walker. 1994. *Ethnonationalism: The Quest for Understanding*. Princeton, N.J.: Princeton University Press.

Eller, Jack David, and Reed M. Coughlan. 1993. "The Poverty of Primordialism: The Demystification of Ethnic Attachments." *Ethnic and Racial Studies* 16, no. 2: 183–201.

Greenfeld, Liah. 1992. *Nationalism: Five Roads to Modernity*. Cambridge, Mass.: Harvard University Press.

Jacobs, Norman. 1985. *The Korean Road to Modernization and Development*. Urbana: University of Illinois Press.

Jones, David Martin. 1995. "Democracy and Identity: The Paradoxical Character of Political Development." In *Towards Illiberal Democracy in Pacific Asia*, eds. Daniel A. Bell, David Brown, Kanishka Jayasuriya, and David Martin Jones. London: Macmillan and New York: St. Martin's.

Kell, Tim. 1995. *The Roots of Acehnese Rebellion*. Ithaca, N.Y.: Cornell University Press.

Liddle, R. William. 1970. *Ethnicity, Party, and National Integration: An Indonesian Case Study*. New Haven, Conn.: Yale University Press.

Lloyd, Grayson. 1999–2000. "Indonesia's Future Prospects: Separatism, Decentralization, and the Survival of the Unitary State." *Current Issues Brief* 17. Foreign Affairs, Defence and Trade Group, Parliament of Australia. Available at http://wopared.aph.gov.au/library/pubs/cib/1999–2000/2000cib17.htm. Accessed 13 September 2000.

Merkel, Wolfgang. 1998. "The Consolidation of Post-Autocratic Democracies: A Multi-Level Model." *Democratization* 5, no. 3: 33–67.

Morris, Eric Eugene. 1983. Islam and Politics in Aceh. Ph.D. diss., Cornell University.

Schwarz, Adam. 1999. *A Nation in Waiting*. St. Leonards: Allen and Unwin.

Stanley, [no further name given]. 1998. "Behind the Student Demands." *Inside Indonesia* 55 (July–September). Available at www.insideindonesia.org/edit55/st.htm. Accessed 30 September 2000.

van Klinken, Gerry. 1999. "Digest 89: What is the Free Aceh Movement?" *Inside Indonesia* (25 November). Available at www.insideindonesia.org/digest/dig89.htm. Accessed 30 September 2000.

4

Understanding Contending Nationalist Identities: Reading Ernest Gellner and Benedict Anderson from Taiwan

Chang Maukuei

THE PERSONAL AND THE THEORETICAL

Ernest Gellner's lifelong interest in nationalism is heavily influenced by the circumstances of his life, suggests John A. Hall. He says that it is "utterly impossible" for Gellner to neglect the significance of nationalism because of Gellner's background: a lower-middle class Jew of German Bohemian origin, growing up in a family loyal to the Czech Republic when the Nazis arrived, but disillusioned with postwar Czechoslovakia in its expulsion of the Germans (Hall 1998: 2–3). Indeed, a reading of Gellner's theory of nationalism takes on new meaning once the reader learns of Gellner's background and of the political concerns expressed (or hidden) in his works.

Benedict Anderson, whose work is also central to this chapter, is probably not different in having his background influence his work. Anderson recalled that his interest in the study of nations originated from his own earlier personal experiences. These include his broad overseas experiences during his childhood, his family background (he is of both British and Irish descent), his resentment of British imperial snobbery, his personal encounters with a war of independence and with nationalism in Indonesia under Sukarno (Anderson 1998),[1] and his "funny" accent in daily life in the American-English world.

This does not mean that theories of nation and nationalism are predicated by theorists' political or moral standings, but that they are also the narratives of the authors and their responses to the larger political and social-cultural milieu in which they are situated. In common practice, the academic community is inclined to read theoretical texts as merely some objectified "textual reality," as if they were a body of codified knowledge, abstract and independent from the author's personal subjectivity. This problem can be even more conflated for contemporary non-Western scholars such as me. Despite the lasting influences of modernization and globalization, not only can the sociopolitical context confronting the theories and theorists be foreign to us, but the language used in theoretical writing itself can also be a barrier. It is a problem we have to face all the time in engaging in intellectual dialogue with English-language and other foreign-language writers.[2] Moreover, from time to time, we find gaps and cracks between our specific experiences and the general ideas or abstract theories about nationalism, whether from Western tradition or the subaltern.

I am not advocating a strong relativism that places authentic cultural difference above universalizing tendencies, stressing the oversimplified and straw-man-like dichotomy between the "West" and the "East," nor proclaiming the "uniqueness" of Taiwan issues in the study of nationalism. My position is rather simple: to engage in constructive dialogue between selective theories and "our" particular lived experiences in this nationalistic world, with a strong emphasis on comparison and self-reflection. Theories are really like culturally biased telescopes that, even with their farsightedness, do not capture our historical experiences well because they were made for a different set of concerns. Sometimes, unknowingly, we place ourselves on the wrong side of the telescopes when trying to explore our own place. Reflexive reading of the theories is almost unavoidable. Both reflexive reading and comparison also advance the ideas or the knowledge conceived with the unknown blind spots of authors from "other" cultures. It is therefore my wish, through reading Anderson and Gellner and approaching the analysis of Taiwan's circumstances dialectically, that we not only achieve a better understanding of Taiwan's national problem, but also increase the academic community's stock of knowledge regarding nations and nationalism. Thus, my chapter shows why it was that, in the late 1980s, the struggle for democracy in Taiwan was also a struggle amongst competing nationalisms and differing visions of the representation and participation of "our kind." As we shall see, this outcome is a consequence of the historical conjuncture surrounding Taiwan's particular experiences in confronting the imposition of Japanese colonial domination, Chinese nationalism, and its collective drive for modernization. Through this conjuncture, conflicting imaginings of "we the sovereign people" were given birth, ensuring the intertwining of a democratic movement and nationalist politics in the contemporary era.

Gellner and Anderson were chosen because they are two of the most widely read and quoted scholars in recent literature about nationalism. Anderson, moreover, is particularly influential in recent studies on nationalism in Taiwan. Anderson and Gellner share some similarities in their arguments, but with strongly different emphases. For instance, at the most abstract level, they both subscribe to the rationalistic assumption of nationalism, arguing against the naturalist conception of nation and for the artificial construction (or imaginary) process of nation. However, Anderson focuses on the role of the rise of the vernacular, secularization, and the growth of "print capitalism," the latter referring to the development of new technology and markets for newspapers, novels, and books, while Gellner looks at the role of historical processes and the necessities of industrialization.

Because it is not my purpose to provide a full comparison, I shall focus on my own reading of them, examining their theoretical propositions with both my personal experiences and my study of different nationalist camps in Taiwan. I hope to provide an explanation for the origin and making of Taiwanese national identity through both employing and challenging Gellner and Anderson.

THE ORIGIN OF "TAIWANESE PEOPLE"

Some of my major points regarding the origin and transformation of Taiwan's national identity have been expressed elsewhere (Chang 2000). Because my purpose here is to engage Anderson and Gellner, I will provide only a brief summary at appropriate places. The first point I want to raise is about the importance of history and its impact on how people perceive themselves. Basically, the emergence of Taiwanese consciousness (and national identity) is a historical and conjunctural outcome, instead of a structural one.[3] Anderson's book *Imagined Communities* is illuminating in several ways. First of all, his arguments surrounding the importance of people's self-image, the changing mode of thinking about oneself, and the process of consciously making one "nation" collectively, immediately reject the pseudoscientific and naturalistic claims of most nationalist indoctrination. For my research on nationalism, his thesis of the "imagined community" led me first to ask when the people (in Chinese history) perceived of themselves as "one nation" in the modern sense. The official line that the Chinese people have possessed a "oneness" for almost five thousand years cannot go unchallenged.[4]

It was not easy for me to embrace Anderson at first. I was born in Taiwan in 1953 of mainlander parents who had fled their homeland for Taiwan with the Nationalist army and majority of other mainlanders who settled in Taiwan in 1949. Like many first-generation mainlander families, my family had little contact with either the native society or with our mainland relatives. From my early education into college, I received a nationalist education—including literature; Chinese, *not* Taiwanese, history; and civic education—and political indoctrination, such as through studying the thought of Dr. Sun Yat-sen. I grew up under the influence of the Cold War with right-wing, pro-American, strong state-promoted patriotism, and an ideology centered on development and economic prosperity. When the West was troubled by the

Vietnam War and waves of social protests and experiments, we in Taiwan were almost unaffected, as if enclosed in an ideological capsule sealed by the authoritarian government. My own personal and political identity had been categorically nationalistic Chinese and patriotic. My views have changed a great deal since then. Reading Anderson was part of my personal growth, which helped reshape my worldview regarding nations and peoples.

What can Anderson's thesis offer to the understanding of the opposite nationalist claim, namely that the Taiwanese form unequivocally one racial/national group entitled to be an independent nation with their own country? Some of the pioneers of Taiwanese nationalism suggest that Taiwanese people have been a suppressed nation since the seventeenth century, with the Taiwanese nation (*minzu*) constantly ruled by foreign intruders, including the Spanish, the Dutch, the Chinese, and the Japanese (Shi 1980). If Anderson's thesis makes me look at my own Chinese nationalist background with more skepticism, it also makes me look closely at when and how the Taiwanese began to think of themselves as a nation.[5] When and under what historical conditions did this self-awareness or imagination of being Taiwanese start?

In fact, I did not hear the term "Taiwanese nation" (*Taiwan minzu*) until the 1979 Kaohsiung Incident. Taiwan was still under martial law and I was twenty-six.[6] The incident broke out in Kaohsiung, southern Taiwan's largest city. Military police clashed with dissidents marching for human rights in the streets. It was followed by the crackdown on the opposition movement and the arrest of almost every well-known Taiwanese opposition leader of the time. Later, under international pressure, the dissidents faced a show-trial in military court. Soon I began to hear and read materials distributed by overseas dissidents about the Taiwanese nation, an allegedly different "nation" from the Chinese. I was shocked and found this absurd. How could we, the mainlanders, and the Taiwanese people belong to a different "race"?[7] I thought we were all "the same," of Chinese origin, descendants of the Legendary Yellow Emperor, and "kin of the Dragon." When I grew up I had little sense of either a "racial problem" or "meaningful differences" other than accents between my Taiwanese peers and me.

Looking back, my ignorance about the Taiwan *minzu* seems only normal given my mainlander background. It also came from the suppression that occurred under martial law (1951–1987), which silenced many dissidents and made autonomous civic participation almost impossible. There was little chance for me to hear or to learn anything about the Taiwan *minzu*. Nowadays the events surrounding the February 28 Incident—the brutal suppression of a 1947 Taiwanese uprising causing thousands of deaths and the subsequent "white-terror era" against suspected leftists—are widely known to the public. However, only several years ago they were a carefully guarded national taboo. People were forbidden to discuss them openly and prohibited from carrying out any research on related subjects. "Officially" Taiwan existed in its nationalist mission to recover the lost motherland (mainland China), not for its own nationhood.

As many political scientists have described, 1979 was a watershed in Taiwan's political development.[8] One year before, mostly Taiwanese dissidents—with the help of a very small number of democratic mainlanders—had begun pushing for political liberalization and democracy. The Kaohsiung Incident and the trial of the democrats "awakened" many people of Taiwanese origin. People had sunk into an "angry silence" under strict martial law rule (Hsiao 2000). However, the setback only gave the opposition movement broader support in the next elections (Rigger 1999). The suppression triggered outrage amongst overseas Taiwanese groups and, hence, strengthened their mobilization and other "underground" activities against the regime. Exiled dissidents sought channels to help the democratic movement in Taiwan and circulated propaganda calling for an independent state through self-determination and replacing the ruling regime, the Nationalistic Kuomintang (Chen 1992; Geoffroy 1997).

On the other hand, the mainlanders' reaction to the Kaohsiung Incident was quite different. The majority of them were inclined to be proregime and patriotic, believing the government and dismissing the accused as agitators, conspirators, accomplices to the "Communists bandits," and even traitors. The divide between the mainlanders and many Taiwanese was very deep, which also affected greatly my personal life for quite a while.

The timing was really a watershed for me. I was in the United States, about to choose ethnic/racial politics—and later nationalist politics—as my research agenda. My exposure to this subject in the United States started my own early transformation to liberal and multiculturalistic thought from the conservative nationalism of my background.

Let us return to the near present, the year 2000. In a lecture to a Taiwanese audience on 26 April 2000,[9] Anderson said that Taiwan belongs to the kind of "creole nationalism" of North America, Australia, New Zealand, Singapore, Quebec, and many other places. Creole nationalism is formed when children of immigrants in the "New World," despite their cultural inheritance from the motherland, begin to distance themselves from their ancestral homeland (through either alienation or subjugation); or, after going through a "pilgrimage process" to the center, they begin to evolve into a community of expatriates. The emergence of a "mixed blood," *mestizo* generation affects people's self-consciousness. Anderson implies that creole nationalism is inevitable for Taiwan.

However, to me, Anderson's creole nationalism does not explain the emergence of Taiwanese nationalism. Claims of Taiwanese national identity did not aim at separation from the "motherland" nor grow from a pilgrimage

experience. "Mixed blood" people were not a salient issue either until the recent interest in the search for roots among the descendants of plains Aborigines who were thought to have been "assimilated" into the Han (compare
Brown 2001).

What Happened in the Beginning?

To trace the origin of nationalist thinking amongst Taiwanese requires a
knowledge of history. Taiwan was inhabited by Aborigines before the arrival
of outsiders. From the beginning of the seventeenth century until recently,
Han Chinese settlers drove out other settlers and colonialists such as the
Spaniards, the Dutch, and the Japanese. Chinese (or Han) settlers with the
assistance and sometimes the administration of the Manchu government succeeded in pushing the indigenous peoples to Sinicize or relocate to remote,
mountainous areas (Shepherd 1993). Taiwan was at the southeastern frontier
of the Manchu Empire from 1683. Although the island was very different
from southern China in many aspects even before it was ceded to Japan in
1895, those looking for linguistic and cultural similarities between Taiwan
and the mainland can easily find them. As mentioned,[10] one camp of Taiwanese nationalism suggests that the "Taiwanese people" are genetically different from Han Chinese because of the mixing of early settlers with the Aborigines, Dutch, Spaniards, and Japanese. But this contradicts history because
"blood" or "lineage" was less a concern than "civility" for Han Chinese society. Aborigines were not excluded from adopting Chinese civilization. A
higher level of Sinicization was both promoted by the government and
agreeable to the Han immigrants.[11] Also, although mixed marriages were
rather common between Han and Aborigines, the *mestizo* had no cultural or
social significance.[12] Before the Japanese period, state–society relations as a
whole underwent Sinicization, as plain Aborigines were half-encouraged,
half-compelled to adopt Han culture. In short, along with the expansion of
Han culture and Han settlers, and along with the expansion of Manchu government in Taiwan especially prior to its ceding to Japan in 1895, Taiwan
was on its way to being transformed into a province similar to other parts of
southern China, both culturally and politically.

The Manchu were forced to surrender Taiwan to Japan after a humiliating
defeat by the Japanese in the 1895 Sino–Japan War. Under oppressive Japanese rule, the Taiwanese people gradually transformed their traditional Han
Chinese outlook into a more modernistic Taiwanese one, particularly from
1918 into the 1920s. In this period the Taiwanese began to grasp their own
conditions: their "fate" of being both subjects and quasi citizens in the Japanese empire and the new (modern) modes of political thinking, especially the
new term "nation," which could be used to resist the colonialist. Most early
Taiwanese nationalists were Taiwanese elite from well-to-do families who

received a Japanese "modern" and "national" education, often in Tokyo, the center of new ideas and Western modes of thinking in early twentieth-century East Asia. Their acquisition of Taiwanese nationalist sentiments took place in the milieu of the following factors.

First, Chinese settlers in Taiwan suffered from relatively low standing in the Japanese Empire. The Japanese government treated them as people of a different "race" without giving them equal citizenship under the empire's political system. It also looked down upon Taiwanese because of their defeat and their premodern (backward) "cultural traits." Second, exposure to Western ideas about citizenship, equality, justice and colonial conditions were important for Taiwanese consciousness. The first few Taiwanese nationalists learned about the Wilsonian principle of self-determination for colonized people, which became widespread after the World War I, and studied independence movements that had spread even to Korea, another Japanese colony, in 1919. Consciousness of being Taiwanese—the notion of a Taiwanese nation—quickly formed. Third, the softening of the Japanese bureaucratic empire and Japan's transformation to parliamentary politics—which took place during the *Taisho Minshu* (democracy) era (roughly 1918–1932)—also widened their horizons and allowed room for political activities. Fourth, Taiwanese consciousness also meant being self-reliant in resisting the Japanese, as China was divided, weak, chaotic, and incapable of doing anything to help.

As one recent work (Wu Ruei-ren 2001) has shown, the notion that "Taiwan belongs to the [Japanese] empire but also belongs to the Taiwanese people" was clearly stated by Tsai Pei-huo and other young intellectuals in Tokyo (the Taiwan New People Association, or *Taiwan Xin Min Hui*) in 1920. The first part of the sentence refers to the political reality that their struggle was not revolutionary, but a moderate cultural awakening that tested the limits of tolerance prescribed by the authority: Taiwan was part of Japan, and Taiwan independence was not the immediate goal. While the second part stated the wish for home rule (an expression of the idea of self-determination), it was a "polite" demand for recognition of distinct status for Taiwan and its people. Their political action led to the now well-known "Abolition of Bill No. 63" campaign[13] and the "Petition Movement for the Creation of a Taiwan Council," as well as the creation of the first influential political association, the Taiwan Cultural Association (*Taiwan Wenhua Xiehui*, 1921–1931).[14]

Their aim, unlike many examples of creole nationalism, was not to cut ties with or oppose the ancestral homeland. Rather, they found that they were sandwiched between their Han roots and their unequal status under the Japanese. They could not be fully Han Chinese because they belonged to Japan, and they could not be fully Japanese because they were different from Japanese and treated as if a "distinct race" by Japanese authorities. The sociopolitical conditions for creole nationalism were not there.

However, the call for "elevating people's cultural consciousness" implied a Taiwanese modernist standpoint, abandoning part of their old Han customs.[15] This "progressiveness" was prompted by their own comparisons to the modernized colonialist and the outside world. It moved away from conservative Han traditionalism, but not from Han Chinese identity just yet. This is important because this self-awakening process and the related political acts of resisting colonial conditions and modernization set Taiwanese consciousness apart from the Chinese nationalism of their compatriots, which was peaking at the same period. But it needs to be reemphasized that, prior to 1945, this Taiwanese consciousness was not formed to deny their Han Chinese roots, as some contemporary Taiwanese nationalist rhetoric tends to suggest.

Class differences also mattered when Taiwanese tried to define their own fate and the meaning of their existence in opposing the Japanese. The New Cultural (and patriotic) movement in China (i.e., the May Fourth Movement, 1919) incited a short-lived yet rich New Literature Movement from 1920 (but mainly between 1924–1926) in Taiwan. The Republican revolution and the Communist advancement also influenced the Taiwan Communist Party,[16] formed secretly in Shanghai in 1928. It was actually the first group that espoused outright national independence and liberation for Taiwanese *minzu* (Wu Ruei-ren 2001). Inspired by Leninism, which called for a united front of all oppressed and colonized nations to overthrow feudalism, colonialism, and other oppression, it aimed to "awaken" the Taiwanese and ally them with other colonized nations to overthrow the colonialists.

Unlike the other more moderate Taiwanese elite youth, the leftist group promoted class struggle against not only Japanese colonialism and conglomerates but also conservative Taiwanese landlords and bourgeoisie. Their political actions merged with the then newly rising urban workers and sugarcane farmers[17] and led to island-wide farmers' protests (1926–1932) and workers' strikes (1927–1931). Communist relations to the more elitist, reform-oriented, and "moderate" national movement were cooperative when the major goal was to "awaken" the masses and mobilize a unified anticolonial movement. Yet they often fought over how to lead the anticolonial and liberation movement—and over who should be the leader (Chen 1998).

For both the Right and the Left, the Taiwanese nation and nationalism were created at the juncture of rapid change after World War I. The prevalent progressive ideas and strategies like self-determination, class struggle, national liberation, and modernization had filtered through Taiwanese elites and activists and became part of their new self-imagination in their struggles against oppression. Both elite and leftist activists reflected on their own historical situation and their humiliation and suffering in the world context, using the new global theoretical languages of nationality, race, citizenship, assimilation, and equality. They were not only searching for a new

meaning for their existence and identity, but also devising political strategies to change their own circumstances. Thus, the nationalist theme of this
"moment of departure," paraphrasing Partha Chatterjee (1993: 54), was already divided by class origin and in relation to moral frames of reference
concerning social reforms.

To summarize, early Taiwanese nationalism was created in specific historical and global conditions by different groups occupying different positions
in the social hierarchy. Their nationalism was not aimed at independence
from celestial China, their ancestral homeland. Unlike with other creole nationalism, the pilgrimage to motherland was not possible because of Japan's
colonization. Neither was there oppression from the ancestral homeland
against the children of the settlers. The motherland was just not the target of
the resistance. Instead, it was a source of intellectual inspiration and identification that Taiwanese relied on from time to time to differentiate themselves from their colonial masters.

On Transforming the General Public:
The Colonial State, Activists, and the Masses

This portion of Taiwan history was not part of my formal education, which
was dominated by Chinese nationalism. Taiwanese nationalism only very recently became a topic of scholarly research. It had been primarily a topic for
lay "historians" (mainly of Taiwanese origin) inclined to Taiwanese independence. It was common for them to hail the moderates' resistance as "the
good and the righteous, and an exemplary demonstration of Taiwanese
identity." By emphasizing Taiwanese identity, they hence played down the
importance of the Communist activists who, as noted, had been very active
during that period. This was because the term "Communist" carried a con-
notation of Chinese nationalism or the motherland's influence. They also
tended to overlook the impact on Taiwan of the Republican revolution in
China (e.g., see Wang Yude 1993). As for the contemporary Chinese nationalists (the prounification inclined) in Taiwan, they had shown little interest
in this Taiwan home-rule movement from the 1920s. If they were interested
at all, it was largely because they could fit this portion of history into the
larger Chinese nationalist resistance against Japanese imperialism. Of course,
both right- and left-wing nationalists have attempted to play down the historical significance of the Taiwan *minzu* independence claim in 1927, each
for their own purposes. I will not address these further here.

To search for the origin of nationalist ideas, political programs, and Taiwan's pioneering activists is one thing, but to reconstruct similar changes in
the general public is another. We can study the former through documents
and records, but to reconstruct the latter self-transformation requires more
effort and a phenomenological interpretation of ordinary people who left

few personal records. The worldview of the majority of Taiwanese before 1895 was "racialized" as a dichotomy of "the civilized versus the savages" and the "Great Han versus the Foreign Devils." The Japanese were clearly the foreign intruders, while the Aborigines were still uncivilized savages. Ordinary people were also confined to local allegiances and ancestral lineages, such as *Hokkien* and *Hakka*. Moreover, Han settlers in Taiwan before 1915 were not very different from their counterparts in China. More than 80 percent of adults were poorly educated peasants. I must contend that they were very Han Chinese people who practiced folk beliefs and studied Han literature if they were given the opportunity. Confined to their localities and to poverty, their transformation process cannot be equated to the elite and activists. In short, most Chinese in Taiwan during the early years of Japanese rule were still premodern and prenationalistic in their worldview. What were the sociocultural or political factors that transformed them into an imagined national community? Were the elites and activists successful in helping to transform the rest of the people? Was there Japanese influence?

The greatest obstacle for activists trying to reach these illiterate masses was the suppression of political activities and police surveillance by the Japanese police. There was also a communication gap between the elite and the masses. Only one newspaper—published by activists in Taipei and with a daily circulation of a few thousand copies at its peak—was a major forum for public discourse. Its effect on the general public is hard to assess and should not be exaggerated. Then, after 1937, the Taiwanese were forbidden to use Chinese characters completely. Ironically, Japanese gradually became the lingua franca for both activists and other people in Taiwan.

This is not unusual for colonial people. Anderson thinks likewise. The new lingua franca helped to break down localism and brought diverse people into one larger imagination. However, the Han Chinese were unlike the "natives" or the tribal populations Anderson mentioned, such as in the Philippines, the Indies, or on other islands. The Han Chinese indeed already shared a writing system and a culture, involving, for example, folk religions, ancestor worship, Confucian teachings, and the classical literary tradition. However, Japanese became not only a new communication system, but also a new "high culture" sanctioned by the colonial power: the influence of the colonial state writ large not just in the linguistic landscape, but also in the peoples' worldviews.

The Effect of Colonial Governance on Collective Image

In 1994, in an interview titled "the Sadness of Being Taiwanese" by the late Japanese writer Shiba Ryotaro, former Taiwanese President Lee Teng-hui was quoted as saying, "I thought that I was a Japanese until I was 20 years old."[18] Lee believed that he was speaking for his generation as a whole, which is a partial truth. The Japanese were very serious and successful in promoting assimilation and patriotism. Modern national education was institutionalized in Taiwan beginning in the 1920s. The enrollment rate of school-aged children was 10 percent in 1915, 25 percent in 1920, and 71 percent in 1944 (Tsurumi 1977: 148). In the competition for Taiwanese' minds, the Taiwanese resistance did not seem to have the upper hand. The question now becomes: After 1920, did Taiwanese begin to image themselves as Taiwanese with a national destiny striving for political independence, or did some begin to embrace the idealized notion of being Japanese as well? Can Anderson's thesis help us understand this?

In his revision of *Imagined Communities*, Anderson modified his earlier interpretation about official nationalism, which assigned importance to official indoctrination in postcolonial states. Now he suggested that colonial era censuses, maps, and museums paved the way for the postcolonial state to forge a newly imagined nationess (Anderson 1991: 163–85). These colonial institutions are conducive to breaking down isolation and localized regionalism (confined to traditional tribal dialects or regional feuds) by providing new, larger political "boundaries" and general "icons" that in turn change people's self-image, and the image of "others." These provided a sense of "bounded seriality" (Anderson 1998: 35) and a new "lineage" of nationhood.

The Japanese were indeed the first rulers of Taiwan to use population surveys locally. The "entire" population (at least of the portion of the island under effective Japanese control) was counted periodically, beginning in 1905.[19] The beginning of human inhabitation in Taiwan was represented and narrated in the first Taiwan museum in Taipei City in 1908. The government also launched "scientific" surveys of the Aborigines in the name of ethnography. The classification system for Han Chinese subpopulations was completed in 1905, and for the Aborigine "race" in 1915.

But before more concrete evidence can be produced, I hesitate to contend that these measures were important then in building people's collective imagination of being distinctive Taiwanese. If they were important, I would think that the learning of Japanese as *the* "national" and *the* "higher" form of language by Taiwanese would be even *more* important because it penetrated the daily interlocution of people who otherwise spoke different dialects and had different ethnic origins. The learning of Japanese as a national language was also accompanied by the suppression of Chinese, with successive bans on the teaching of Chinese in 1932, the use of Chinese in newspapers in 1937, and then the import of Chinese printed material to Taiwan in 1940. The successful Japanization of the linguistic landscape should have had a much bigger impact on the imagination of people than censuses, museums, and maps.

I am not saying that Anderson is wrong, just that the cultural artifacts and icons representing the community in bonded territory and seriality could not create the meaning or the feeling of the community by themselves. They need to be worked on, narrated, interpreted, constructed, or even fabricated intellectually. Their adoption into the nation-building project can take place only *after* colonialism under the newly emerging independent state. Museums and maps and other ruling techniques were used to promote not a larger notion of being Taiwanese, but the greatness of Japan, and to manufacture more docile subjects (by consenting to their inferior status) in the great Empire.

Gellner and the High Culture Sanctioned by the State

The state's ideological work can weigh heavily on people. In this sense, Gellner may have a much stronger case than Anderson in attributing importance to the state in the forming of a collective consciousness. He adopted a more modernistic and universalistic theory of nationalism, reflected in his argument on the historical stages of societal development—from preagrarian to agrarian to industrial society—and by his functionalistic conceptualization of nationalism as the necessary invention of industrialization. Nationalism was pursued by the rational calculation of state and power elites trying to impose a national "high culture" to homogenize ethnic and other differences. Gellner was not speaking about the colonial context, but of a phenomenon of the larger world (the West?), that is, industrialization, sometimes modernization. For Gellner the colonial condition was at most understood as the intrusion of "foreign" rulers. His work can be easily faulted for its implicit Eurocentrism.[20]

Still, to me, Gellner directs our attention to the link between the state and modernization, on the one hand, and nationalist culture on the other, namely, the imposition of a uniform national high culture through communication and uniform language policy and education. Unless we grasp the role of the state, the techniques of governance it employs, and the cultural institutions it relies on to nurture nationalist narratives and collective ancestry *consciously*, we cannot grasp fully its power to imprint a national image on a diverse populace.

Gellner helped me see the change in Taiwanese under the Japanization promoted to serve the national interests of Japan. Taiwan under Japan had achieved by 1920 the highest industrialization level in Asia outside of Japan itself. Tap water, modern medicine and professions, public schools, agricultural inventions, science, and so on helped to improve the living standards of Taiwanese. North–south roads, railways, telecommunications, electricity, radio, and unified monetary and measurement systems helped to develop a collective imagination of the islanders and the Taiwanese as one larger community, but with an "institutional" Japanese national identity and mixed feelings of belonging to the Empire. This is not necessarily the "Taiwanese identity" with strong self-assertion that people are thinking of today (Lamley 1994).

The "science" employed by the government for administration was not confined only to this material side; it also tried to persuade people to abandon their Chinese heritage. This was not just because of the needs of industrialization of which Gellner speaks, but also because of the Empire's need for loyalty and sacrifice, especially in the late 1930s when Japan began building Taiwan as her base to expand into the South Pacific. The persuasive measures included not just formal education but also social campaigns and elaborate displays of honor and citizen loyalty (Lamley 1994: 215–16). Especially from 1935 to 1945, Taiwanese were under heavy pressure to Japanize. The governor general of Taiwan implemented a carefully orchestrated sociocultural campaign, known as the *Kominka* Movement, to mobilize the general population. Police surveillance was common. People were monitored through civic registration and the established neighborhood watch organizations (the *Ho-ko* system). The overarching goal was to change the mindsets of Taiwanese to facilitate industrialization and colonial rule and expansion. As a result of *Kominka*, some Taiwanese toward the end of Japanese rule were even eager to compete for the chance (and honor) to devote their lives to the "fatherland" (Japan) by joining the imperial armed forces voluntarily.[21]

It is difficult to assess the Japanese legacy on Taiwanese consciousness, especially for those who grew up then. Former President Lee Teng-hui's remarks are a good illustration, though. Two Taiwanese nationalist intellectuals exiled to Japan in the 1950s, Dr. Ong Jok-tik and Dr. Huang Zhaotang, also had ambivalent feelings about their former colonial master. Dr. Ong said that the most abhorrent part of Japanese education was the indoctrination of patriotism and of loyalty to the emperor. But Japanese education also lifted Taiwan from a superstitious and feudalistic society to modernity. In his assessment, the Taiwanese became a learned and modernized people because of Japanese education (Wang 1993: 127–38). Dr. Huang, now a university professor in Japan, wrote that the Taiwanese had a bloody hatred for the Japanese, and that he could never forget the shame that Japanese had brought upon Taiwan through racist colonialism. But he was also quick to point out that the Taiwanese were much better off materially under Japan than they had been before (Huang 1998: 48–50). He also believes that being assimilated and educated Japanese–Taiwanese, and a part of the great empire, gave Taiwanese pride as they abandoned their old low-status Chinese identity (Huang 1998: 10, 11, 17).

So the governance of Japan did matter a great deal in shaping the Taiwanese collective image. Firstly, it created a number of activists who became "modernized" and "enlightened" through their awakening process and who started the first wave of anticolonial struggles invoking a new self-image of the Taiwanese. Secondly, colonial governance created an indisputable high culture against which commoners were measured for their merits. The state was in fact the most influential institutional force in reshaping the "moral horizons" of Taiwanese people. It also created, through enticements, persuasion, and coercion, a largely compliant population that supported the system.

Thus, Taiwan had all the favorable cultural conditions, suggested in Anderson's thesis, for developing a Taiwanese imagination: the spread of a national language; new communication technology, such as press and radio; and new skills of cultural representation. But the meaning of Taiwanese identity is far from settled. I think that it is a loophole in Anderson's thesis that he did not separate the "conditions favorable for national imagination" from "what imagination actually means." I am suggesting that Taiwan started to develop its conditions for national imagination because of its collective experiences under Japanese colonial governance. But what kind of identity can we ascribe to that imagined collectivity? I hope I have demonstrated the complexities and the vicissitudes: people were reacting and choosing to act differently. Feeling sandwiched in between, some chose to be nationalistic Taiwanese holding onto their Han Chineseness with a modern bent; some became patriotic Japanese; some became left-wing Taiwan nationalists; and some sided with the moderate middle-class reformists. In this way, Gellner makes us to look at the imposition of high culture, but his analysis is limited by missing the colonial context and the effect of the combination of colonial domination, expanding imperialism, and modernization.

CONTENDING NATIONALIST VIEWS AND DEMOCRATIZATION

Anderson and Gellner share one fundamental research question: Under what circumstances or historical conditions do people become consciously aware of their collective existence and act in the name of a nation? Their answers to these questions provide us with useful frameworks. But, they are much less successful in understanding how and why in some places and at some times this consciousness fails to materialize. And, they offer little to explain the rise of conflicting nationalist imaginations, nor about why contending nationalist imaginations could emerge under the same nation-state roof. This is because they pay more attention to the operating principles or political functioning of nations and nationalism than to how people become engaged in real politics. Regarding this, Brubaker (1996) is right to remind us that "nationalism is a form of doing politics." It is precisely to the concrete "politics" and the analysis thereof that I turn.

The Failure of the Authoritarian–Nationalistic State

The Chinese nationalist regime (the Republic of China) on Taiwan has failed (or succeeded only partially, for some) to create a unifying Chinese nationalism. It has also helped to provoke the further development of a separatist identity: Taiwanese nationalism. The Republic of China on Taiwan, prior to 1985, was described as a "strong" or "hard" state for its authoritarian and developmental characteristics. It has been very dedicated to manufacturing a genuinely patriotic population with a strong Chinese national identity when pursuing the goal of industrialization and, most importantly, the mission for national unification (i.e., of Taiwan and mainland China, the latter "stolen" by the Communist "bandits" in 1949). My own schooling and passed-on family narratives testify to that. But when one starts to look into the reasons why the competition between Taiwanese and Chinese nationalist thinking took place, the weaknesses of both Anderson's and Gellner's theses for analyzing real politics become obvious.

In an earlier article (Chang 2000) I attempted to solve this question in terms of the following factors. First, the people in China and the people in Taiwan, despite their elements of common heritage, have undergone separate transformations and followed different trajectories since their forced separation in 1895. As we have seen, the notion of self-determination and demands for recognition were already prevalent among the Taiwanese elite, to say the least. The arriving mainland Chinese from the ancestral homeland, however, were very much wrapped in their nationalistic fervor of trying to "unite" all people of different "Chinese" origins in order to rebuild the war-torn motherland and also, more immediately, to prevent communists or other postwar national "opportunists" from rising up against the "Chinese nation."

This gap of mutual expectations between the mainlanders and Taiwanese was created by their respective historical conjunctures. In fact, their respective self-transformation processes took place in reaction to each other's own circumstances without much direct participation from the other side until 1945, when Japan returned Taiwan. Before then, Taiwan and China existed as two separate political fields. As I said earlier, the Taiwanese were people sandwiched between the Japanese Empire and their ancestral homeland. To resolve this dilemma, some resisted Japan through campaigning for "cultural elevation," "awakening," and "recognition for the right to home-rule," while others identified with the Japanese. In any event, their frames of meaning and their references to the Japanese legacy were very different from the mainlanders, who came to "replace" the Japanese. For the newly arrived Chinese with their strong nationalistic fervor, this so-called Taiwanese self-consciousness, with its expectations for autonomous rule and social justice, did not meet the "needs" of a strong and unified Chinese nation. In addition, in the first two years of rule by the motherland after 1945, officials were commonly authoritarian, abusive, and corrupt. Chinese nationalism was in this sense used to justify the privilege of the mainlanders over the Taiwanese. As a result, what was supposed to be a decolonization process after the war ended in 1945 became instead a kind of domestic colonization.[22]

A collision of moralities and an uprising of some kind become inevitable when "outsiders" are perceived as dominating an established community. This background helps explain why the February 28 Incident of 1947 had such a great impact on the later development of Taiwanese consciousness. We also understand more about why, after the eruption, the present-day Taiwan independence movement was started almost exclusively by Taiwanese and not mainlanders, and why so many Taiwanese—but not mainlanders—felt so strongly for the opposition leaders given life sentences after the Kaohsiung Incident some three decades later. Scholars and politicians who want to play down the ethnonationalist significance of these events often list "misunderstanding" and "oppressive governing" as the two major causes. In fact, these events were really related to the collision of two "peoples," who (despite their common origin and shared cultural facets) had embarked on different routes to self-transformation, but were then forcefully united under the banner of Chinese nationalism at its 1945 high tide. Secondly, because the early Taiwanese independent movement was based amongst Taiwanese exiles, its influence on domestic politics and ordinary people before 1978 was not significant.[23] Independence was at most an implicit, not explicit, program of the opposition movement suppressed by authoritarian rule, until at least 1985. For the same reason, authoritarian rule increased the frictions and deepened the difference between Taiwanese and mainlanders. Though the regime evolved from "hard" to "soft" when Chiang Ching-kuo succeeded his father in 1971 (Winckler 1984), it continued to limit the representation of Taiwanese and maintain the asymmetrical distribution of power between the two groups.[24] It is thus no surprise that Taiwan's democratic movement was predominantly led by activists of Taiwanese origin, along with only very few exceptional mainlanders. Before the independence program surfaced in the late 1980s, fighting for democracy was also fighting for equal participation and representation of "our kind." After all, democratic politics is not just about the representation of interests, it is also about the relationship between representations of "interest" and "identity." After a long period of enforced silence, ethnic division and (Taiwanese) mobilization started to warm up on the eve of the Kaohsiung Incident and moved on to surge in the late 1980s after political liberalization (Wang Fu-chang 1996; Hsiao 2000).

Thirdly, the Japanese regime only partially succeeded in assimilating Taiwanese. It had failed to secure national hegemony by the end of the war. The same thing happened to the Nationalist Chinese. Like the Japanese government—but even more anxious to build patriotism among Taiwanese because of the imminent Chinese communist threat—the nationalist state actively imposed on Taiwanese an "appropriate" nationalism and nationalistic high culture. This included campaigns like the Speak Mandarin Movement, the Cultural Renaissance Movement, the Anti-Leftist Campaign, and many other policies about patriotism and loyalty (Chun 1996). Nationalistic education was most successful with mainlanders and their children, but had an uneven impact on those of Taiwanese origin. For instance, highly educated Taiwanese and members of the older generation who grew up under the Japanese were more likely to develop reservations about or distaste for official Chinese nationalism (Chang and Wu 2001). This can be attributed to their greater demand for recognition and respect. Therefore, nationalist teachings under authoritarianism may also have unintentionally provoked resistance from some Taiwanese by making them feel humiliated and defeated in both real politics and in terms of their self-image. Taiwan's democratization movement, and the force of Taiwanese opposition, has arguably grown out of the cracks of and reactions against the authoritarian regime and the nationalism it attempted to impose on people of Taiwanese origin.

Regime Transformation and the "Ethnicization" of Politics

Regime transformation from authoritarian rule to liberal democracy was not the concern of either Gellner or Anderson.[25] In reality, the issue of nation or national identity is often salient in the process of democratization. It has been inextricably intertwined with electoral mobilization and social justice rhetoric in political competition in Taiwan (e.g., Wachman 1994; Wu Naiteh 1994, 1996), but also in South Korea, Canada (especially in Quebec), Australia, and, of course, postcommunist Europe (both Eastern and Western). Whether we agree with Anderson that nation is conceived in the mode of consciousness of the ordinary people, or with Gellner that nation is a useful cultural construct for both the state and the elite to pursue industrialization and other objectives, then the "uses" of nation in real politics and regime transformation processes must be normal and prevalent. But this was apparently not their primary problematic.

My position has been that we need to study the historical context and historical conjuncture factors, not generate an overarching theory in searching for the roots of nation, its origin, and transformation. Likewise, we need to examine its relation to and effect on political processes. It would be difficult for me to imagine the route of Taiwan's regime transformation solely in terms of modernization theory, which stresses economic development or the growth of the middle class as the major factor contributing to democracy. Nor it is possible to imagine the transformation only in terms of the theory of state elites, which assigns primary importance to the adaptability of the regime or the will of some "wise" dictators such as Chiang Ching-kuo. In Taiwan, as Ernest Renan once said in another context, there are two things that constitute the nation: "One lies in the past, the other in the present. One is the possession in common of a rich legacy of memories, the other is present-day consent, the desire to live together, the will to perpetuate the value of the heritage that one has received in an undivided form" (Renan 1882: 19).

For early Taiwanese opposition activists, both common memories and consent to the regime and its national bent were absent. Therefore, the regime transition, the challenge from the opposition, and the regime's adaptation to this challenge have involved not just forging democracy to replace authoritarianism, but also building a new imagining of a nation-state to replace the existing one.

NATIONALISM AND PRAGMATISM

Comparative studies have found that Taiwan's transition from authoritarianism to democracy has been relatively peaceful compared to those of neighboring Asian countries or some of the Latin American regimes (e.g., Huntington 1991; Fukuyama 1995). The question is, will rival nationalist claims in Taiwan become more and more ethnic-prone, intolerant, and eventually lead to violence? Or, will the Taiwanese elite eventually fall for the lure of a proclaimed independent nation-state and stir up a new wave of ethnonationalist conflict between Taiwanese and mainlanders, or between Taiwan and China? Indeed, Snyder has pointed out in his acclaimed *From Voting to Violence* (2000: 20) that a multiethnic country can easily fall victim to nationalist violence during the democratization period if political elites were to find ethnonationalism appealing and useful in the postauthoritarian eras, as in Rwanda, Sri Lanka, and former Yugoslavia.

My view regarding Taiwan is an optimistic one. I think Taiwan is more likely to continue its peaceful movement toward a mature democracy despite its lack of "national" unity.[26] My arguments have to do with the prevalence of routine politics and the existence of a well-established electoral system in Taiwan. As mentioned earlier, early political liberalization in Taiwan began with Chiang Ching-kuo in 1971. This process gradually built up its momentum, albeit very slowly and bumpily. This "softening" of authoritarianism was accompanied by Chiang's willingness to reform his party and for the ruling apparatus to accommodate the new political conditions (e.g., Winckler 1984; Cheng 1993). The well-known "Taiwanization" policy he spearheaded was one of many examples. In addition, the previous opposition, now the ruling DPP elite, have not had much interest in generating violence in domestic politics and have been confined by the rules of the game and the electoral systems. From an institutional perspective, the tendency toward Taiwanization was characterized by a gradual and slow expansion of elections, which have been effectively institutionalized at some levels since 1951. The system has evolved from a democracy "show" dominated by the KMT and manipulated under an authoritarian regime, to the "election holidays" for the dissidents (*xuanju jiaqi*) of the late 1970s and 1980s (e.g., Copper 1981; Li 1984). The system for political competition has generally been open and credible since 1994, when popular elections for the presidency were institutionalized in the revised constitution (Diamond et al. 1997).

For the first twenty-some years, this slow process of opening-up, even though the authority persistently denied all-out institutional change, gave the opposition parties in Taiwan incentives to support the system even while striving to change it. In other words, they participated and hence legitimized, but were not openly admitted to a system that they believed could be democratized and localized through gains in winning elections and popular support. The opposition used various strategies including publishing magazines, protesting in the street, negotiating, and, above all, routinely participating in the not very just electoral politics prescribed by the authority. They did not use radical means, such as an all-out revolution or an all-out nationalistic attack on this "outsider regime." The opposition movement before 2000 drew together many issues, including social activism, human rights, anticorruption, antiefficacy, and the "collective sufferings" of the Taiwanese people (Wu Nai-teh 1994). Because the outcry for Taiwan's independence and Taiwanese nationalism was still punishable by law before 1991, it was therefore "hidden" under many other issues. Thus, although politics was almost always about nationalism, it was not exclusively so. This has made for two intertwined movements, one for democratization and the other for nationalism. Although closely allied with each other neither one has completely absorbed the other.

The democratic institutions have passed the fierce test of the 2000 presidential campaign, when the long-ruling KMT lost to the DPP's pro-Taiwan independence candidate Chen Shui-bian. For almost five days, from the late evening of March 18 when the election result was reported, a part of Taipei City, near the KMT headquarters, was occupied by several thousand KMT (ex)loyalists denouncing Lee Teng-hui (president and in 1989–1999 KMT party chairman) for breaking up the party and precipitating the disgraceful election loss. The angry crowd finally left the streets after Lee agreed to resign the chairmanship a few days later. However, other than this incident, the overall transition of power has been relatively peaceful, suggesting a firmly held belief in freedom of speech, civic liberties, and due process.

This is particularly so if we look at the issues of freedom to express different views on nationalism. Since 1991, publicly advocating either Taiwanese independence or unification with the mainland motherland has been essentially legal. In 1992, the treason article of the Criminal Act was formally revoked. Prior to 1991, even after the lifting of martial law in 1987, people expressing political opinions regarded as contrary to the nation-state's interest—such as Taiwan independence or unification with the Chinese communists—could be arrested and given a life sentence or even the death penalty for treason and conspiracy. It took almost two years of

heated, polarizing, and partisan debate, rallies, and cross-party maneu-
vering before these two rival nationalist discourses could become "normal." The legal change had the immediate effect of bringing conflicting
nationalist arguments into the routine politics of democratic processes and
institutions. Now, popular support for a particular nationalist ideology depends on the effectiveness of political organizations in competing for audience. There is indeed a political "market." By contrast, intimidation,
threat, violent conflict, terrorism, and so forth are less attractive and more
risky as they are outlawed and extremely difficult to justify in a relatively
open system.

A consequence of the well-established electoral system and freedom of
expression has been peaceful regime transition under the same old constitution. Today, the national constitution of the Republic of China, itself a source
of fierce conflict amongst political groups with different interests and nationalist outlooks, is still the ultimate law and font of legitimate power for all
governments. In other words, even if Taiwan's new democracy is awkward,
hard to steer (Clark 2000; Rigger 2001), and constantly hindered by nationalist disputes and strong partisanship paralleling the mainlander–Taiwanese
cleavage, and even if people of different backgrounds sometimes disagree
and distrust each other quite strongly, Taiwan, the Republic of China, is more
likely peacefully to resolve nationalist differences rather than turn toward violence.

Would there not be someone wanting to corrupt this competitive "political market" for his or her own interests? Yes. However, for them to succeed, the larger political framework, including the constitution and myr-
iad of public and civic laws associated with it, would need to be
discarded. Many people would have to feel strong enough to take the
risks involved in abandoning the daily routines, habitual political practices, and beliefs in legitimacy in which so much is at stake. The prevalence of pragmatism regarding politics and nationalism make this only a
remote possibility. That is the third reason I believe Taiwan is unlikely to
move toward a violent nationalist conflict.

Snyder (2000) suggests that the level of economic prosperity may be negatively related to the likelihood that ordinary people will fall prey to nationalist elite manipulation.[27] In other words, if the citizens of a country are well
enough off that they feel they have something to lose by supporting a conflict, they are less likely to do so. Not only has the level of economic prosperity been continuously increasing for the past decade, Taiwan also experienced a development "take-off" prior to early liberalization in the 1970s.
The growth of a moderate and somewhat conservative middle class (mainly
at the civic, professional, and managerial level) has limited the rise of both a
strong labor movement and extreme nationalism (e.g., Chang 1993, 1994).
The resulting pragmatism is also evident in the large proportion of middle-

of-the-roaders; the DPP's unwillingness to declare Taiwan independent (despite its proindependence party platform); and since 1995 its "great reconciliation" policy toward the formal right-wing Chinese nationalists and mainlander elites (see Laliberté in this book; Guo 1998; Chen 2000).

Because of the prevalence of political pragmatism, before closing I want to add a strong note of caution concerning the "Taiwanese–mainlander" dichotomy in Taiwan, a central theme of this chapter. There has been some rising polarization: that is, if one is truly a Taiwanese patriot, one cannot be a respectful Chinese and vice versa. However, political attitude studies from 1992 to 2000 reveal that the largest proportion of people elect to be in the "middle" category. When asked: "How would you answer if you were asked if are you Chinese or Taiwanese?" and given the following choices: (1) I am Chinese, (2) I am both, or (3) I am Taiwanese, the proportion for "I am Chinese" ranged from 11 to 19 percent, for "I am both" (the compromise category) from 37 to 46 percent, and for "I am Taiwanese" from 27 to 39 percent.[28] At least one-fourth of the population appears to have contingent identities, depending on the situation and the context.[29]

Pragmatism is also very significant if we look at the increasing Taiwanese investments in mainland China, despite political tensions between Taipei and Beijing, and despite the Taiwan government's continuous warnings. The total trade dependence of Taiwan on China (excluding Hong Kong and Macau) increased from 2 percent in 1987 to 17.5 percent in 1999.[30] Trade and tourism between mainland China and Taiwan has also grown dramatically.[31] This is occurring without amiable political ties between the two governments, and without the convenience of direct flights across the Taiwan Strait. Therefore, some scholars have gone as far as to identify Taiwan as a postnational society, unconstrained by nationalist ideas and projects (e.g., see Shi Zhiyu 1995).[32]

In the beginning of this chapter, I mentioned the importance of being reflexive in reading theories. The prevalent theoretical view of nation—seeing it as a state-led or class-based creation and everything else as fabrication—neglects the capacity of people to reflect and act upon their political and economic circumstances. Also, authoritarian elites may be able to impose "order" and "peace," but cannot "impose" nationalism on the majority of the people over a long period. At present it would be even more difficult for an authoritarian elite to do so, especially when confronted with today's fast expanding global economy. Is nationalism coming to an historical end all over the world? My study of Taiwan tells me "no" and that this question is too general to be meaningful. Today, in relatively well-to-do places like Taiwan, Quebec, South Korea, Scotland, Israel, Greece, or even Australia, for differing reasons, citizens still feel the strong power of nationalism at all levels of politics, even while it is held in check by institutional politics and, on many occasions, overriding pragmatic concerns.

NOTES

1. During Anderson's 2000 visit to Taiwan, we were surprised to find out that, although a preeminent professor from Cornell who had lived in the United States for more than forty years and well-versed in different languages, he always travels with his Irish passport. He said casually "it is just a 'habit.'"

2. During my college years at Taiwan University, we used Paul B. Horton and Chester L. Hunt's *Sociology* (McGraw Hill 1968) for our sophomore "English" class. Learning sociology and learning English, though critics often say sociology is written in incomprehensible English, was actually combined in those days. Not long ago, one of my graduate students, very frustrated by English, asked me why we must heavily rely on Western theories (referring to the English works chosen for the class).

3. By conjuncture, I mean the convergence of many forces of social relations at a particular time in history. It is different from the "structural," which implies the outcome is somewhat determined by objective social relations.

4. On demythologizing the Chinese nation, see Duara (1993); Shen (1997).

5. In 1993, I was one of the earliest scholars to apply Anderson's thesis to understanding the Chinese nation in Taiwan. I said the "authenticity" of the Chinese nationalism taught to students was part of national mythology, more an agreed-on imagination than reality. What really matters is what we think of ourselves. My study of Taiwanese nationalism came after this.

6. While I was studying sociology at Purdue University in the United States I received newsletters distributed by a local Formosan Student Association that supported the general outcry against the arrests.

7. I am referring to the notion of Taiwan *minzu* characterized by Dr. Liao Wenyi, the pioneer of the Taiwan independence movement, but since largely abandoned. He said in the 1950s that Taiwan *minzu* consists of people of mixed-blood lineage from the Spaniards, Dutch, Aborigines, and Han settlers.

8. On the February 28 Incident, see Lai, Myers and Wei (1991). On the Kaohsiung Incident, see Tien (1989: 95–100) and Chu (1992: 38–40).

9. The title of the paper was "Western Nationalism and Eastern Nationalism: Is There a Difference That Matters?" As the title suggests, Anderson is inclined to a general understanding of nationalism beyond the "East" and "West" division.

10. See note 8 above.

11. The general opinion today is that the plains Aborigines were deprived of their land and culture and forced to Sinicize, but according to Shepherd (1993) the Manchu government was in effect quite rational and conscientious in managing land issues when Aborigine interests were involved, though it failed to protect the Aborigine population in the end.

12. Brown (2001: 153–64) also demonstrates that "culture is more important than ancestry in classifying people" with respect to the Aborigines and Han people in adjacent communities in southern Taiwan.

13. Under Bill No. 63 (1896–20) later modified as Bill 3–1, the *Taiwan Sotoku* (Governor General) was now accountable to neither the Imperial Diet (the Congress) of Japan nor to the Taiwanese.

14. The Left and Right split openly in 1927, and the association turned Left after a series of internal fights.

15. In 1920, progressive Taiwanese youth envisioned their cause in terms of women's liberation, the proletarian movement, suffrage, and the national-awakening movements. That is, woman, class, and nation were the three main issues for Taiwan (Young 1993: 86–7).

16. It was first created as the Division of the Taiwan Nation in the Japanese Communist Party, receiving instructions from both Moscow and Tokyo. Its relation to the Chinese Communists was not very significant until later in the 1940s.

17. Sugar cane farmers were contract tillers and workers under the Japanese sugar industry conglomerates.

18. He was born in 1923. His father and eldest brother both worked for the Japanese government, the latter selected as an outstanding Taiwanese youth and placed in the "voluntary army." Lee studied in Japan for two years and returned to Taiwan in 1945.

19. After 1915, the census was carried out every five years.

20. Later he studied post-Communist nationalism in the Eastern Bloc and relations among Islam, industrialization, and nationalism.

21. The *Kominka* movement included social, cultural, and linguistic policies to facilitate the rapid learning of Japanese, the sciences, and Japanese virtues. All sectors of society were mobilized to glorify the Empire and the Emperor. The total number of Taiwanese in the Japanese military was at least 200,000. During the last year of the war, more than 40,000 Taiwanese were also drafted (involuntarily) to join the military.

22. The late Dr. Wang Yude, a Taiwanese independence activist, wrote: "Only now [referring to the abusiveness of Chinese officials in Taiwan], Taiwanese began to miss the Japanese period. Taiwanese despised Japanese and had called them 'dogs.' 'Dogs' bark, but 'dogs' will watch the door for you. Chinese are 'pigs.' 'Pigs' only know how to glut themselves" (Wang 1996: 157).

23. With political liberalization and their defiant return to Taiwan in the late 1980s, their influence grew.

24. Ordinary mainlanders were also excluded from participating in politics because of the nature of the regime, but they seemed to be overrepresented in the higher circle and power elite and, unlike the Taiwanese, were relatively supportive of KMT rule before its split in 1992 (Chang 1989).

25. Earlier studies of regime transformation (O'Donnell et al. 1986), mentioned little about nationalist politics. Chu (1992) argued for its importance when analyzing Taiwan's democratization. For more recent works challenging this view, see Snyder (2000) and Sakwa (1999).

26. My optimistic arguments would be hard to maintain if China invaded, provoked by a move toward independence. This external factor, constituting both a national security and economic threat for Taiwan, has exerted tremendous pressures on Taiwanese domestic politics. Beijing's sovereignty claims over Taiwan and calculated favorable or unfavorable treatment of different Taiwanese political parties also complicates and poses a challenge to the established democratic virtue. However, because of space limits, I cannot fully deal with this topic in this chapter. My observations primarily end in 2000, when, in defiance of Beijing's direct warnings, Chen Shui-bian was elected as president.

27. Snyder is not clear about the difference between "relative poverty," the gap between the rich and the poor, and "absolute poverty," the level of income.

28. The percentages were taken from regular opinion surveys conducted by the ROC government between February and March 2000 (see Mainland Affairs Council 2000a).

29. Another reason is the prevalence of intermarriage. Sociologists estimate that 50 percent of the "mainlanders" born between 1950 and 1960, and up to 80 percent of those born between 1960 and 1970, came from parents of different origins. This phenomenon alone makes the ethnic "divide" questionable. Given the high level of urbanization and industrialization, everyday life in Taiwan is much too complicated to allow a hostile cleavage to get in the way all the time. Political tolerance can be essential for daily life to continue normally.

30. The Taiwan government registered as much as U.S.$16.1 billion, or 22,616 cases, of approved investment from Taiwan to China from 1991 to October 2000 (see Mainland Affairs Council 2000b). However, these official statistics probably underestimate the reality.

31. It is estimated that from 1988 to 1998 mainland authorities issued an average of 1.2 million entry visas to Taiwanese every year (see Ministry of the Interior 1999).

32. I am very skeptical of Shi Zhiyu's viewpoint. The fluidity and diversity of identity politics in Taiwan, and the mixture of many different (and contradictory) ideas and behaviors connected with them, can be better interpreted as market-driven pragmatism without attributing anything to postmodern thinking.

REFERENCES

Anderson, Benedict O. 1991. *Imagined Communities: Reflections on the Origin and Spread of Nationalism*. London: Verso.
——. 1998. *The Spectre of Comparison: Nationalism, Southeast Asia, and the World*. New York: Verso.
Brown, Melissa J. 2001. "Reconstructing Ethnicity: Recorded and Remembered Identity in Taiwan." *Ethnology* 40, no. 2 (Spring): 153–64.
Brubaker, Rogers. 1996. *Nationalism Reframed: Nationhood and the National Question in the New Europe*. Cambridge: Cambridge University Press.
Chang, Maukuei. 1989. "The Formation of Partisan Preferences in Taiwan's Democratization Process, 1986–1987." In *Taiwan: A Newly Industrialized State*, eds. H. M. Hsiao et al. Taipei: National Taiwan University.
——. 1993. "Middle Class and Social and Political Movements in Taiwan." In *Discovery of the Middle Classes in East Asia*, ed. Hsiao Hsin Huang. Taipei: Institute of Ethnology, Academia Sinica.
——. 1994. "Toward an Understanding of *Sheng-chi Wen-ti* in Taiwan, Focusing on Changes after Political Liberalization." In *Ethnicity in Taiwan: Social, Historical, and Cultural Perspective*, eds. Chen Chung-min, Chuang Ying-Chang, and Huang Shu-min. Taipei: Institute of Ethnology, Academia Sinica.
——. 2000. "On the Origin and Transformation of Taiwan Identity." *China Perspective* 28: 51–70.
——, and Wu Hsin-yi. 2001. "*Guanyu minzu yu zuqun luenshu zhong de rentong yu qingxu—zuenzhong yu chengren de wenti*" ("About identification and emotion

issues in the national and ethnic discourse—issues of dignity and recognition"). In *Minzu zhuyi yu Liangan Guanxi* (Nationalism and cross-strait relations), eds. Chia-lung Lin and Yongnian Zheng. Taipei: Xin Ziran.

Chatterjee, Partha. 1993. *Nationalist Thought and the Colonial World: A Derivative Discourse.* Minneapolis: University of Minnesota.

Chen, Fangming. 1998. *Zhimindi Taiwan: zuoyi zhengzhi yundong shiluen (Taiwan the colony: historical essays on the leftist movement).* Taipei: Maitian.

Chen, Mingcheng. 1992. *Hai wai taidu sishi nian (The forty years of the overseas Taiwan independence movement).* Taipei: Zili.

Chen, Shui-bian. 2000. *The Son of Taiwan: The Life of Chen Shui-Bian and His Dreams for Taiwan.* trans. David Toman. Taipei: Wang Chenfeng.

Cheng, Tun-jen. 1993. "Taiwan in Democratic Transition." In *Driven by Growth: Political Change in the Asia-Pacific Region*, ed. James W. Morley. Armonk, N.Y.: M.E. Sharpe.

Chu, Yun-han. 1992. *Crafting Democracy in Taiwan.* Taipei: Institute for National Policy Research.

Chun, Allen. 1996. "From Nationalism to Nationalizing: Cultural Imagination and State Formation in Postwar Taiwan." In *Chinese Nationalism*, ed. Jonathan Unger. Armonk, N.Y.: M.E. Sharpe.

Clark, Cal. 2000. *The 2000 Taiwan Presidential Elections.* New York: Asia Society.

Copper, John F. 1981. "Taiwan's Recent Election: Progress Toward a Democratic System." *Asian Survey* 21, no. 10 (October): 1029–39.

Couture, Jocelyne, Kai Nielsen, and Michel Seymour, eds. 1998. *Rethinking Nationalism.* Calgary: University of Calgary Press.

Diamond, Larry, et al., eds. 1997. *Consolidating the Third Wave Democracies: Themes and Perspectives.* Baltimore: Johns Hopkins University Press.

Duara, Prasenjit. 1993. "De-Constructing the Chinese Nation." *The Australian Journal of Chinese Affairs* 30: 1–26.

Fukuyama, Francis. 1995. "Confucianism and Democracy." *Journal of Democracy* 6: 20–33.

Gellner, Ernest. 1983. *Nations and Nationalism.* Ithaca, N.Y.: Cornell University Press.

———. 1994. *Encounters with Nationalism.* Oxford: Blackwell.

———. 1997. *Nationalism.* London: Weidenfeld & Nicolson.

Geoffroy, Claude. 1997. *Taiwan duli yundong (The Taiwan independence movement)*, trans. Huang Fadian. Taipei: Qianwei.

Guo, Zheng-liang. 1998. *Minjindang zhuanxing zhitong (The DPP's transformation ordeal).* Taipei: Tianxia.

Hall, John A., ed. 1998. *The State of the Nation: Ernest Gellner and the Theory of Nationalism.* Cambridge: Cambridge University Press.

Hsiao, A-qin. 2000. *Contemporary Taiwanese Cultural Nationalism.* London: Routledge.

Huang, Zhaotang. 1998. *Taiwan na xiang na li si wen (Taiwan nationalism).* Taipei: Qianwei.

Huntington, Samuel P. 1991. *The Third Wave: Democratization in the Late Twentieth Century.* Oklahoma City: University of Oklahoma Press.

Jiang, Yihua. 1998. *Ziyou zhuyi, minzu zhuyi yu guojia rentong (Liberalism, nationalism, and national identity).* Taipei: Yangzhi Publishers.

92 *Chang Maukuei*

Lai, Tse-han, Ramon H. Myers, and Wei Wou. 1991. *A Tragic Beginning, the Taiwan Uprising of February 28, 1947*. Stanford, Calif.: Stanford University Press.

Lamley, Harry J. 1994. "Taiwan Under Japanese Rule, 1895–1945: The Vicissitudes of Colonialism." In *Taiwan: A New History*, ed. M. Rubinstein. Armonk, N.Y.: M.E. Sharpe.

Li, Hsiao-feng. 1984. *T'ai-wan min-chu yun-tung* (*Taiwan's democratic movement*). Taipei: Zili.

Mainland Affairs Council. 2000a. "Minzhong dui ziwo rentong de kanfa" ("The public's views on self-identity"). Executive Yuan, ROC Government, March 2000. Available at www.mac.gov.tw/big5/mlpolicy/pos/8903/8903_3.gif. Accessed 4 June 2003.

———. 2000b. "Liangan jingji jiaoliu zhongyao zhibiao" ("Leading cross strait economic exchange indicators"). *Monthly Report for Cross-Straits Economy* 98 (October). Taipei: Executive Yuan, ROC Government. Available at www.chinabiz.org.tw/maz/eco-month/home.htm. Accessed 4 June 2003.

Ministry of the Interior. 1999. "Liangan renmin jiaoliu" ("Statistics on cross strait exchanges"). Taipei: Executive Yuan, ROC Government. Available at www.moi.gov.tw/w3/stat/topic/topic3.5.html. Accessed 4 June 2003.

O'Donnell, Guillermo, Philippe C. Schmitter, and Laurence Whitehead, eds. 1986. *Transitions from Authoritarian Rule: Latin America*. Baltimore: Johns Hopkins University Press.

Renan, Ernest. 1882. *Qu'est-ce qu'une nation?* trans. Ida Mae Snyder. Paris: Calmann-Levy.

Rigger, Shelley. 1999. *Politics in Taiwan—Voting for Democracy*. London: Routledge.

———. 2001. *From Opposition to Power: Taiwan's Democratic Progressive Party*. Boulder, Colo.: Lynne Rienner.

Sakwa, Richard, ed. 1999. *The Experience of Democratization in Eastern Europe: Selected Papers from the Fifth World Congress of Central and East European Studies, Warsaw*. New York: St. Martin's Press; London: Macmillan.

Shen, Sung-chiao. 1997. "The Myth of *Huang-ti* (Yellow Emperor) and the Construction of Chinese Nationhood in Late Qing." *Taiwan: A Radical Quarterly in Social Studies* 28: 1–76.

Shepherd, John. 1993. *Statecraft and Political Economy on the Taiwan Frontier, 1600–1800*. Stanford, Calif.: Stanford University Press.

Shi, Ming. 1980. *Taiwan ren si bainian shi* (*The four-hundred-year history of the Taiwanese*). San José: Peng Lai Dao.

Shi, Zhiyu. 1995. *Houxiandai de guojia rentong* (*Postmodern national identity*). Taipei: Shijie.

Snyder, Jack. 2000. *From Voting to Violence: Democratization and Nationalist Conflict*. New York: W.W. Norton.

Tien, Hung-Mao. 1989. *The Great Transition: Political and Social Change in the Republic of China*. Stanford, Calif.: Hoover Institute, Stanford University.

Tsurumi, E. Patricia. 1977. *Japanese Colonial Education in Taiwan, 1895–1945*. Cambridge, Mass.: Harvard University Press.

Wachman, Alan. 1994. *Taiwan: National Identity and Democratization*. Armonk, N.Y.: M.E. Sharpe.

Wang, Fu-chang. 1996. "*Fandui yundong de gongshi dongyuan: 1979–1989 nian liang po tiaozhan gaofeng de bijiao*" ("The consensus mobilization of the opposition movement: A comparison of the 1979 and the 1989 surging"). *Taiwanese Political Review* 1: 129–209.

Wang, Horng-luen. 2000. "Rethinking the Global and the National: Reflections on National Imaginations in Taiwan." *Theory, Culture, and Society* 17, no. 4: 93–117.

Wang, Yude (or Ong, Jok-tik). 1993. *Taiwan kumen de lishi (The suffocating history of Taiwan)*. Taipei: Qianwei.

Winckler, Edwin A. 1984. "Institutionalization and Participation on Taiwan: From Hard to Soft Authoritarianism?" *China Quarterly* 99: 481–99.

Wu, Nai-teh. 1994. "Social Cleavages and Political Competition: Why Is There No 'Stunt Election' in Taiwan?" *Bulletin of the Institute of Ethnology* 78: 101–30. Taipei: Academia Sinica.

———. 1996. "Liberalism, Ethnic Identity, and Taiwanese Nationalism." *Taiwanese Political Science Review* 1: 5–38.

Wu, Ruei-ren. 2001. "Taiwan Must Belong to Taiwanese—the Discourses of Anticolonial Struggles and Taiwanese Nation-State, 1919–1923." In *Minzu zhuyi yu Liangan Guanxi (Nationalism and cross-strait relations)*, eds. Chia-Lung Lin and Yongnian Zheng. Taipei: Xin Ziran.

Young, Cui. 1993. *Riju shidai Taiwan funyu jiefang yundong (The Taiwanese women's liberation movement under Japanese rule)*. Taipei: China Times Publishing.

5

The Political Economy and Cultural Politics of Ethnic Conflict in Asia

Katharine N. Rankin and Kanishka Goonewardena

DEMOCRACY VERSUS ETHNIC CONFLICT?

A paradox hovers over this book: in the present Asian context, democratization and ethnic conflict go hand in hand. If the recent discourse on "Asian values" is any measure, it seems that an authoritarian politics—by way of the state or through civil society—could better "manage" Asian political struggles rooted in ethnocultural identity than have emergent democratic regimes (for a discussion, see Bell 2000). An apparently straightforward empirical description of the Asian geopolitical landscape here becomes, not without a hint of liberal trepidation, a handy political and policy prescription: more authoritarianism, less identity conflict. It is difficult to imagine a similar judgment being issued in North America during the Civil Rights movement in the United States or on the eve of the Night of the Long Knives in Canada. Here the solutions would have involved—and did involve—not less, but more democracy, along with minority rights (called "affirmative action" in the United States and "positive discrimination" in India, the largest democracy in the world). But so long as we are in Asia, why not inner peace according to Singapore, instead of internecine violence à la Sri Lanka? Leaving aside the question of exactly how democratic Sri Lanka is for now, we argue that the paradox noted is false and the good intentions premised upon it misleading.

Before authoritarianism is considered—explicitly or implicitly—as a solution to ethnic conflicts in Asia, two questions suggest themselves. Does democratization really cause ethnic conflict, in Asia or elsewhere? Or do democratic governments and ethnic conflict happen to coexist today within the bounds of some nation-states? We answer the first in the negative, for the want of evidence, or more precisely, in the view of evidence to the contrary, the implications of which are explored below. We respond to the second question affirmatively, while noting the global scope of the phenomenon in question, which encompasses Europe, the Middle East, Africa, and the Americas—thus eschewing any narrowly culturalist explanations and offering instead grounds for addressing ethnic conflicts that not only reject authoritarianism, patrimonialism, ethnoreligious fundamentalism, and other forms of domination, but also are more *radically* democratic than the actually existing democracies in Asia.

In fairness to those whose views differ from ours on these matters—both in this volume and (more frequently) elsewhere—we should note at the outset what is usually meant by democracy in this context (see Swift 2002). Not surprisingly, it refers to liberal bourgeois democracy: universal suffrage, periodic elections amidst civil liberties (individual rights as well as, in officially multicultural countries, minority rights), and the rule of law. The formal separation of the state and the church too is often part of this conception, though not always. As Daniel Bell suggests in chapter 2, "liberalism" is the "least controversial" (i.e., the most hegemonic) standard against which countries can be measured with respect to democracy—and their ability to curb ethnic conflict. This more or less liberal-bourgeois approach to democracy (and politics more generally), however uncontroversial, overlooks the larger political-economic context within which ethnic conflicts, particularly those fueled by ethnoreligious fundamentalisms, are being played out as we write—within or outside Asia. It is oblivious, in particular, to the manner in which nationalism today functions as a response to, or indeed as a modality of, globalization: i.e., how, in Fredric Jameson's (1996) words, "religious fundamentalism . . . only comes into significant being when the traditional Left alternatives . . . have suddenly seemed unavailable." By virtue of its hegemony, moreover, the "least controversial" standpoint equates democracy with liberal democracy as such, foreclosing any thought as to how the former might be reformulated and extended beyond the limits set by the latter in order more effectively to address identity conflict within the present political–economic conjuncture. Our position, which is not overly constrained by the limits of actually existing democracy, is different. On the one hand, we caution against counseling Asian states to respond to ethnic conflict with a choice between liberal bourgeois democracy and authoritarianism; and on the other, we advocate deepening democracy beyond the barriers erected by liberal democracy as a means to address the socioeconomic causes of ethnic conflict in particular and fundamentalisms ignited by globalization more generally.

Our premise for asserting this position can be simply stated. If, in keeping with feminist and socialist strands of democratic theory, we adopt a deeper understanding of democracy as expanding the scope of human freedom in all spheres of life—political and economic, public, and private—then more meaningful and substantive possibilities emerge for mitigating ethnic and, indeed, other forms of conflict and violence. With such an understanding, we could also challenge more forcefully the skepticism with which the very notion of democracy has too often been regarded in relation to ethnic conflict in Asia and elsewhere, even (or especially) by those whose humanistic values are not in question. The goal in this chapter is thus to explore criteria for achieving greater degrees of democracy within multiethnic Asian societies by examining the following issues confronting those societies today: the contradictions of late-capitalist democracy, ethnoreligious nationalism, and the competing politics of recognition and redistribution.

THE CONTRADICTIONS OF LATE CAPITALISM

Few chapters in this book address the historical conjuncture within which several Asian countries, such as Indonesia and Nepal, have recently embarked on the path of political democracy, while others such as India and Sri Lanka have struggled to maintain democratic regimes in the face of authoritarian challenges: namely, the integration of the Asian region (among others) to the capitalist world economy by means of economic liberalization initially in the wake of the global recession of 1973. Yet these political-economic coordinates pose fundamental challenges for democratization, of which ethnic conflict is but one among several. During this period, neoliberal economic ideology has been institutionalized on a global and regional scale by the World Bank, International Monetary Fund (IMF), World Trade Organization (WTO), Association of South-East Asian Nations (ASEAN), and South Asian Association for Regional Cooperation (SAARC) programs of structural adjustment (SAPs) and "free" trade. The outcome has been the subordination and displacement of Asian "national development projects" by the ever more global imperatives of capitalist accumulation, according to rules and regulations determined in large measure by the United States and the G-7 (Gowan 1990; McMichael 1995). These trends have exerted two powerful yet contradictory forces on the nation-state. On the one hand, Asian states rendered increasingly impotent vis-à-vis their creditors and donors (even those East Asian pioneers of "alternative" paths to economic adjustment—South Korea, Taiwan, and Japan) must now, in the wake of the Asian financial crisis, relinquish "corrupt" state control of the economy and instead install more laissez-faire self-regulatory mechanisms tailor-made for the accumulation of capital according to neoliberalism; on the other hand, if they wish to retain legitimacy *as* nation-states, they must also play an ever greater role in both containing, indeed masking, the class conflict inherent in orthodox neoliberal capitalism and in managing the inevitable social costs and uneven benefits of corporate globalization.

The expectation within economic theories and political rhetoric promoting these trends is that economic liberalization itself acts as a "civilizing force" fostering the conditions propitious for political democracy. As political economist Stephen Gill (1996: 211) has pointed out, market freedoms are assumed—as routinely announced by G-7 leaders—to generate political freedoms: "through the growth of an 'enterprise culture' and through 'market discipline,' the virtues of prudence, responsibility, good governance, and social progress will arise in partly spontaneous fashion." Yet the past two decades have unequivocally demonstrated that economic liberalization and political democracy stand in a contradictory relationship. To wit: globalization has produced "democratic deficits" in two specific respects. First, the New World Order ruled by free trade regimes has spawned an antidemocratic trend in state–society relations, dubbed by Gill "the new constitutionalism." Opening national economies to financial integration has entailed not merely the removal of restrictive national-protectionist regulations, not merely *de*-regulation, as neoliberal ideology would have it. Rather, it has involved a re-regulation through the construction of legal frameworks to insulate from public scrutiny new economic institutions within and beyond states (e.g., WTO, ASEAN). As Philip McMichael (1995: 38, 43) has argued within the debates about globalization and state capacity, "it is the *nation*-state that is losing its salience, not the state itself," as national regulation shifts from "national coherence to enterprise competitiveness in a global market." Asian states making the transition to democracy or attempting to maintain established democratic regimes are doing so at a time when statecraft has been streamlined and steamrolled by transnational forces, with scant respect for either political party ideologies—which in any case exhibit all signs of neoliberal convergence—or popular will.

Second, while Asian states play a role in enforcing the rules of the global economy within their own borders, their capacity (and obligation, if not will) to shield the domestic economy and the people who inhabit it from the deleterious effects of globalization has diminished. For accompanying economic liberalization has been the erosion of redistributive policies and other forms of social protection (Cox 1996; Gill 1996). In this policy environment the social costs of economic adjustment—rising unemployment and inflation, decreased buying power, growing class disparity—fall mainly on the socially weak segments of the population: women and the poor, but also ethnic minorities, such as the Sri Lankan Tamils (Benería et al. 1987; Gill 1996; Mittleman 1996). Thus, while the architects of the New World Order claim to promote political democracy through economic liberalization, the social and material basis for greater political equality has been undermined in many Asian countries (Bagchi 1995, 1998, 1999). In the face of rapidly liberalizing Asian economies, consequently, the institutions of formal democracy merely apply a veneer of political equality over increasingly severe forms of social inequality (Bagchi 2000).

The persistence of such inequality in the context of narrowly defined political equality has in fact been a defining feature of liberal capitalism over time and across cultures. How has this hypocrisy survived in the midst of the political freedoms that liberal democracy promises? It has been able to survive only by means of a hegemonic separation of the "political" and "economic" spheres within liberal capitalism, as Marx observed most explicitly in his trenchant essay "On the Jewish Question" (Tucker 1978). Cannier conservatives such as Carl Schmitt (1976) and François Furet (1989) have drawn subsequently on Marx and been quite explicit, in *their* critiques of liberal democracy, about how "political sovereignty was split off from the economy, or, better put, [how] its internal logic depended on the exclusion of the economy from any visible position within the imaginary political terrain" (Buck-Morss 2000: 15–23). What this "split" entailed was also clear to them: a "fundamental respect for private property" (Schmitt, cited in Buck-Morss 2000: 15–16). More recently, Ellen Wood (1995: 14) has incisively noted, the consequences of this separation in terms of the *structural* limits to *liberal-bourgeois* democracy:

> If the defining characteristic of capitalism as a political terrain is the formal "separation of the economic and the political," or the transfer of certain "political" powers to the "economy" and "civil society," what consequences does this have for the nature and scope of the state and citizenship? Since capitalism entails, among other things, new forms of domination and coercion, which are outside the reach of instruments designed to check traditional forms of political power, it also reduces the salience of citizenship and the scope of democratic accountability. Capitalism, to put it simply, can afford a universal distribution of political goods without endangering its constitutive relations, its coercions and inequities. This, needless to say, has wide-ranging implications for our understanding of democracy and the possibilities of its expansion.

The implications are as follows: liberal democracy tolerates social and economic inequality and presents no fundamental challenge to the basic dynamics of capitalism or class relations. "It is, in fact, a specific feature of capitalism," writes Wood, "that a particular kind of universal equality is possible which does not extend to class relations—that is, precisely, a formal equality, having to do with political and legal principles and procedures rather than with the disposition of social or class power" (1995: 259). The owners of private property, moreover, can carry out surplus extraction (economic coercion) without wielding direct political power in the conventional liberal sense—sheltered from lines of political accountability or any obligation to perform social responsibilities. The insulation of economic coercion from popular sovereignty creates a structural impediment to actualizing democratic principles in the "fortresses and earthworks" of civil society: "the transformation of political into economic conflicts and the location of struggles at the point of production . . . tend to make class struggle . . . *local* and *particularistic*"—mitigating the potential for the economically disenfranchised to organize across space and ethnicity to demand more powerful forms of accountability (Wood 1995: 45; italics in original).

Today Marxists are of course not alone in registering the contradiction between actually existing democracy and capitalism, with special attention to the contemporary hegemony of neoliberalism. For example John Gray (1998a), a leading conservative political philosopher in the United Kingdom—erstwhile admirer of and counsel to Margaret Thatcher—has written influentially and prolifically on the deepening instability of global capitalism, with a call to heed the advice of Karl Polanyi (1944) on the deleterious social consequences of freewheeling markets. The country that solicits the sharpest criticism from Gray, it should be noted, is the United States—for attempting to universalize a political-economic system that cannot work in its own backyard, so to speak. Even Hayekian liberals have acknowledged the essential contradiction between capitalism and democracy that is heightened by globalization (Gray 1998b). A recent feature on "the future of the state" in *The Economist* framed the issue with characteristic clarity. "The fundamental question," announced *The Economist*, "is not, as many suppose, whether democracy is compatible with globalization, but whether democracy is compatible with liberty." How so?

> [F]reedom and democracy are linked, of course—but so are freedom and capitalism. And, unfortunately, the pessimists [critics of free-market globalization] are right to question whether capitalism can continue to get along happily with democracy. . . . Democratic states, indulgent of anti-liberal values, may make such demands of capitalism, and place such burdens and restrictions upon it, that it will slowly fade away, along with freedom.[1]

Here is a point for critics of Asian countries to consider: as far as democracy is concerned, not all is quiet on the Western front either. Nor is this disquiet of recent origin, as Polanyi (1935: 391) testified in a famous exchange with Austrian economist (and Hayek's colleague) Ludwig von Mises, during the infamous fascist "resolution" of the crisis of liberal capitalism in Europe: "the mutual incompatibility of Democracy and Capitalism is almost generally accepted to-day as the background of the social crisis of our time" (cited in Cangiani n.d.). In fact, as Polanyi's studies of markets across cultures further demonstrate, the danger today is everywhere the same: it is that capitalist markets—socially constructed and legally sanctioned—will generate such catastrophic social costs as to generate *spontaneous* mobilizations to demand social protection—as evidenced in Asia and elsewhere (Bagchi 1995, 1998, 1999, 2000; Gill 1996; Mittleman 1996, 2000; Klein 2002). The issue is thus not whether or not democracy undermines capitalism, but whether the countermovements for social protection spawned by capitalist markets will generate democratic or antidemocratic outcomes, given the range of politico-ideological forms they may assume. In multiethnic Asian societies, especially where left political forces have been weakened, the contradiction between democracy and economic globalization has often prompted an affirmation of religious and ethnic identity (along with other essentialized articulations of difference) as the privileged ideological form for demanding social security and well-being. As discussed below for the cases of Sri Lanka and India, these kinds of identity politics have readily exploited the existing structures of parliamentary democracy to galvanize ethnoreligious nationalisms at the expense of minority communities (Ahmad 1996; Jeganathan and Ismail 1995; Sivanandan 1990)—some of which in turn have spawned their own countermovements of separatist nationalism (Ali 2001; Cheran 2000).

Yet, it would be a mistake to view such ethnic conflict as the consequence of *democratization*, and then to envisage authoritarian forms of governance by the state or within civil society as a means for restoring—or enforcing—ethnic harmony. More fruitful would be to dwell on the underlying contradictions—between liberal democracy and capitalism, political equality and economic inequality. The project of democracy in Asia could then identify the limits of actually existing democracy and begin *extending* democracy beyond the walls of the "political" cast in the liberal-bourgeois mold into the "social" realm, not excluding the domain of the "economic." In Peter Osborne's (1991: 221) words, the task at hand is this: "*socialization of the political* and *politicization of the social.*" Only then will it be possible to institute democracy in a deeper sense, instead of restricting its scope to a bourgeois political category. To return to Karl Polanyi in the context of contemporary neoliberalism, this task above all involves the re-embedding of capitalist economic institutions within society so that economic matters, and not just political issues in a narrow sense, would be meaningfully accountable to the will of the people. This entails not just redistributing goods and services (economic democracy à la Robert Dahl [1985]), but engaging democratic principles as the driving mechanism of the economy and economic rationality and, thereby, subjecting the latter to the popular control of freely associated producers (Cangiani n.d., 1997, 1998; Wood 1995).

RELIGIOUS AND ETHNIC NATIONALISM

Having established the political-economic determinant of ethnic conflict, we can now turn to its ethnoreligious substance. The contributors to this book not surprisingly present contradictory evidence regarding the relationship between ethnic and religious diversity and the scope for democracy in Asia.

Bell argues that democracy could be inappropriate for some multiethnic, multireligious Asian societies with weakly developed nation-states, based on the concern that religious and ethnic diversity can actually spawn conflict and abuse of minority rights in the absence of authoritarian rule. Brown, Wurfel, and Bertrand approach the issue of ethnic conflict by examining the role of patrimonialism in democratization processes; they raise the possibility that a reconfigured patrimonialism could function in a benign way to mitigate ethnic conflict. For Brown, this prospect is especially promising, though he notes the risk patrimonialism poses for democracy. Stainton (2001) and Silverstein (2001), as well as Laliberté in this volume reveal that the Taiwanese and Burmese cases, respectively, suggest an alternative scenario: in multiethnic democratizing societies, religions that cut across ethnic differences can play a unifying role at the national scale, while leaving intact—even strengthening— liberal democratic structures. What patterns can we detect across the Asian region? And what, if any, more specific conclusions can be drawn about the scope for democracy in multiethnic Asian nations? Drawing on evidence from the South Asian context for comparative perspective, we will argue the following: (a) only when nations attempt to resolve the present crisis of economic structure with recourse to ethnonationalist ideology does majority rule become a threat to the rights of minority ethnic groups; and (b) religion (or any other pan-ethnic association within civil society) can play a unifying role vis-à-vis multiple ethnic groups only in the context of secular rule, i.e., in the absence of religious or ethnic forms of nationalism that are constitutionally enshrined in the very structure of the state.

Our analysis must begin, once again, with reference to the political-economic conjuncture. In the context of economic liberalization, the market mechanism integrates the national into the global economy, but fragments its social base, as a wide range of critics of globalization and neoliberalism have amply demonstrated. It does so by breeding socioeconomic inequalities and sociocultural insecurities (Bourdieu 1998; Bourdieu et al. 1999). The contradiction of market integration and social disintegration thus exacerbates the fundamental paradox of democratic governance concerning the contributors to this volume: the task of reconciling the claims of universality made by liberal citizenship with the particularities of specific groups of citizens (civic nationalism with ethnocultural and multicultural nationalisms, in Brown's formulation). And that contradiction is bound, as Aijaz Ahmad (1996: 288) observes, "to precipitate the crisis of the hyphen that equates the nation with the state in 'nation-state'":

> If the state no longer represents the interest *of* the nation in the international system of nation-states, but represents the interests of global finance *to* the nation, and if the majority of the nation cannot see in the state an agency that seeks to reconcile the competing interests of various classes and other social forces within the nation, then the very premise of the nation-state becomes questionable.

There are two likely outcomes of this scenario relevant for assessing the scope for democracy in multiethnic Asia. Individuals, increasingly differentiated in economic terms, seek shelter from the inequities of the market in less explicitly economic and more particularistic networks of identity, often articulated in terms of ethnic solidarities. That is, where state formation is weakly developed and ethnicity diverse, the Polanyian "countermovement" against the excesses of the "self-regulating market" takes on a fiercely identitarian character. Meanwhile, the ruling classes step in to mobilize these identitarian solidarities to create a nationalist ideological cement geared toward unifying the nation on *cultural* (ethnic, religious, linguistic) rather than social grounds (premised on redistributive justice). As the cases of India and Sri Lanka demonstrate, the outcomes for ethnic or religious minorities in this scenario are patently antidemocratic (Ahmad 1996; Goonewardena 2000; Gunasinghe 1996; Sivanandan 1990).

In both cases a liberal, it should be noted, and secular democracy had coexisted for several decades with ethnic and religious diversity in the postindependence period. This is not to say that ethnic tensions did not exist, but they were contained within broadly redistributive economic policies executed by liberal democratic regimes. India is particularly remarkable in this respect: although the state was formed "in the crucible of communal holocaust," political leaders opted for a secular polity (Ahmad 1996: 284). In both cases, universal suffrage had been successfully introduced amidst high levels of poverty; and unity had been accomplished through an anticolonial nationalist ideology, planned and independent economic development, and a balance of market exchange and social regulation characteristic of the "welfare state." This redistributive nationalist compact has since been destined to the dustbin of history by neoliberal orthodoxy. Thus, the erosion of liberal-secular legitimacy—relating in both instances to a growing marginalization of ethnic communities in the political process—has come in the wake of a significantly diminished scope for domestic redistributive justice within the context of local as well as global economic liberalization. All of this started to happen in Sri Lanka in the late 1970s and in India in the early 1990s, corresponding well to the timing of the recent escalation of ethnic conflicts in these two countries.

In the vacuum left by the shrinkage of redistributive justice, that is to say, the space was found for a nationalism based on ethnoreligious identity. To clarify how ethnonationalist forces could fill this vacuum with a cultural chauvinism of fascistic orientation, Ahmad proves incisive once again with reference to the Indian experience:

> Policies of liberalization can only succeed if Indian nationalism can be detached from its historic anticolonial origins and redefined in culturalist, irrationalist, racist terms, so that national energies are expended not on resistance against

imperialism but on suppression of the supposed enemy within: the denomina-
tional minority, the Communist Left, the "pseudo-secularist," any and all opposi-
tions to "Tradition" as defined by *Hindutva* and its accomplices among the indigenist sophists. I might add that in this redefinition of nationalism, "religion" serves
in the Islamicist and Hinduizing ideologies much the same function—of exclusion
of the other, purification of the self—that "race" has historically had in the making
of imperialist and fascist ideologies in Europe (Ahmad 1996: 294; e.g. Jalal 1995).

In Nepal (where democracy is only a decade old and has never approached
the redistributive accomplishments of India and Sri Lanka), ethnic nationalist
movements have not achieved electoral dominance. However, neither have
they sparked *ethnic* violence in the wake of the mid-1980s economic liberal-
izations, that is, following the conventional SAP recipe of currency devaluation
and convertibility, financial sector reform, privatization of state-owned enterprises, removal of price controls, and liberalization of trade (Sharma 1997).
Krishna Bahadur Bhattachan (1995) attributes the relative lack of ethnicized
conflict in Nepal to the alliance of ethnonationalist movements with a Maoist
insurgency articulating a radical rejection of capitalist imperialism. To the extent that Nepal has suffered political violence, in other words, it has not been
along ethnic lines. In this South Asian nation-state, claims for cultural recognition have been conjoined with demands for radical economic restructuring.

In Sri Lanka and India, where the Left has not mounted a systematic assault
on post-Fordist economic liberalization, the social community forged
through liberal redistributive policies of the postindependence era is collapsing amidst expanding class divides, but the experience of this reality in
everyday life is articulated in Sinhala-Buddhist and Hindu nationalism—
Jathika Chinthanaya and *Hindutva* respectively—"as nostalgia for a past
that never was and must therefore be made afresh with all the resource and
ambition of a remorseless upward mobility" (Ahmad 1996: 287). The increase in literacy rates, commodification of the economy, and expansion of
communication grids unleashed by economic and political modernization,
meanwhile, have created the material conditions making it possible to replace secular redistributive nationalism with a symbolic unity rooted in an
ethnoreligious national identity—and the "invention of a belief system that
can be widely shared, easily packaged, reduced to a linear explanatory narrative . . . through TV serialization and mass spectacle" (Ahmad 1996: 295).
Ahmad (1996) and Goonewardena (2000) have noted the conditions of possibility for neofascist styles of politics immanent within the rise of such culturalist forms of nationalism in India and Sri Lanka respectively: the hysteri-
cal religiosity and appeal to tradition; the vacuum in left-liberal leadership;
the large army of unemployed and increased militancy among the immiser-
ated; and the demonization of ethnic minorities (for example, Tamils in Sri
Lanka and Muslims in India) and political radicals amidst economic decay
and national demise. For the present purpose of assessing the relationship

between democracy and ethnic conflict the significant point to note is that, in South Asia, it has been specifically *clerical* forms of *bourgeois* democracy attempting to reconcile the promises of economic liberalization with the actualities of economic inequality that have spawned violent ethnoreligious conflict—not the kind of "deep democracy" we advocate.

The problem for Asian societies could then be posed, not as a choice between democracy and ethnic harmony, but as an injunction to nurture a modern civil society based on equal and effective citizenship through constitutionally guaranteed secularism. In the absence of secularism, formal liberal democracy can foster cultural domination every bit as much as economic oppression. While secularism is certainly no guarantee of freedom from cultural domination, it must certainly be a condition—just as much as subjecting the economy to democratic principles—for achieving "greater degrees of democracy" as advocated by democratic theorists such as Frank Cunningham (1987) and C. B. Macpherson (1973). Here again, the history of Western democracy proves instructive, notwithstanding claims to the contrary by South Asian cultural nationalisms or their postcolonial "indigenist" intellectuals (Chatterjee 1986, 1993; e.g., Vanaik 1997). For, as Ahmad points out, secularism was introduced in medieval Europe—fragmented by monarchical states, divided along religious lines, but also containing persecuted religious minorities—as a compact:

> First of all to obtain the peace between neighboring states founded on prior histories of religious conflict; second, to obtain a modicum of safety for the religious minorities, dissidents and smaller sects . . . ; and third, to gain for the newly constituted centralized states a modicum of freedom from the Vatican even inside the world of Catholicism (1996: 313).

Secularism thus "contained the seeds of democracy" even in the context of centralized monarchial rule: for already the issue of minority protection had become instrumental to the idea of citizenship in territorially defined states, highlighting minority rights as a key principle to be articulated with an ideal of popular sovereignty. To return to the economic base for social harmony, the idea of radically restructuring the economy in egalitarian fashion is also already immanent in the principle of democracy—for citizens with unequal power over the economy cannot be equal participants in formal democratic processes.

THE POLITICS OF RECOGNITION AND THE LIMITS OF CIVIL SOCIETY

The foregoing analysis suggests that both socioeconomic justice and cultural recognition must be equally important pillars in the construction of democratic polities devoid of violent ethnic conflict. The experience of ethnic conflict in Asia reveals the many forms that oppression can assume: violence is its most overt expression, but, prior to manifest violence, oppression takes the form of economic exploitation, on the one hand, and cultural imperialism, marginalization, and powerlessness on the other (Young 1990). Injustice, as feminist political philosopher Nancy Fraser (1997a) has cogently argued, assumes both socioeconomic and cultural forms (see also Henders and Lie, chapter 1 and chapter 6). In South Asia, left-liberal democracies had never adequately confronted these two faces of oppression—or the relationship between them. The commitment in postindependence Sri Lanka, for example, to economic redistribution through universal healthcare, education, and social welfare was accompanied by a failure to address dilemmas of recognition—mainly by its marginalization of the Tamil community in the political process. By the same token, the suggestion by David Brown that "the patrimonial politics of the transition from authoritarian rule can facilitate the emergence of new pluralist ethnocultural and multicultural visions of the nation" overlooks the cultural dimension of justice. However "responsive" a restructured patron class may be, the patrimonial framework leaves intact an underlying cultural valuational structure that creates injustices of misrecognition: clients will always suffer the stigma of dependency and disadvantage. The challenge here must not simply be to avert ethnic conflict with recourse to redistributive politics, but also to recognize cultural domination, nonrecognition, and disrespect as pressing forms of injustice to be addressed through democratic political processes.

As Fraser (1997a) suggests, however, economic disadvantage and cultural disrespect require two different political remedies: redistribution or political-economic restructuring, on the one hand, and recognition or cultural-symbolic revaluation on the other. Ethnic conflict stems both from socioeconomic inequality and from authoritative constructions of norms that privilege dominant ethnic groups; thus neither political economic redistribution nor cultural recognition alone can alleviate the oppression of marginal ethnic groups. Yet conjoining remedies of redistribution with those of recognition can pose formidable challenges because the former approach seeks to abolish difference by establishing equal access to resources, while the latter aims to affirm the value of ethnic difference and resist cultural homogenization. Remedies of distribution can, moreover, exacerbate cultural misrecognition—as with targeted assistance programs that stigmatize the poor and marginal (such as microfinance programs, which originated in Bangladesh but have now become a development orthodoxy throughout Asia and beyond). Acknowledging such problems, Fraser (1997a) argues that a politics of recognition can be effectively compatible with a politics of redistribution only if both are "transformative"— if they both aim to correct inequitable outcomes by restructuring the underlying socioeconomic and cultural frameworks.

Feminist philosophers have also pioneered in exploring how these political recommendations for responding at once to the demands of both redistribution and recognition could translate into principles for constructing a democratic polity. Anne Phillips (1996, 1991), for example, argues for a "politics of presence" over a "politics of ideas." She notes that liberal democracy has grappled with the issue of difference since its inception—already in 1787 the Founding Fathers of the U.S. Constitution were debating the "tyranny of the majority" before such luminaries as Tocqueville and Mill established the tension between majority rule and minority protection as a fundamental challenge to democracy. Yet liberal democracy has dealt with difference, both theoretically and programmatically, as "difference of ideas, opinions, and beliefs" to be accounted for through a politics of representation. Writes Phillips, "the role of the politician is to carry a message: the messages will vary, but it hardly matters if the messengers are the same" (1996: 141). An awareness of cultural forms of injustice such as has been presented here, however, suggests that we need a more complex understanding of the relationship between knowledge and experience (Mohanty 1997; Moya and Hames-García 2000). Large-scale struggles for recognition, such as the women's and Civil Rights movements in North America, for instance, have historically shifted the emphasis in political process

> from an objectively defined set of interests (that just needed more vigorous pursuit) to a more exploratory notion of possibilities thus far silenced and ideas one had to struggle to express. In this latter understanding of the processes that generate needs and concerns and ideas, it is harder to sustain the primacy of ideas over political presence. If it is simply a question of representing a given range of ideas and interests, it may not much matter who does the work of representation. But if the range of ideas has been curtailed by orthodoxies that rendered alternatives invisible, there will be no satisfactory solution short of changing the people who represent and develop the ideas (Phillips 1996: 142).

Phillips cites several precedents for reconciling liberal democracy with a politics of presence: such as the quota systems adopted by some Asian and European political parties to achieve greater gender parity in elected assemblies; redrawn electoral districts that raise the number of minority politicians elected in the United States; and "power-sharing practices of European consociational democracies that have distributed executive power and economic resources between different religious and linguistic groups" (1996: 147). Within a Habermasian framework of communicative rationality, the underlying principle for a politics of presence is that differences in social position and identity are a vital resource for the critical articulation of public reason, rather than a "diversity" the state must somehow "manage" (Young 1996: 127). In "communicative democracy," then (to borrow Young's expression), democratic deliberation depends crucially on the development of "subaltern counterpublics"—enclaves of resistance such as politicized ethnic minorities, without which the democratic process would "privilege the expressive norms of one cultural group over those of others, thereby making discursive assimilation a condition for participation in public debate" (Fraser 1997b: 84). The point here is that majority rule and minority rights, socioeconomic redistribution and cultural recognition, can coexist peacefully and grow together, but only if each is constitutionally established as a key element in the construction of a democratic polity.

Several contributors to this book have expressed optimism about civil society as a locus for containing the tensions of multiethnic Asian societies—or reconciling a politics of redistribution with a politics of recognition (e.g., Laliberté, Wurfel). Their optimism reflects a general trend today among scholars and policy-makers alike of investing civil society with a capacity to correct past state and market failures in allocating goods and services as much as in fostering participation in democratic processes. The expectation has been that civil society represents a zone of freedom outside the purview of the state, where voluntary associations and a plurality of social relations may thrive in the pursuit of the public good. The progressive potential in recent theories of civil society lies in their recognition of the *social* dimensions of economic growth and political democracy. Yet there are several reasons to exercise considerable caution (see also Rankin 2002).

Firstly, those optimistic about civil society—ranging from the World Bank, to liberal scholars, to development practitioners, to social movement leaders—too often fail to consider adequately how the present political–economic conjuncture (namely, the consolidation of neoliberal economic ideologies and programs on a global scale) jeopardizes the very promise of associational networks and generates new forms of incivility. State restructuring has too often withdrawn the very social infrastructure upon which the poor (who typically belong to marginal ethnic groups) must depend if they are to survive as social citizens before they can hope to become culturally empowered minorities. In this context, there are structural limits to what civil society can achieve in the way of social justice once the state has been let off the hook concerning its social responsibilities. Secondly, it is no coincidence that the "career" of civil society is one that has flourished at this particular neoliberal political–economic conjuncture (Mayer and Rankin 2002). For the ideal of civil society, as presently construed, enables the architects of neoliberalism to cast their reengineering of state-society relations in seemingly progressive terms—"freedom" from state oversight coupled with voluntary associational networks, local capacity-building, cultures of respect and tolerance—with hardly a hint of how these last are now being drawn inexorably into the vortex of laissez-faire market forces increasingly immune from popular sovereignty (see Goonewardena and Rankin 2000). Yet, civil society is now expected to fill the vacuum—or shoulder the burden—left by neoliberal state restructuring ("structural adjustment") in Asia and around the world. It thus offers an opportunistic economic—or, better, a moral—justification for reducing the state's role in providing basic social protection.

Finally, the coercive dimensions of civil society itself too often get obscured by the veneers of "freedom," "networks," "trust," and "local self-reliance." Patrimonial relations embedded in Indonesian civil society, for example, no matter how much they may cut across ethnic groups, are founded on hierarchical social structures and corresponding ideologies whose function is to maintain, not radically challenge and transform, socioeconomic inequality and cultural disrespect. Gestures of kindness and giving from patron to client function as a form of domination, a "symbolic violence" with the pernicious effect of binding the oppressed to their oppressors through feelings of trust and obligation (see Bourdieu 1977). As Pierre Bourdieu has extensively argued, the shared values, trust, social capital, and norms of reciprocity that constitute the "wealth" of civil society themselves have exploitative and ideological dimensions. The benefits and costs of participation in civil society are not distributed equally: some benefit at the expense of others. Ellen Wood (1995: 255–56) sums up the political danger in overlooking the inherently conflictual and contradictory nature of civil society in capitalist societies:

> The current theories of civil society do, of course, acknowledge that civil society is not a realm of perfect freedom or democracy. It is, for example, marred by oppression in the family, in gender relations, in the workplace, by racist attitudes, homophobia, and so on. . . .
>
> Yet these oppressions are treated not as constitutive of civil society but as dysfunctions in it. In principle, coercion belongs to the state while civil society is where freedom is rooted; and human emancipation, according to these arguments, consists in the autonomy of civil society . . . from the state. What tends to disappear from view . . . is the relations of exploitation and domination, which irreducibly constitute civil society, not just as some alien and correctible disorder, but as its very essence.

Our support for interventions in civil society must therefore be suitably qualified: we advocate expanding and enriching civil society only to the extent that it asserts an adversarial relationship with capitalism and a transformative politics of recognition.

BEYOND LIBERALISM: DEEPENING DEMOCRACY

Many, including several contributors to this book, have opted to consider the threat of ethnic conflict in Asia in light of the "least controversial definition of democracy," construed in the liberal sense of procedural guarantees of free and fair elections and basic civil liberties. This approach may be most pragmatic, given the limits to actually existing democracy all over the world. But it also overlooks the structural causes of ethnic conflict in Asia, by sequestering the economic and social spheres from political accountability in both theory and practice. Reducing democracy to political liberalism can, in its most extreme interpretation, narrow the issue for multiethnic Asian societies to a choice between political democracy and ethnic harmony. We reject this interpretation, or any more moderate variant of it, and opt instead, also for pragmatic reasons, to adopt Frank Cunningham's (1987) view of democracy as a "matter of degrees."

We also categorically reject relativist interpretations that characterize democracy, including liberal democracy, as exclusively "Western" and thus inappropriate for "other" cultures (e.g., Bell and Jayasuriya 1995; Tax 1999). The goal of furthering minority rights and promoting cultural diversity while ensuring a good life for all cultivates in us a commitment opposed to relativism. We argue that certain universal and, indeed, modern principles of human "dignity" and "intrinsic worth" (to which diverse peoples from all over the world have contributed) are essential in Asia, as much as elsewhere, for the well-being of democratic polities striving to actualize the potential of Kantian rational agents who "legislate . . . universal laws while being [themselves] subject to these laws" (Kant 1994 cited in Mohanty 1997: 199). We therefore insist, following Kant (1991, 1994), Hegel (1989), Wood (1995), and Marx (see Tucker 1978)—as well as contemporary students of "difference" and "multiculturalism" such as Fraser (1997a, 1997b) and Mohanty (1997)—that moral universalism and cultural pluralism are not only complementary, but also require each other. For universalism, contrary to widespread misunderstanding propagated by lax brands of postmodern theory (Eagleton 1990, 1996), is not antithetical to the just valorization of cultural difference; what fails to do justice to the latter is not universalism as such, but those particularisms (ethnocentric or other) that *masquerade* as universals, i.e., the ones on which Hegel was particularly fond of heaping scathing scorn (Anderson 1992: 290–91). Satya Mohanty (1997: 250) is right: "the respect we accord (in principle) to other humans [and cultures] is . . . the respect for the 'humanity' in *all of us*, which is the *rational capacity to be free and self-legislating members of a radically democratic polity.* Thus the universalist moral and political ideal is *opposed* in principle to ethnocentrism"—including, we might add for the record, Eurocentrism—and *presupposed* by genuine multiculturalism (emphases added).

The imperative then, surely, is to deepen democracy within any given political-economic context, with due attention to claims of both redistribution and recognition (Fraser and Honneth 2003). Accordingly, we wish to assert a "controversial" definition of democracy that would extend popular sovereignty beyond the merely "political" realm of actually existing liberalism to encompass the economy and civil society as well. For in our view, fundamental contradictions undermine liberal democracy because it operates on the basis of a separation of the "economic" from the "political," within which citizens who are unequal in economic relations and cultural respect cannot be equals in the political realm—except, of course, in ideological fantasy. In this manner, liberal democracies have historically allowed both socioeconomic and cultural forms of injustice to flourish—and assume the shape of ethnic conflict—even, or especially, in the midst of "political equality." Resolving these contradictions, while radicalizing democratic polities in Asia, demands a radical reorientation of democracy toward social justice, not its mutation into authoritarian forms.

NOTES

The authors wish to thank B. S. Goonewardene for his close reading and expert criticism on an earlier draft of this chapter.

1. Clive Crook, "The Future of the State," *The Economist*, 20 September 1997.

REFERENCES

Ahmad, Aijaz. 1996. *Lineages of the Present: Political Essays*. New Delhi: Tulika.
Ali, Tariq. 2001. "Bitter Chill of Winter." *London Review of Books*, 19 April. Available at www.lrb.co.uk. Accessed 19 April 2001.
Anderson, Perry. 1992. "The Ends of History." In *A Zone of Engagement*. London: Verso.
Bagchi, Amiya Kumar, ed. 1995. *Democracy and Development*. New York: St. Martin's Press.
———. 1998. "The Growth Miracle and Its Unravelling in East and South-East Asia." *Economic and Political Weekly* 33, no. 18: 1025–42.
———. 1999. "Globalization, Liberalization, and Vulnerability: India and the Third World." *Economic and Political Weekly* 34, no. 45: 3219–30.
———. 2000. "Neoliberal Economic Reforms and Workers of the Third World at the End of the Second Millennium of the Christian Era." *International Journal of Comparative Sociology* 61, no. 1: 71–88.
Bell, Daniel A. 2000. *East Meets West: Human Rights and Democracy in East Asia*. Princeton, N.J.: Princeton University Press.
———, and Kanishka Jayasuriya. 1995. "Understanding Illiberal Democracy: A Framework." In *Towards Illiberal Democracy in Pacific Asia*, eds. Daniel A. Bell, David Brown, Kanishka Jayasuriya, and David Martin Jones. Houndmills: Macmillan/St. Antony's College.
Bened́a, Lourdes et al., eds. 1987. *The Crossroads of Class and Gender: Industrial Homework, Subcontracting, and Household Dynamics in Mexico City*. Chicago: University of Chicago Press.

Bhattachan, Krishna Bahadur. 1995. "Ethnopolitics and Ethnodevelopment: An Emerging Paradigm in Nepal." In *State, Leadership, and Politics in Nepal*, ed. Dhruba Kumar. Kathmandu: Center for Nepalese and Asian Studies.

Bourdieu, Pierre. 1977. *Outline of a Theory of Practice*. Cambridge: Cambridge University Press.

——. 1998. *Acts of Resistance: Against the Tyranny of the Market*, trans. Richard Nice. New York: The New Press.

——, et al. 1999. *The Weight of the World: Social Suffering in Contemporary Society*. trans. Priscilla Parkhurst Ferguson et al. Stanford, Calif.: Stanford University Press.

Buck-Morss, Susan. 2000. *Dreamworld and Catastrophe: The Passage of Mass Utopia in East and West*. Cambridge, Mass.: The MIT Press.

Cangiani, Michele. n.d. "The Transformations of the Market Society: Karl Polanyi's Point of View." Unpublished Manuscript. Universita degli Studi di Venezia, Italy.

——, ed. 1997. *The Milano Papers: Essays in Societal Alternatives*. Montréal: Black Rose Books.

——. 1998. *Economia e democrazia: saggio su Karl Polanyi*. Padova: Poligrafo.

Cheran, Rudramuthi. 2000. Changing Formations: Nationalism and National Liberation in Sri Lanka and the Tamil Diaspora. Ph.D. diss., York University, Canada.

Chatterjee, Partha. 1986. *The Nation and Its Fragments*. Princeton, N.J.: Princeton University Press.

——. 1993. *Nationalist Discourse the Colonial World: A Derivative Discourse*. London: Zed Books.

Cox, Robert W. 1996. "A Perspective on Globalization." In *Globalization: Critical Reflections*, ed. James H. Mittleman. Boulder, Colo.: Lynne Rienner.

Cunningham, Frank. 1987. *Democratic Theory and Socialism*. Cambridge: Cambridge University Press.

Dahl, Robert. 1985. *A Preface to Economic Democracy*, New Haven, Conn.: Yale University Press.

Eagleton, Terry. 1990. "Nationalism: Irony and Commitment." In *Nationalism, Colonialism, and Literature*, eds. Terry Eagleton, Fredric Jameson, and Edward W. Said. Minneapolis: University of Minnesota Press.

——. 1996. *The Illusions of Postmodernism*. Oxford, U.K.: Blackwell Publishers.

Fraser, Nancy. 1997a. "From Redistribution to Recognition? Dilemmas of Justice in a 'Postsocialist' Age." In *Justice Interruptus: Critical Reflections on the "Postsocialist Condition."* New York: Routledge.

——. 1997b. "Rethinking the Public Sphere: A Contribution to the Critique of Actually Existing Democracy." In *Justice Interruptus: Critical Reflections on the "Postsocialist Condition."* New York: Routledge.

——, and Axel Honneth. 2003. *Redistribution or Recognition? A Philosophical Exchange*. London: Verso.

Furet, François. 1989. *Interpreting the French Revolution*, trans. Elborg Foster. New York: Cambridge University Press.

Gill, Stephen. 1996. "Globalization, Democratization, and the Politics of Indifference." In *Globalization: Critical Reflections*, ed. James H. Mittleman. Boulder, Colo.: Lynne Rienner.

Goonewardena, Kanishka. 2000. "'National Ideology' in Sri Lanka: A Question Concerning Technology, Modernity, and the West?" Paper presented at the conference

Democracy and Identity Conflicts in Asia: Human Security, Human Rights, and Cultural Diversity in an Age of Globalization. University of Toronto, 5–6 December.

———, and Katharine Rankin. 2000. "The Desire Called Civil Society." Paper presented the Forty-second Annual Conference of the Association of Collegiate Schools of Planning (ACSP). Atlanta, 2–5 November.

Gowan, Peter. 1990. *The Global Gamble: Washington's Faustian Bid for World Dominance*. London: Verso.

Gray, John. 1998a. *False Dawn*. New York: The New Press.

———. 1998b. *Hayek on Liberty*. 3d ed. London: Routledge.

Gunasinghe, Newton. 1996. *Newton Gunasinghe: Selected Essays*, ed. Sasanka Perera. Colombo: Social Scientists' Association.

Hegel, G. W. F. 1989. *Hegel's Science of Logic*. trans. A. V. Miller. Atlantic Highlands, N.J.: Humanities Paperback Library.

Jalal, Ayesha. 1995. *Democracy and Authoritarianism in South Asia: A Comparative and Historical Perspective*. New York: Cambridge University Press.

Jameson, Fredric. 1996. "Five Theses on Actually Existing Marxism." *Monthly Review* 47, no. 11: 1–10.

Jeganathan, Pradeep, and Qadri Ismail, eds. 1995. *Unmaking the Nation: Politics of Identity and History in Modern Sri Lanka*. Colombo: Social Scientists' Association.

Kant, Immanuel. 1991. "An Answer to the Question: 'What is Enlightenment?'" In *Kant: Political Writings*, 2d ed. enlarged, ed. Hans Reiss. trans. H.B. Nisbett. Cambridge: Cambridge University Press.

———. 1994. *Grounding for the Metaphysics of Morals*, trans. James W. Ellington. Indianapolis: Hackett Publishing Company.

Klein, Naomi. 2002. *Fences and Windows: Dispatches from the Front Lines of the Globalization Debate*. Toronto: Vintage Canada.

Macpherson, C. B. 1973. *Democratic Theory: Essays in Retrieval*. Oxford: Oxford University Press.

Mayer, Margit, and Katharine Rankin. 2002. "Social Capital and (Community) Development: A North/South Perspective." *Antipode* 34, no. 4: 804–8.

McMichael, Philip. 1995. "The New Colonialism: Global Regulation and the Restructuring of the Interstate System." In *A New World Order?: Global Transformations in Late Twentieth Century*, eds. David A. Smith and Jozsef Borocz. Westport, Conn.: Greenwood Press.

Mittleman, James H. 1996. "The Dynamics of Globalization." In *Globalization: Critical Reflections*, ed. James H. Mittleman. Boulder, Colo.: Lynne Rienner.

———. 2000. *The Globalization Syndrome*. Princeton, N.J.: Princeton University Press.

Mohanty, Satya. 1997. *Literary Theory and the Claims of History: Postmodernism, Objectivity, Multicultural Politics*. Ithaca, N.Y.: Cornell University Press.

Moya, Paula M. L., and Michael Hames-García, eds. 2000. *Reclaiming Identity: Realist Theory and the Predicament of Postmodernism*. Berkeley: University of California Press.

Osborne, Peter. 1991. "Radicalism without Limit? Discourse, Democracy, and the Politics of Identity." In *Socialism and the Limits of Liberalism*, ed. Peter Osborne. London: Verso.

Phillips, Anne. 1991. *Engendering Democracy*. University Park: The Pennsylvania State University Press.

———. 1996. "Dealing with Difference: A Politics of Ideas, or a Politics of Difference?" In *Democracy and Difference: Contesting the Boundaries of the Political*, ed. Seyla Benhabib. Princeton, N.J.: Princeton University Press.

Polanyi, Karl. 1935. "The Essence of Fascism." In *Christianity and the Social Revolution*, eds. J. Lewis, K. Polanyi, and D. K. Kitchin. London: Gollancz.

———. 1944. *The Great Transformation*. Boston: Beacon Press.

Rankin, Katharine N. 2002. "Social Capital, Microfinance, and the Politics of Development." *Feminist Economics* 8, no. 1: 1–24.

Rebeck, Judy. 2000. *Imagine Democracy*. Toronto: Stoddart.

Schmitt, Carl. 1976. *The Concept of the Political*, trans. George Schwab. New Brunswick, N.J.: Rutgers University Press.

Sharma, Shankar Prasad. 1997. "Market-Led Development Strategy in Nepal." In *Developmental Practices in Nepal*, eds. Krishna B. Bhattachan and Chaitanya Mishra. Kathmandu: Central Department of Sociology and Anthropology, Tribhuvan University.

Silverstein, Josef. 2001. "Ethnicity, Elitism, and the Problems of Reestablishing Democracy in Burma." Paper presented at the conference Democracy and Identity Conflicts in Asia: Human Security, Human Rights, and Cultural Diversity in an Age of Globalization. University of Toronto, 5–6 December.

Sivanandan, Ambalavanar. 1990. "Sri Lanka: A Case Study." In *Communities of Resistance: Writings on Black Struggles for Socialism*. London: Verso.

Stainton, Michael. 2001. "'Through Love and Suffering': The Presbyterian Church, Ethnic Identity, and Democracy in Taiwan." Paper presented at the conference Democracy and Identity Conflicts in Asia: Human Security, Human Rights, and Cultural Diversity in an Age of Globalization. University of Toronto, 5–6 December.

Swift, Richard. 2002. *The No-Nonsense Guide to Democracy*. Toronto: The New Internationalist/Between the Lines.

Tax, Meredith. 1999. "World Culture War." *The Nation*, 17 April. Available at www.thenation.com/doc.mhtml?i=19990517&s=tax&c=1. Accessed on 10 April 2003.

Tucker, Robert C., ed. 1978. *The Marx-Engels Reader*. New York: W. W. Norton and Company.

Vanaik, Achin. 1997. *Communalism Contested: Religion, Modernity, and Secularization*. New Delhi: Vistaar Publications.

Wood, Ellen Meiksins. 1995. *Democracy against Capitalism: Renewing Historical Materialism*. Cambridge: Cambridge University Press.

Young, Iris Marion. 1990. *Justice and the Politics of Difference*. Princeton, N.J.: Princeton University Press.

———. 1996. "Communication and the Other: Beyond Deliberative Democracy." In *Democracy and Difference: Contesting the Boundaries of the Political*, ed. Seyla Benhabib. Princeton, N.J.: Princeton University Press.

II

REFLECTING ON EAST ASIA

6

The Politics of Recognition in Contemporary Japan

John Lie

In 1986 Prime Minister Nakasone Yasuhiro declared, "Japan has one ethnicity (*minzoku*), one state (*kokka*), and one language (*gengo*)" (Terazawa 1990: 64–65). In his ethnic allegory, ethnic and cultural homogeneity contributed to Japan's economic efflorescence, whereas multiethnicity—particularly the presence of poor ethnic minorities—accounted for the decline of the United States. Nakasone's speech generated protest from the United States, which ironically was about to enter a period of intense debates on the virtues of multiculturalism. Regardless of the virtues or vices of multiethnic or multicultural nation-states, however, nary a voice was raised to question Nakasone's bedrock assumption: the putative ethnic homogeneity of Japan. Indeed, it has been a truism within and without Japan that Japan is remarkable for its ethnic homogeneity. Many Japanese take it for granted that they live in a monoethnic society, and the same assumption is shared not just by scholars of Japan and Japanese themselves, but also by virtually everyone else. In a book devoted to the subject of multiethnicity, the historian William H. McNeill (1986: 18) remarks: "More than any other civilized land . . . the Japanese islands maintained ethnic and cultural homogeneity throughout their history."

In *Multiethnic Japan* (Lie 2001), I argue that Japan has been and remains a multiethnic society. The presence of discriminated minority groups—including the indigenous *Ainu* and Okinawans, colonial-era immigrants from the Korean peninsula and Chinese mainland, *Burakumin* (descendants of premodern outcastes), and others—readily refutes the claim of monoethnic Japan. At the turn of the millennium, the active and vocal organizations of various minority groups render implausible the very assumption of Japanese monoethnicity.

In this chapter, I explore the trajectory of the politics of ethnic recognition in post–World War II Japan, a period in which Japan (re)democratized and adjusted to the loss of much of its empire. I survey the origins of ethnic minority groups in Japan and the reasons why ethnic mobilization was minimal in the 1950s and 1960s. I then analyze the social and discursive origins of popular mobilization qua ethnic groups since the 1970s. In doing so I argue that, as an essentially contested concept, political democracy has distinct connotations. In the prewar period, Japan's expansive empire promoted an inclusionary idea of democracy that included imperial subjects. In this vision of imperial democracy, not only ethnic Japanese but also ethnic Koreans, Chinese, and others were legally Japanese citizens. Though they usually could only advance as *individuals* through Japanization, imperial Japan, nevertheless, did recognize the existence of distinctive ethnic *groups*. In the post–World War II period, the prewar era was widely criticized as undemocratic, and the new order sought to institute a "true" democracy. Ironically, the establishment of an American-style democracy led to the exclusion of ethnic others in the name of a "small," democratic Japan. In the process, an inclusionary idea of citizenship was replaced by an exclusionary one that was narrowly restricted to ethnic Japanese. The self-consciously anti-imperialist position thereby generated an ethnically discriminating polity. The establishment of a "true" democracy is, ironically, one of the sources of monoethnic Japan.

THE HISTORICAL CONTEXT OF MULTIETHNIC JAPAN AND MONOETHNIC IDEOLOGY

To be recognized as a group inevitably involves that group's differentiation from others. That is, the formation of minority groups implies the existence of a majority group, or a dominant ethnic identity. It would seem obvious that people who have resided in the Japanese archipelago have always regarded themselves as Japanese, but that is almost certainly not the case. I argue that the formation of Japanese national or ethnic identity was coeval with the making of modern Japan. That is, the widespread sense of being Japanese among people living in Japan was the product of modern state-making, with its infrastructural and ideological innovations. More specifically, I make three interrelated points. First, Japanese national identity before the Meiji Restoration was not widely shared. Second, modern state-making disseminated Japanese identity but, simultaneously, rendered it as a multiethnic society. Finally, monoethnic ideology became popular in the post–World War II period.

If the dissemination of Japanese identity is a modern phenomenon, the product of post–Meiji Restoration nation-building, then it follows that there was an absence of a widely dispersed national identity before the late nineteenth century. This argument contradicts the commonsense presupposition that people who live in present-day Japan have always felt themselves to be Japanese. However, it has a prima facie plausibility given other historical works on national identity, such as the work of Eugen Weber (1975), who asserts the late nineteenth-century formation of widespread French national identity (see also Hobsbawm 1990; Calhoun 1997).

To put my argument in a more systematic way, modern national identity requires the modern state's infrastructural and ideological development. On the one hand, a well-developed state infrastructural capacity—nation-wide systems of transportation, communication, and education—is necessary to transmit and reproduce an identity over a large territory. Beyond the tangible solidity of localized social interactions—villages and regions—state-led institutions, ranging from compulsory military service to mass schooling, spread the message of national identity, and state-led infrastructural developments, such as nation-wide circuits of transportation and communication, construct the medium to spread it across the nation.

On the other hand, equally significant is the ideological transformation of the modern state. In premodern Japan, as in all premodern, status-based societies, the ruling elite did not promote an inclusive political identity that was consonant with the polity. The reason is simple: a rigidly stratified society is incompatible with an inclusive and inclusionary identity. Indeed, individuals of different status groups are frequently seen as different kinds of people. Recall in this regard Ernest Gellner's (1983: x) influential definition of nationalism as "a theory of political legitimacy, which requires that ethnic boundaries should not cut across political ones, and—ethnic boundaries . . . should not separate the power-holders from the rest." The ideology of premodern polities tended not to insist on such a bond between the rulers and the ruled; the former were, whether because of gods or genes, superior to the latter.

In contrast, modern polities, as Gellner suggested, insist on the bond between the rulers and the ruled. In part due to the heightened demand of political legitimacy—necessitated in turn by mass conscription, for example—modern polities, whether democratic or authoritarian, promote one or another form of nationalism, thereby often asserting ethnoracial isomorphism among the populace. This tendency is all the more striking in late and, therefore, more consciously developing countries, such as Germany or Japan (e.g., Plessner 1959).

My second point is that Japanese modern state-making, with its infrastructural development and an inclusionary ideology, widely disseminated national identity and patriotic nationalism. This is not surprising in a country that fought wars virtually continuously and relied heavily on mass or citizen conscripts. In the form of the emperor ideology, the nation was literally transmogrified as the children of the emperor, constituting the family-state. The Japanese nation, in other words, became one large family with the emperor as the divine patriarch.

Nevertheless, simultaneous with the development of patriotic nationalism was the making of multiethnic Japan. Ironically, precisely when it became possible to talk of widespread Japanese national identity, the modern nation-state became irrefutably multiethnic. The fundamental mechanism was colonialism, or territorial expansion. Hokkaido, the northernmost large island of the Japanese archipelago, came under Japanese sovereignty. The modern Japanese state thereby conquered an indigenous population. The *Ainu* constituted a heterogeneous group, with significant linguistic and cultural diversity, but became conflated as an Aboriginal group that became the target of enforced assimilation to the Japanese norm.

In the 1870s, the Japanese state also colonized Ryûkyû, or Okinawa. The southern group of islands, with its own diversity of languages and cultures, had been an independent kingdom, albeit with tributary relations to the Qing and Tokugawa rulers. Almost overnight, however, it became part of the ever-expanding Japanese empire. Like the *Ainu*, Okinawans became objects of enforced assimilation.

Beyond Hokkaido and Okinawa, Japan also colonized a series of territories in Asia. Beginning with Taiwan in 1895, Japan went on to control Korea, Manchuria, and other parts of the Chinese mainland, the southern Pacific islands (*Nan'yô*), and so on. In so doing, not only did the territory of Japan expanded fourfold, but also the Japanese polity became irreducibly multiethnic. This was the case not only because of the empire, but also because the empire, so to speak, came home. Owing especially to wartime labor shortages, the massive influx of colonial labor—as well as the entry of *Burakumin* and Okinawans into the mainstream labor market—rendered Japan as a profoundly multiethnic society. In other words, modern Japanese state-making made Japan multiethnic.

Given that prewar Japan was an empire and multiethnic, it should not be surprising that the state or national ideology of Imperial Japan was not monoethnic. All empires, after all, are multiethnic. The dominant group may claim their superiority over the colonized, but that does not gainsay that the polity is multiethnic. For example, the British may have regarded themselves as superior to the benighted masses in India, but the British empire was multiethnic and British imperial ideology was far from monoethnic nationalism. Similarly, Imperial Japan occasionally featured arguments about monoethnic nationalism, but the dominant ideological tenor was to highlight is multiethnic constitution. Japan may be a family-state, but Koreans and Chinese were also part of the extended family. Koreans, for example, were the emperor's baby (*tennô no sekishi*), and Koreans and Japanese were said the hail from the same ancestors (*Nissen dôsoron*). Indeed, the Japanese racial ideology asserted racial isomorphism, or at least kinship, among the conquered peoples throughout East and Southeast Asia.

Thus, the claim that Japan has been and remains monoethnic became dominant only after the collapse of the Japanese empire. This was true in a crude demographic sense: having lost its expansive empire, postwar Japanese society was considerably less ethnically heterogeneous than it had been. Also, with the empire went the imperial ideology, including its presumption of multiethnic Japan. While ideologists of Imperial Japan described and explained Japanese multiethnicity, the postwar period condemned not only imperialism, but also its inevitable correlate: ethnic heterogeneity. Moreover, the idea of a small Japan went well with the ideals of democracy and monoethnic nationalism. Especially in comparison to the multiethnic U.S.—the singular source of comparison for postwar Japanese intellectuals—Japan appeared to be and thought it should be monoethnic. The newfound popularity of monoethnic Japan was also founded in large part on the advancing cultural integration of Japan. By the 1960s, the urban–rural divides had nearly disappeared and the status distinction largely withered away. Japan appeared to be a culturally integrated and homogeneous society. That is, the claim of monoethnic Japan had a prima facie cogency.

The ideology of monoethnicity justified the neglect of ethnic minorities by the government and the public. The government recognized no *Burakumin* neighborhoods in Tokyo, for example (Yagi 1984: 175), despite their significant presence (e.g., Honda 1990). The putative nonexistence of ethnic minorities legitimated passivity on the part of local and national government. The ideology of monoethnicity, in other words, released the Japanese government from addressing the demands of various minority groups. The Korean-Japanese scholar Pak Kyông-sik (1992: 81) has observed: "When we demand equality, we get 'mono-ethnic state-society.'" The dominant belief was that "passivity and silence" would eliminate *Burakumin* discrimination (Yagi 1984: 250). Korean Japanese, in this regard, were expected to return imminently to their "home" in North or South Korea.

BETWEEN PASSING AND RETURNING

What has allowed so many Japanese to believe that they have lived and continue to live in a monoethnic society is the silence of the actually existing minority groups. The *Ainu* were not only few in number, but also the culture was devastated by a century of Japanization efforts. They were also almost exclusively concentrated in Hokkaido and, therefore, outside of popular consciousness, particularly in Tokyo where mass media institutions were concentrated. Until 1972, Okinawa was under U.S. control and most Okinawans resided in Okinawa. The silence of these two groups is, therefore, not difficult to explain. Given their geographical distance and isolation, they were mere scratches on most Japanese people's mind. But how about the two larger groups: *Burakumin* and Koreans? Why were they not seen and heard?

First, both groups were socially isolated. In the postwar period, many *Burakumin* and Korean Japanese remained residentially segregated. Furthermore, employment discrimination minimized the opportunities for *Burakumin* and Koreans to work alongside Japanese. Hence, most Japanese, especially in Tokyo, were unlikely to encounter large groups of *Burakumin* or Korean Japanese either in their neighborhood or workplace.

Secondly, and more importantly, both groups complemented the ideology of Japanese monoethnicity. For the major postwar Burakumin organization, the Burakumin Liberation League, the principal strategy was to cease social stigmatization by claiming their essential Japaneseness. Rather than a politics of ethnic recognition, then, the privileged path of *Burakumin* activism was to seek assimilation. In contrast, the major Korean organizations—divided by their conflicting allegiances to the two Koreas—sought to identify themselves with their respective homelands. In other words, they were to be recognized as Koreans, who were moreover intending to return to either North or South or unified Korea in due course.

The Path toward Passing

The *Burakumin* claim about their essential Japaneseness needs to be placed in the context of their racialization during the prewar period. Although they became an essentialized identity only after the Meiji Restoration, their newfound unity prodded efforts to seek their distinct genealogy and racial origins from mainstream Japanese people. Numerous theories were floated to account for their fundamental differences from the dominant Japanese ethnicity. Some scholars claimed that they hailed from the Korean peninsula, whereas others suggested that they were descendants of Christian and other religious heretics in the premodern period. These theories converged, however, in designating *Burakumin* as a racially distinct group of people. In the early twentieth-century "popular notion," *Burakumin* were said to have "one rib-bone lacking; they have one dog's bone in them; they have distorted sexual organs; they have defective excretory systems; if they walk in moonlight their neck will not cast shadows; and, they being animals, dirt does not stick to their feet when they walk barefooted" (Ooms 1996: 303).

The proximate origin of *Burakumin* was the 1871 Emancipation Decree, which transformed the outcastes into formally free new commoners (*shin heimin*). Rather than rigid status distinctions that proscribed occupational mobility and interstatus marriage during Tokugawa rule, the Meiji state guaranteed occupational mobility, residential freedom, the right to surnames, and other features of formally egalitarian citizenship. The Decree granted the new commoners the same rights as the commoners (*heimin*). Thus, there was a transition from caste—defined by customary or legal proscription on occupational mobility or exogamy—to ethnicity. Social discrimination and cultural stigma did not disappear against the new commoners. The very fact that the family registry system (*koseki*) distinguished *heimin* from *shin heimin* allowed a simple documentary basis for differentiation. More importantly, the new commoners, who lived in special villages (*tokushu buraku*), were considered a breed apart from mainstream Japanese.

The Meiji state not only destroyed the legal basis of discrimination, but also, simultaneously, withdrew protective measures, such as monopolies over several occupations, that had sustained the livelihood of *Burakumin* ancestors. *Burakumin* therefore lost their principal sources of livelihood and were forced to cultivate meager plots of land, engage in low-waged crafts, such as making footwear and matches, or work in the secondary labor market, especially in construction and coal mines. The Meiji state was slow to expand schooling, transportation, and communication to *Burakumin* villages. In short, *Burakumin* held the worst jobs and housing of modern Japanese society. Legal discrimination was replaced by economic competition and class reproduction.

The ferment of social reformism in the 1890s contributed to the stirring of *Burakumin* liberation. Some younger *Burakumin* became educated and began to agitate. *Suiheisha* (Leveling Society), an organization devoted to ending discrimination against *Burakumin*, was organized in 1922 and had 53,000 members by 1928. Despite wartime repression, *Suiheisha* remained the largest left-leaning organization in existence, with 40,000 members in 1940 (Neary 1989: 50–56, 91). Its principal activity was a campaign of denunciations (*kyûdan tôsô*) (Neary 1989: 85). Leftist and communist supporters dominated the organization before and after 1945 (Totten and Wagatsuma 1966: 62–63).

The Japanese government engaged in a policy of repression and integration. Liberal social thinking and the fear of popular uprising—symbolized by the 1918 Rice Riots—goaded the government to pursue welfare measures for *Burakumin*—the so-called *yûwa* (assimilation and harmony) policy (Neary 1989: 130–32, 166). The first state aid occurred in 1920 in the form of various improvement projects for *Burakumin* villages (Neary 1989: 59–61). Poverty, geographical segregation, and social stigmatization characterized most *Burakumin*. In the 1930s, *Burakumin* households earned income perhaps one-half of the national average and experienced lower wages and poorer living conditions than Japanese Japanese (Neary 1989: 148–49).

Suiheisha and *yûwa* policy consolidated *Burakumin* identity. On the one hand, *Suiheisha* organized *Burakumin* qua *Burakumin*, thereby entrenching

Burakumin identity. On the other hand, the state, especially via *yûwa* policy, treated *Burakumin* as a distinct group.

In the postwar period, Burakumin continued to occupy a distinct niche in Japanese society. Although no longer called *buraku*, but *dôwa chiku* (assimilated area), many postwar *Burakumin* neighborhoods were socially segregated, with inferior infrastructures (Fukuoka et al. 1987: 18–19). Poverty continued to mark *Burakumin* areas, and *Burakumin* themselves were characterized by low educational attainment and high welfare dependency (de Vos and Wagatsuma 1966: 125–28). Not unlike the Jim Crow U.S. South, *Burakumin* day laborers in rural areas had separate and substandard facilities for dining and sanitation (Neary 1989: 3).

In spite of legal equality, *Burakumin* continued to be excluded from prestigious corporate jobs and marriages with mainstream Japanese people. Many large corporations used name books (*chimei sôkan*) to identify individuals with *Burakumin* ancestry and avoid hiring them (Upham 1987: 114–16). Although some consider the cause to be the groupism or the village mentality (*mura ishiki*) of Japanese bureaucrats and managers, it may have more to do with the association of *Burakumin* with communism and political activism.

In addition to residential and economic segregation, *Burakumin* culture showed distinct characteristics and faced discrimination from the mainstream population. In the early 1960s, the *Burakumin* diet reflected a tradition of meat-eating in the consumption of internal organs that many Japanese abhor, as well as the wearing of distinctive sandals. The Japanese people John Cornell (1967: 347) interviewed in the 1960s regarded *Burakumin* as "rough in speech, crude or brutal in relations with each other, having a low boiling point, quarrelsome, highly sensitive to insult, born traders, and relatively much more cohesive than any other community." In the classic language of otherness, *Burakumin* were "darkly disreputable, mysterious, and substantially unknown" (Cornell 1967: 348). The most common reason that Japanese give for *Burakumin* discrimination is that they act in unison. National and local governments have largely denied or neglected the condition of *Burakumin*, and most Japanese people were indifferent to their plight.

If the political and economic factors contributed to the crystallization of *Burakumin* identity in the early twentieth century, the same causes were leading to their partial dissolution in the late twentieth century. In 1946, *Suiheisha* and the more moderate supporters of *yûwa* policy consolidated to form what came to be known after 1955 as *Buraku Kaihô Dômei* (the Buraku Liberation League). In part in response to *Burakumin* activism, the 1965 Cabinet *Dôwa* Policy pointed to the persistence of discrimination against *Burakumin*. Consequently, the Japanese government initiated special measures from 1969 to improve *Burakumin* residences and neighborhoods. The fundamental spur that integrated many *Burakumin* into the mainstream labor market was, however, rapid economic growth and the tight labor market of the 1960s. It underscores W. Arthur Lewis' (1985: 44) generalization that: "The most effective destroyer of discrimination is fast economic growth."

Nonetheless, the conditions of *Burakumin* in the 1990s had yet to reach the egalitarian ideal. Welfare dependency and discrimination still marked many *Burakumin*. However, significant improvements in educational attainment and employment opportunities had taken place. In particular, the Burakumin Liberation League and other activist organizations have worked closely with international human rights organizations. Their most important activity, however, remains the protest against and denunciation of writers, publishers, and politicians who defame *Burakumin*. The political tactic of the Buraku Liberation League conspires with the ideology of monoethnicity to maintain the silence on and the invisibility of ethnic differentiation and discrimination.

The Dream of Return

Since the 1920s, the principal Japanese strategy was to assimilate Koreans. In effect, Koreans were placed on the path that *Ainu* and Okinawans had been on from several decades before. The Oriental Development Company achieved in a more organized manner what the pioneers had done in Hokkaido. Similar to the imposition of standard Japanese on *Ainu* and Okinawan people, the use of the Korean language was banned. Education sought to instill the Japanese imperialist worldview. In general, the Japanese policy toward Korea sought to extirpate Korean culture and to transform Koreans into the emperor's people (*kôminka*). Especially after the mid-1930s, Japan instituted a policy of complete Japanization. The Korean school curriculum became the same as the Japanese in 1938, while Koreans were forced to adopt Japanese names in 1940. Over time, the Japanese leaders asserted the harmony (*Naisen yûwa*) and unity (*Naisen ittai*) of Japan and Korea. The policy of assimilation reached its ideological height in the idea of Japanese and Koreans sharing the same ancestry (*Nissen dôsoron*). Koreans—as despised as they were by many Japanese—were touted as the emperor's baby (*tennô no sekishi*) and regarded as imperial subjects (*kôkoku shinmin*).

Many Koreans, leaving the impoverished rural areas in search of better opportunities, as well as responding to the insistent Japanese demand for cheap labor, sought employment in Japanese mines and factories. Most of them hailed from the southern part of Korea and were farmers or laborers. After the abolition of entry restrictions in 1922, the number of Koreans in the main Japanese islands increased rapidly. In spite of the limitations placed on the Korean labor influx between 1925 and 1939, their number rose five-fold. For example, 60 percent of coal miners in Hokkaido and 10 percent of all workers in Osaka were Korean by the early 1940s.

As the Japanese war effort intensified in the 1930s, the state recruited Korean workers, at times forcefully. Koreans in Japan played a significant role in the war effort. From 810,000 to 940,000 Koreans were conscripted to work in mining, construction, and other manual labor in the Japanese archipelago between 1939 and 1945. In particular, coal mines and construction work became dominated by Koreans when Japanese men were increasingly dispatched to war fronts. Within the Korean peninsula, some 3.2 million Koreans were relocated. In this regard, the organization of the notorious *teishintai* (*chongsindae* in Korean) was initially designed not to produce sexual serfs for Japanese soldiers, but rather to force Korean women workers into ammunition, textiles, and other factories. By 1944, at its height, the Korean population in the Japanese archipelago reached 2.4 million people. Between 1 and 1.5 million of them were forcefully relocated.

If a low estimate of Korean culture was a pretext to colonize Korea, then actual colonization confirmed it. In Japanese travel accounts of Korea in the early twentieth century, "laziness ranked with backwardness, poverty, and filth among the most salient characteristic of Korean life" (Duus 1995: 404). The nadir of Korean Japanese history occurred in the aftermath of the 1923 Kantô earthquake. The rumor that Koreans were poisoning the water supply unleashed a massive pogrom, leading to thousands of deaths of not only Koreans, but also Okinawans and Chinese.

Korean migrant workers, being predominantly poor farmers, were largely illiterate and ill prepared for urban employment. Neither Japanese-speaking nor skilled, most of them worked in demanding manual work, such as mining and construction. Korean workers, along with *Burakumin* and Okinawans, occupied the lowest tier in the urban labor market. Because of poverty and discrimination, Koreans became concentrated in Korean ghettoes, often in proximity to *Burakumin* and Okinawan neighborhoods.

The proximate origin of the Korean minority in postwar Japanese society is therefore the labor demands of prewar Japan. Although two-thirds of Koreans in Japan returned to the Korean peninsula after 1945, the repatriation effort was hindered by international politics, political confusion in Korea, and Korean Japanese' decision to eke out a living in postwar Japan. In the immediate postwar years, many Koreans, along with *Burakumin*, sought survival and fortune in the black market. The anti-Korean hysteria in 1946 was due in part to the perceived evils of Korean black marketeers. Most significantly, the destructive Korean War and the rapidly improving Japanese economy persuaded many Koreans to stake their immediate future in Japan. The continuing poverty of the two Koreas in the 1960s, in contrast to the rapid growth in Japan, provided enough time for second generations, many of whom grew up without an adequate command of Korean, to settle in Japan.

Until 1965, when the Japan–South Korea Peace Treaty was concluded, the status of Koreans in Japan was ambiguous and under constant siege. Although Koreans were considered Japanese nationals under colonial rule, they were stripped of their citizenship after the end of World War II. The 1950 nationality law decreed patrilineality as the fundamental basis of Japanese citizenship; the 1952 law decreed the governmental registration and surveillance of foreigners. With the 1965 Peace Treaty, South Korean citizenship was imposed on most ethnic Koreans in Japan. However, both the Japanese government and leading Korean organizations regarded Koreans in Japan as foreigners or sojourners. The postwar Japanese government, in contrast to its prewar counterpart, assiduously sought to differentiate Japanese from Koreans. It constantly interfered in Korean ethnic education and sought to suppress Korean ethnic organizations. The ethnic Koreans in Japan identified themselves as Koreans and regarded their residence in Japan as temporary. The sojourner status and the conflicting allegiance to the two Koreas—represented by the North Korea–affiliated *Sôren* (*Chongryun*) and the South Korea–allied *Mindan*—have stunted their identification as Korean Japanese. Although most Koreans in Japan hailed from southern Korea, many of them have identified themselves ideologically with North Korea. They leaned, like *Burakumin*, to the left and participated in labor unions as well as the Communist Party.

In the postwar period, Korean Japanese faced all manner of discrimination. Because of their status as foreigners, many Korean Japanese are ineligible for government and corporate jobs. Indeed, the vast majority had to seek self-employment, such as in petty manufacturing, recycling, and the restaurant and pachinko trades, or secondary or informal sector jobs in construction, cleaning, and so on. Many Japanese in turn regarded Korean Japanese with considerable prejudice, not only because of the colonial legacy, but also because of their impoverished state. Surveys from the 1950s consistently showed Koreans to be the most disliked national group in Japan. Hence, Richard Mitchell (1967: 158) concluded his mid-1960s study on a pessimistic note: "The traditional Japanese dislike for Koreans remains strong, and may even have increased."

There were indisputable improvements in the postwar period, however. The improved situation of Korean Japanese stems in part from a series of legal and political struggles, including the 1974 Hitachi employment discrimination lawsuit and the 1980s effort to amend the foreign registration law (the anti–finger printing movement). Generational shifts—from first-generation Koreans to second- and third-generation Koreans in Japan, or Korean Japanese—underlie the politics of ethnic recognition and inclusion. By the mid-1970s, over three-fourths of Korean Japanese were Japanese-born and Japanese-educated, and 70 percent of Korean Japanese marriages were to Japanese Japanese by 1985. Korean-Japanese names can be found in prestigious professions: to cite one example, the Bill Gates of Japan is a Korean Japanese, Son Masayoshi.

The De Facto Assimilation

Thus, the politics of assimilation and return superceded ethnic mobilization. For members of both groups, then, the dominant response was to pass as ordinary Japanese. Given the fact of discrimination, individual *Burakumin* and Korean Japanese sought to assimilate into mainstream society. In the postwar period, these two groups were not racialized—they were not physiologically or culturally distinct from the dominant Japanese population. Most *Burakumin*, as I have noted, share the contemporary Japanese view that they are ethnically Japanese. One consequence of ethnic denial is the virtual ignorance about *Burakumin*, especially in the Tokyo area. The Japanese-American sociologist I. Roger Yoshino found "few in the Tokyo area who had any knowledge of the *Burakumin*" (Yoshino and Murakoshi 1977: v). Indeed, more Japanese were aware of the U.S. Black liberation movement than the *Burakumin* liberation movement in their own country.

Most Korean Japanese, in contrast, did not regard themselves as in any way Japanese. The prevailing self-identification until the 1960s was as sojourners. To the extent that they participated in Japanese economic and social life, they found it easier to pass as Japanese. Even in the 1990s less than a tenth used their Korean names. Their collective political energy was focused on homeland politics and their Japanese manifestation in the division between *Chongryun* and *Mindan*.

Passing as a widespread individual strategy closed the vicious circle of monoethnic ideology. Assimilation is possible only for selected individuals as long as discrimination is widespread. By not seeking a collective challenge to monoethnic ideology and ethnic discrimination, the status quo was sustained. Both *Burakumin* and Koreans could become Japanese as individuals, but, in so doing, they could not, as collectives, become part of Japan.

THE ASSERTION OF NON-JAPANESE IDENTITIES

By the 1980s, however, the situation of different ethnic groups had transformed sufficiently to usher in discourses and movements for the recognition of Japanese multiethnicity. The transformation of ethnic politics stemmed from changing social situations. Residential and employment segregation weakened. In particular, the labor shortages of the 1960s incorporated *Burakumin* to the mainstream Japanese labor market.

Precisely when assimilation advanced, ethnic identity was asserted. Although almost all *Ainu*, *Burakumin*, Chinese, Koreans, Okinawans, and other ethnic minorities in Japan are culturally indistinguishable from their Japanese counterparts, a powerful centrifugal force against assimilation emerged from the 1960s. For Korean Japanese, the first generation's concern for homeland politics became superseded by the second and third generations' interest in Japanese politics. As early as the late 1940s, perhaps a third of Koreans in Japan could not speak Korean fluently. Among third or fourth generation Korean Japanese, Korean-language fluency is extremely rare, and there is little memory of homeland. Younger Korean Japanese are culturally Japanese, albeit with some Korean identification.

Furthermore, various social movements and intellectual currents encouraged ethnic mobilization. Both the New Left and the new social movements in Japan took up the causes of various oppressed social groups. The global dissemination of human rights and antidiscrimination, both as ideas and as organizations, accelerated after the 1960s. Many Korean Japanese people I met were extremely curious about the fate of the Korean diaspora in the U.S. in general and the idea of being Korean American in particular. One such collective expression was the effort to construct a Koreatown in Kawasaki, which was in part inspired by the existence of a Koreantown in Los Angeles.

CONCLUSION

One may very well wonder whether it would not be more sensible to ignore ethnic diversity altogether. Would it not be more sensible, as postwar modernization theorists and Marxists did, to assume that particularistic identities will wither away in favor of more universalistic ones? Should we not take Article 14 of the Japanese Constitution for granted: "All of the people are equal under the law and there shall be no discrimination in political, economic or social relations because of race, creed, sex, social status or family origin"? Do we not risk reifying the ethnic categories, thereby fomenting interethnic conflict and suppressing intraethnic differences? Should we not attempt to free ourselves from the alienated categories of peoplehood, such as ethnicity or nation? Although I am profoundly sympathetic to universalistic ideals and cosmopolitan concerns, I am afraid that abstract universals such as democracy cannot emerge without concrete struggles for recognition and inclusion.

The pursuit of abstract universals carries the danger of empty formalism, thereby reproducing the discourse of monoethnicity and the phenomena of passive racism and passing. When Japanese students were asked whether they would marry *Burakumin*, most claimed that they would. Very few, however, were willing to do so after they were shown a video on *Burakumin* discrimination. The converse of passive racism is the prevalence of passing. Many Korean Japanese who have become Japanese citizens nonetheless continue to hide the fact of naturalization and live in fear of exposure of their Korean ancestry. Although police officers are taught in police school to ignore ascriptive characteristics, such as nationality and *Burakumin* status (Bayley 1976: 85–86), several Korean Japanese told me that they are frequently harassed by the police. In the meantime, well-meaning Japanese, steeped as they may be in the ideology of universal human rights and democracy, reiterate the ideology of monoethnic Japan. Consider in this regard the shortcomings of the Japanese social sciences. In nearly 700 pages, contributors to a volume on contemporary Japanese society had nothing to say about minorities in Japan (Watanabe 1996). The critical overview of Japanese society by the progressive sociologist Mita Munesuke (1996) similarly bypasses ethnic questions. When Western postmodern and postcolonial scholars revived the issues of nation and ethnicity in the 1980s, some Japanese scholars followed the fashion. Their writings are replete with *katakana* (a script used for foreign words)—*nêshon* and *esunishitî*, not *kokka* and *minzoku*—but devoid of actually existing Japanese minorities (e.g., Ôsawa 1996). Non-Japanese Japanese are not mentioned even when a book argues for the multiethnic nature of contemporary Japanese society (Yamauchi et al. 1991: 10).

Abstract universals such as democracy must be achieved through concrete particulars. As alienated and particularistic as ethnic categories may be, we cannot wish them away. Rather, we need to struggle through concrete concerns of prejudice, discrimination, and denial in hope of overcoming them and building a more ethnically inclusive citizenship as the foundation of an ethnically inclusive democracy.

REFERENCES

Bayley, David H. 1976. *Force of Order: Police Behavior in Japan and the United States*. Berkeley: University of California Press.

Calhoun, Craig. 1997. *Nationalism*. Minneapolis: University of Minnesota Press.

Cornell, John B. 1967. "Individual Mobility and Group Membership: The Case of the *Burakumin*." In *Aspects of Social Change in Modern Japan*, ed. R. P. Dore. Princeton, N.J.: Princeton University Press.

De Vos, George, and Hiroshi Wagatsuma. 1966. "The Ecology of Special Buraku." In *Japan's Invisible Race: Caste in Culture and Personality*, eds. George de Vos and Hiroshi Wagatsuma. Berkeley: University of California Press.

Duus, Peter. 1995. *The Abacus and the Sword: The Japanese Penetration of Korea, 1895–1910*. Berkeley: University of California Press.

Fukuoka, Yasunori, Hiroaki Yoshii, Atsushi Sakurai, Shûsaku Ejima, Haruhiko Kanegae, and Michihiko Noguchi, eds. 1987. *Hisabetsu no bunka, hansabetsu no ikizama (Culture of discrimination, life of anti-discrimination)*. Tokyo: Akashi Shoten.

Gellner, Ernest. 1983. *Nations and Nationalism*. Oxford: Blackwell.

Hobsbawm, E. J. 1990. *Nations and Nationalism since 1780: Programme, Myth, Reality*. Cambridge: Cambridge University Press.

Honda, Yutaka. 1990. *Burakushi kara mita Tokyo* (*Tokyo from the standpoint of Burakumin history*). Tokyo: Aki Shobô.

Lewis, W. Arthur. 1985. *Racial Conflict and Economic Development*. Cambridge, Mass.: Harvard University Press.

Lie, John. 2001. *Multiethnic Japan*. Cambridge, Mass.: Harvard University Press.

McNeill, William H. 1986. *Polyethnicity and National Unity in World History*. Toronto: University of Toronto Press.

Mita, Munesuke. 1996. *Gendai shakai no riron: jôhôka, shôhika shakai no genzai to mirai* (*Theory of modern society: the present and the future of informatizing and commoditizing society*). Tokyo: Iwanami Shoten.

Mitchell, Richard H. 1967. *The Korean Minority in Japan*. Berkeley: University of California Press.

Neary, Ian. 1989. *Political Protest and Social Control in Pre-War Japan: The Origins of Buraku Liberation*. Atlantic Highlands, N.J.: Humanities Press International.

Ooms, Herman. 1996. *Tokugawa Village Practice: Class, Status, Power, Law*. Berkeley: University of California Press.

Pak, Kyông-sik. 1992. *Zainichi Chôsenjin, kyôsei renkô, minzoku mondai* (*Koreans in Japan, enforced migration and ethnic problems*). Tokyo: San'ichi Shobô.

Plessner, Helmuth. 1959. *Die Verspätete Nation: Über die politische Verführbarkeit bürgerlichen* (*The belated nation: on the political seduction of bourgeois spirit*). Geistes, 2d ed. Stuttgart: Verlag W. Kohlhammer.

Terazawa, Masako. 1990. "Nihon shakai no heisasei to bunka" ("The closed character of Japanese society"). In *Gaikokujin rôdôsha no jinken* (*The human rights of foreign workers*), ed. Gyôzaisei Sôgô Kenkyûsho. Tokyo: Ôtsuki Shoten.

Totten, George O., and Hiroshi Wagatsuma. 1966. "Emancipation: Growth and Transformation of a Political Movement." In *Japan's Invisible Race: Caste in Culture and Personality*, eds. George de Vos and Hiroshi Wagatsuma. Berkeley: University of California Press.

Upham, Frank K. 1987. *Law and Social Change in Post-war Japan*. Cambridge, Mass.: Harvard University Press.

Weber, Eugen. 1976. *Peasants into Frenchmen: The Modernization of Rural France, 1870–1914*. Stanford, Calif.: Stanford University Press.

Yagi, Kôsuke. 1984. "Buraku sabetsu no genjitsu to mondaiten" ("The reality and problems of Burakumin discrimination"). In *Kôza sabetsu to jinken*, Vol.1: *Buraku I* (*Lectures on discrimination and human rights*, Vol. 1), eds. Eiichi Isomura, Yasuko Ichibangase, and Tomohiko Harada. Tokyo: Yûzankaku.

Yamauchi, Masayuki, and Minzoku Mondai Kenkyûkai, eds. 1991. *Nyûmon sekai no minzoku mondai* (*Introduction to the ethnic problems of the world*). Tokyo: Nihon Keizai Shinbunsha.

Yoshino, I. Roger, and Sueo Murakoshi. 1977. *The Invisible Visible Minority: Japan's Burakumin*. Osaka: Buraku Kaiho Kenkyusho.

7

Ethnic Identity in China: The Rising Politics of Cultural Difference

Dru C. Gladney

Foreigners and the Chinese themselves typically picture China's population as a vast monolithic Han majority with a sprinkling of exotic minorities living along the country's borders. This understates China's tremendous cultural, geographic, and linguistic diversity—in particular the important cultural differences within the Han population. This ignores the fact that China is officially a multinational country with fifty-six recognized "nationalities." More importantly, recent events suggest that China may well be increasingly insecure regarding not only these nationalities, but also its own national integration. The World Trade Center and Pentagon attacks of September 11, 2001, actually brought China and the United States closer together in an antiterrorism campaign that has made the case of *Uyghur* separatism in China much more prominent in the Western press.

At the same time, China is now seeing a resurgence of local nationality and culture, most notably among southerners such as the Cantonese and *Hakka*, who are currently classified as Han. These differences may increase under threats from ethnic separatism, economic pressures such as inflation, the growing gap between rich and poor areas, and the migration of millions of people from poorer provinces to those with jobs. Chinese society is also under pressure from the officially recognized minorities such as *Uyghurs* and Tibetans. For centuries, China has held together a vast multicultural and multiethnic nation despite alternating periods of political centralization and fragmentation. But cultural and linguistic cleavages could worsen in a China weakened by internal strife, inflation, uneven growth, or a struggle for political succession. The National Day celebrations in October 1999, celebrating fifty years of the Communist Party in China, underscored the importance of China's many ethnic peoples in its national resurgence. Recent crackdowns

133

on antiseparatism and antiterrorism underscore the Chinese government's increasing concern regarding national security and the integrity of its border areas.

Thus, just as the legitimacy of the Communist Chinese government has always rested on the construction of a Han majority and of selected minority nationalities out of Sun Yat-sen's shifting "tray of sand," the prospects for and implications of democratization in China are closely tied to the ongoing constitution of collective identities. In China's increasingly assertive cultural diversity—intensely sharpened by economic liberalization—lies a new and perhaps precarious pluralism. As I argue below, it is too early to claim that this tolerance of diversity within authoritarian political unity carries the seeds of democracy. Nevertheless, it does reflect a heightened search for party–state legitimacy in the face of the increasing social, economic, and cultural strains brought on by globalization.

THE SOVIET UNION AS CHINA'S PROLOGUE?

At the beginning of the last decade, not a single observer of international politics predicted that the former Soviet Union would now be fragmented into a mélange of strident new states and restive ethnic minorities. When Russian troops marched on Chechnya in hopes of keeping what remains of its former empire together, few analysts drew parallels to China's attempts to reign in its restive Muslim *Uyghur* minority. Considering worldwide Muslim support for the liberation struggles of Muslims in Bosnia and Kosovo, and with growing support among world—notably Asian—Muslims for the Palestinian "anticolonial" struggle against Israel, it is not surprising to find growing Muslim concern regarding the "plight" of China's Muslims.[1]

China is thought to be different. It is rarely supposed to be shaken by ethnic or national disintegration.[2] Cultural commonality and a monolithic civilization are supposed to hold China together. While ethnic nationalism has generally been absent from Western reporting and perspectives on China, the peoples of the People's Republic have often demonstrated otherwise. Continuing separatist activities and ethnic unrest have punctuated China's border areas since a major Muslim uprising in February 1996, which led to bombings in Beijing and frequent eruptions on its periphery.[3] Quick and violent responses to thwart localized protests, with twenty-seven "splittists" reportedly killed in an uprising in December 1999 outside of Khotan in southern Xinjiang *Uyghur* Autonomous Region, indicate rising Chinese government concern over the influence of separatist sentiment spilling over from the newly independent Central Asia nations into China's Muslim areas. The more than 20 million Turkic *Uyghurs*, *Kyrgyz*, *Kazaks*, and other Muslims who live in these areas are a visible and vocal reminder that China is linked to Eurasia. For *Uyghur* nationalists today, the direct lineal descent from the *Uyghur* Kingdom in seventh-century Mongolia is accepted as fact, despite overwhelming historical and archeological evidence to the contrary, and they seek to revive that ancient kingdom as a modern Uyghuristan.[4] Random arrests and detentions continue among the *Uyghur*, who are increasingly being regarded as China's Chechens. A report in the *Wall Street Journal* of the arrest on 11 August 1999 of Rebiya Kadir, a well-known *Uyghur* businesswoman, during a visit by the U.S. Congressional Research Service delegation to the region, indicates the Chinese government's suspicion of the *Uyghur* people continues.[5]

China is also concerned about the "Kosovo effect," fearing that its Muslim and other ethnic minorities might be emboldened to seek outside international (read Western) support for continued human rights abuses. Just prior to its National Day celebrations in October 1999, the State Council hosted its first three-day conference on "the nationalities problem" in Beijing and issued a new policy paper, "National Minorities Policy and its Practice in China."[6] Though this White Paper did little more than outline all the "good" programs China has carried out in minority areas, it did indicate increasing concern and a willingness to recognize unresolved problems, with several strategic think tanks in Beijing and Shanghai initiating focus groups and research programs addressing ethnic identity and separatism issues.[7]

But ethnic problems in the China of Jiang Zemin and, now, Hu Jintao go far deeper than the "official" minorities. Sichuanese, Cantonese, Shanghainese, and Hunanese cafés are avidly advocating increased cultural nationalism and resistance to Beijing central control. As the European Union experiences difficulties in building a common European alliance across these linguistic, cultural, and political boundaries, we should not imagine China to be less concerned about its persistent multiculturalism.

If the Holy Roman Empire were around today, it would look much like China. Two millennia ago, when the Roman Empire was at its peak, so was the Han dynasty—both empires barely lasted another 200 years. At the beginning of the last millennium, China was on the verge of being conquered by the Mongols and divided by a weakened Song dynasty in the south and the Liao dynasty in the north. Their combined territory was equal only to the five northern provinces in today's PRC. Indeed, it was the Mongols who extended China's territory to include much of what is considered part of China today: Tibet, Xinjiang, Manchuria, Sichuan, and Yunnan. Over the last two millennia China has been divided longer than it has been unified: can it maintain national unity until the next century? History suggests otherwise. Indeed, with the reacquisition of Macau in late 1999, China is the only country in the world that is *expanding* its territory instead of reducing it. Will China be able to continue to resist the inexorable forces of globalization and nationalism?

Just as linguistic diversity within China leads Chinese linguists such as John DeFrancis to speak of the many Chinese languages, attention to cultural diversity should force us to give further weight to the plurality of the Chinese peoples in national politics. A former American president once claimed to know the mind of "the Chinese." This is as farfetched as someone claiming to know the European mind. Have any U.S. policy-makers spent time talking to disgruntled entrepreneurs in Canton and Shanghai, impoverished peasants in Anhui and Gansu, or angry Central Asians in Xinjiang, Mongolia, and Tibet? While ethnic diversity does not necessitate ethnic separatism or violence, growing ethnic awareness and expression in China should inform policy that takes into account the interests of China's many peoples, not just those in power. China's policy, including toward issues of political liberalization and democratization, should represent more than the interests of those in Beijing.

NATIONALITY IN CHINA

Officially, China is made up of fifty-six nationalities: one majority nationality, the Han, and fifty-five minority groups. Initial results from the 2000 census suggest a total official minority population of nearly 104 million, or approximately 9 percent of the total population. The peoples identified as Han comprise 91 percent of the population from Beijing in the north to Canton in the south. They include the *Hakka*, Fujianese, Cantonese, and other groups (Mackerras 1994: 25). These Han are thought to be united by a common history, culture, and written language; differences in language, dress, diet, and customs are regarded as minor and superficial. The rest of the population is divided into fifty-five official "minority" nationalities that are mostly concentrated along the borders, such as the Mongolians and *Uyghurs* in the north and the *Zhuang, Yi (Lolo)*, and *Bai* in southern China, near Southeast Asia. Other groups, such as the *Hui* and Manchus, are scattered throughout the nation, and there are minorities in every province, region, and county. An active state-sponsored program assists these official minority cultures and promotes their economic development (with mixed results). The outcome, according to China's preeminent sociologist, Fei Xiaotong, is a "unified multinational" state (Fei 1981: 20). But even this recognition of diversity understates the divisions within the Chinese population, especially the wide variety of culturally and ethnically diverse groups within the majority Han population (Honig 1992). These groups have recently begun to rediscover and reassert their different cultures, languages, and history. Yet, as the Chinese worry and debate over their own identity, policy-makers in other states still take the monolithic Han identity for granted.

The notion of a Han person (*Han ren*) dates back centuries and refers to descendants of the Han dynasty, which flourished at about the same time as the Roman Empire. But the concept of Han nationality (*Han minzu*) is an entirely modern phenomenon that arose with the shift from the Chinese empire to the modern nation-state (Duara 1995: 47). In the early part of this century, Chinese reformers had been concerned that the Chinese people lacked a sense of nationhood, unlike Westerners and even China's other peoples such as Tibetans and Manchus. In the view of these reformers, Chinese unity stopped at the clan or community level rather than extending to the nation as a whole. Sun Yat-sen, leader of the republican movement that toppled the last imperial dynasty of China (the Qing) in 1911, popularized the idea that there were "Five Peoples of China"—the majority Han being one and the others being the Manchus, Mongolian, Tibetan, and *Hui* (a term that included all Muslims in China, now divided into *Uyghurs, Kazakhs, Hui*, etc.). Sun was a Cantonese, educated in Hawaii, who feared arousing traditional northern suspicions of southern radical movements. He wanted both to unite the Han and to mobilize them and all other non-Manchu groups in China (including Mongols, Tibetans, and Muslims) into a modern multiethnic nationalist movement against the Manchu Qing state and foreign imperialists. The Han were seen as a unified group distinct from the above mentioned "internal" foreigners as well as the "external" foreigners on their frontiers, namely the Western and Japanese imperialists. Dikotter (1992) has argued that there was a racial basis for this notion of a unified Han *minzu*, but I suspect the rationale was more strategic and nationalistic—the need to build national security around the concept of one national people, with a small percentage of minorities supporting that idea. The Communists expanded the number of "peoples" from five to fifty-six, but kept the idea of a unified Han group. The Communists were, in fact, disposed to accommodate these internal minority groups for several reasons. The Communists' 1934–1935 Long March, a 6,000-mile trek across China from southwest to northwest to escape the threat of annihilation by Chiang Kai-shek's Kuomintang (KMT) forces, took the Communists through some of the most heavily populated minority areas. Harried on one side by the KMT and on the other by fierce "barbarian" tribesmen, the Communists were faced with a choice between extermination and promising special treatment to minorities—especially the *Miao, Yi*, Tibetans, Mongols, and *Hui*—should the party ever win national power. The Communists even offered the possibility of true independence for minorities. Chairman Mao frequently referred to Article 14 of the 1931 Chinese Communist Party (CCP) Constitution, which "recognizes the right of self-determination" of the national minorities in China and their right to complete separation from China and to the formation of an independent state for each minority. This commitment was not kept after the founding of the People's Republic (Gladney 1996: 60–75). Instead, the party stressed

maintaining the unity of the new state at all costs. The recognition of minorities, however, also helped the Communists' long-term goal of forging a
united Chinese nation by solidifying the recognition of the Han as a unified
"majority." Emphasizing the difference between Han and minorities helped to
de-emphasize the differences within the Han community. The Communists incorporated the idea of Han unity into a Marxist ideology of progress with
the Han in the forefront of development and civilization, the vanguard of
the people's revolution (Gladney 1994a: 97). The more "backward" or
"primitive" the minorities were, the more "advanced" and "civilized" the
so-called Han seemed and the greater the need for a unified national identity. Cultural diversity within the Han has not been admitted because of a
deep (and well-founded) fear of the country breaking up into feuding
warlord-run kingdoms as happened in the 1910s and 1920s. China has historically been divided along north/south lines, into Five Kingdoms, War-
ring States, or local satrapies, as often as it has been united. Indeed, China
as it currently exists, including large pieces of territory occupied by Mongols, Turkic peoples, Tibetans, etc., is three times larger than China was
under the last Chinese dynasty, the Ming, which fell in 1644. Ironically, geographic "China" as defined by the People's Republic was actually established by foreign conquest dynasties, first by the Mongols and finally by
the Manchus. A strong, centralizing Chinese government (whether of foreign or internal origin) has often tried to impose ritualistic, linguistic, and
political uniformity throughout its borders. The modern state has tried to
unite its various peoples with transportation and communications networks and an extensive civil service. In recent years these efforts have
continued through the controlled infusion of capitalistic investment and
market manipulation. Yet even in the modern era, these integrative mechanisms have not produced cultural uniformity, which, as we shall see, has
implications for economic and political liberalization as well as democratization.

HAN NATIONALITY AS INVENTED NATIONAL UNITY

Although presented as a unified culture—an idea also accepted by many
Western researchers—Han peoples differ in many ways, most obviously in
their languages. The supposedly homogenous Han speak eight mutually unintelligible languages (Mandarin, *Wu*, *Yue*, *Xiang*, *Hakka*, *Gan*, Southern
Min, and Northern *Min*). Even these subgroups show marked linguistic and
cultural diversity; in the *Yue* language family, for example, Cantonese speakers are barely intelligible to *Taishan* speakers, and the Southern *Min* dialects
of Quanzhou, Changzhou, and Xiamen are equally difficult to communicate
across (Norman 1988: 27). Chinese linguist Y. R. Chao has shown that the

mutual unintelligibility of, say, Cantonese and Mandarin is as great as that of Dutch and English or French and Italian (Chao 1976: 83). Mandarin was imposed as the national language early in the twentieth century and has become the lingua franca, but, like Swahili in Africa, it must often be learned in school and is rarely used in everyday life in many areas. Cultural perceptions among the Han often involve broad stereotypical contrasts between north and south (Blake 1981). Northerners tend to be thought of as larger, broaderfaced, and lighter-skinned, while southerners are depicted as smaller and darker. Cultural practices involving birth, marriage, and burial differ widely; Fujianese, for example, are known for vibrant folk religious practices and ritualized reburial of interned corpses, while Cantonese have a strong lineage tradition, both of which are almost nonexistent in the north. One finds radically different eating habits from north to south, with northerners consuming noodles from wheat and other grains, open to consuming lamb and beef, and preferring spicy foods, while the southern diet is based upon rice, eschews such meats in favor of seafood, and along the coast is milder. It is interesting in this regard that Fei Xiaotong (1989: 12) once argued that what made the Han people different from minorities was their agricultural traditions (i.e., minorities were traditionally not engaged in farming, though this failed to take account of groups like the Koreans and *Uyghur* who have farmed for 1400 years). Yet Fei never considered the vast cultural differences separating rice-eaters in the south from wheat-eaters in the north. As other chapters in this volume also demonstrate, this process of national unification based on an invented majority at the expense of a few isolated minorities is one widely documented in Asia and not unique to China (see Gladney 1998a).

IDENTITY POLITICS AND NATIONAL MINORITIES

China's policy toward minorities involves official recognition, limited autonomy, and unofficial efforts at control. The official minorities hold an importance for China's long-term development that is disproportionate to their population. Although totaling only 8.04 percent of the population, they are concentrated in resource-rich areas spanning nearly 60 percent of the country's landmass and exceed 90 percent of the population in counties and villages along many border areas of Xinjiang, Tibet, Inner Mongolia, and Yunnan. While the 1990 census recorded 91 million minorities, the 2000 census is estimated to report an increase in the minority population to 104 million (Zhang Tianlu 1999).

Shortly after taking power, Communist leaders sent teams of researchers, social scientists, and party cadres to the border regions to "identify" groups as official nationalities. Only 41 of the more than 400 groups that applied were recognized, and that number had reached only 56 by 1982. For generally political reasons, most of the nearly 350 other groups were identified as Han or lumped together with other minorities with whom they shared some features. Some are still applying for recognition. The 1990 census listed almost 750,000 people as still "unidentified" and awaiting recognition—meaning they were regarded as ethnically different, but did not fit into any of the recognized categories. In recognition of the minorities' official status as well as their strategic importance, various levels of nominally autonomous administration were created: five regions, thirty-one prefectures, ninety-six counties (or, in Inner Mongolia and Manchuria, banners), and countless villages. Such "autonomous" areas do not have true local political control, although they may have increased local administration of resources, taxes, birth planning, education, legal jurisdiction, and religious expression. These areas have minority government leaders, but the real source of power is still the Han-dominated Communist Party. As a result, they may actually come under closer scrutiny than other provinces that have large minority populations but not "autonomous" status, such as Gansu, Qinghai, and Sichuan. While autonomy seems not to be all that the word might imply, it is still apparently a desirable attainment for minorities in China. Between the 1982 and 1990 censuses, eighteen new autonomous counties were established, three of them in Liaoning Province for the Manchus, who previously had no autonomous administrative districts. Although the government is clearly trying to limit the recognition of new nationalities, there seems to be an avalanche of new autonomous administrative districts. Besides the eighteen new counties and many villages whose total numbers have never been published, at least eight more new autonomous counties are to be set up. Five will go to the *Tujia*, a group widely dispersed throughout the southwest that doubled in population from 2.8 to 5.8 million from 1982 to 1990.

The increase in the number of groups seeking minority status reflects what may be described as an explosion of ethnicity in contemporary China. Indeed, it has now become popular, especially in Beijing, for people to "come out" as Manchus or other ethnic groups, admitting they were not Han all along. While the Han population grew a total of 10 percent between 1982 and 1990, the minority population grew 35 percent overall—from 67 million to 91 million. The Manchus, a group long thought to have been assimilated into the Han majority, added three autonomous districts and increased their population by 128 percent from 4.3 to 9.8 million, while the population of the *Gelao* people in Guizhou shot up an incredible 714 percent in just eight years. Clearly these rates reflect more than a high birthrate; they also indicate "category-shifting," as people redefine their nationality from Han to minority or from one minority to another. In interethnic marriages, parents can decide the nationality of their children, and the children themselves can choose their nationality at age eighteen. One scholar predicts that, if the minority populations' growth rate continues, they will total 864 million in 2080 (Zhang 1999). Recent reports regarding the 2000 census already mentioned suggest a 9.1 percent increase in the total population. China has recently begun to limit births among minorities, especially in urban areas, but it is doubtful that authorities will be able to limit the avalanche of applications for redefinition and the hundreds of groups applying for recognition as minorities. In a recent fascinating book, Ralph Litzinger (2000: 238) has suggested that the "politics of national belonging" have led the *Yao* willingly to participate in the process of Chinese nationalization. Similarly, Louisa Schein's (2000: 30–31) book on the *Hmong* minority argues that "internal Orientalism" has led to a resurgence of interest in the exoticized minority "Other."

Why was it popular to be "officially" ethnic in 1990s China? This is an interesting question given the negative reporting in the Western press about minority discrimination in China. If it is so bad to be a minority in China, why are their numbers increasing? One explanation may be that, in 1982, there were still lingering doubts about the government's true intent in registering the nationalities during the census. The Cultural Revolution, a ten-year period during which any kind of difference—ethnic, religious, cultural, or political—was ruthlessly suppressed, had ended only a few years before. By the mid-1980s, it had become clear that those groups identified as official minorities were beginning to receive real benefits from the implementation of several affirmative action programs. The most significant privileges included permission to have more children (except in urban areas, minorities are generally not bound by the one-child policy), pay fewer taxes, obtain better (albeit Chinese-language) education for their children, have greater access to public office, speak and learn their native languages, worship and practice their religion (often including practices such as shamanism that are still banned among the Han), and express their cultural differences through the arts and popular culture. Indeed, one might even say it has become popular to be "ethnic" in today's China. Mongolian hot pot, Muslim noodle, and Korean barbecue restaurants proliferate in every city, while minority clothing, artistic motifs, and cultural styles adorn Chinese bodies and private homes. In Beijing, one of the most popular new restaurants is the Thai Family Village (*Dai Jia Cun*). It offers a cultural experience of the Thai minority (known in China as the *Dai*), complete with beautiful waitresses in revealing *Dai*-style sarongs and short tops, sensually singing and dancing, while exotic foods such as snake's blood are enjoyed by the young Han nouveau riche. As predicted, it is not unusual to learn of Han Chinese prostitutes representing themselves as Thai and other minorities to appear more exotic to their customers (Gladney 1994a). Surprisingly, the second most popular novel in China in 1994 was *The History of the Soul* (*Xin ling shi*), which concerned personal and religious conflicts in a remote Muslim region in northwest

China and was written by Zhang Chengzhi, a *Hui* Muslim from Ningxia. This rise of "ethnic chic" is in dramatic contrast to the antiethnic homogenizing policies of the late 1950s anti-Rightist period, the Cultural Revolution, and even the late-1980s "anti-spiritual pollution" campaigns.

Foreign policy considerations have also encouraged changes in China's treatment of minority groups. China has one of the world's largest Muslim populations—nearly 20 million, more than the United Arab Emirates, Iraq, Libya, or Malaysia—and has increasing contacts with trade partners in the Middle East and new Muslim states created on its borders. China provides the Middle East and Central Asia with cheap labor, consumer goods, weaponry—and increasing numbers of Muslim pilgrims to Mecca (Gladney 1994b). These relations will be jeopardized if Muslim, especially *Uyghur*, discontent continues over such issues as limitations on mosque building, restrictions on childbearing, uncontrolled mineral and energy development, and continued nuclear testing in the Xinjiang region. Foreign policy considerations also argue for better treatment of Korean minorities because South Korean investment, tourism, and natural resources have given China's Koreans in Liaoning and Manchuria a booming economy and the best educational level of all nationalities (including the Han). Another factor has been international tourism to minority areas, including the "Silk Road" tourism to Xinjiang and marketing of package tours to the "colorful" minority regions of Yunnan and Guizhou for Japanese, Taiwanese, and Southeast Asian Chinese tour groups. The most striking change in China's policy toward a single minority as a result of international relations has been the initiation, just after the improvement in Sino–Israeli relations in 1992, of discussions about granting official nationality status to the Chinese Jews (*Youtai ren*), once thought to have disappeared entirely. As Sino–Israeli relations improve, and China seeks increased tourism dollars from Tel Aviv and New York, one might imagine that the Chinese Jews will once again reappear as an official nationality in China.

The creation, on China's Central Asian frontier, of several new states that have ethnic populations on both sides of the border has also made ethnic separatism a major concern. The newly independent status of the Central Asian states has allowed separatist groups in Xinjiang to locate some sources of support, leading to more than thirty reported bombing incidents in the Xinjiang Region in 1999, claimed by groups militating for an "Independent Turkestan." At the same time, freer travel across the Central Asian borders has made China's Muslims well aware of the ethnic and political conflicts in Azerbaijan and Tajikistan, and also that many of them are better off economically than their fellow Muslims across the border. Several meetings of the "Shanghai Five" (PRC, Kazakhstan, Kyrgyzstan, Tajikistan, and Russia) since April 1997 have concluded treaties strengthening border security and the refusal to harbor separatist groups. In April 1999, the Kazakhstan authorities returned to China three *Uyghurs* accused of separatism. Beijing's challenge is to convince China's Muslims that they will benefit more from cooperation with their national government than from resistance. In the south, a dramatic increase in cross-border relations between Chinese minority groups and Myanmar (Burma), Cambodia, and Thailand has led to a rising problem of drug smuggling. Beijing also wants to help settle disputes in Cambodia, Vietnam, and Myanmar because of the danger of ethnic wars spilling over the border into China. In Tibet, frequent reports of ongoing resistance and many arrests continue to filter into the media despite the best efforts of Beijing "spin control."

INTERNAL DIVISIONS AMONG THE HAN MAJORITY

Not only have the "official" minorities in China begun to assert their identities more strongly, pressing the government for more recognition, autonomy, and special privileges, but different groups within the so-called Han majority have begun to rediscover, reinvent, and reassert their ethnic differences. With the dramatic economic explosion in South China, southerners and others have begun to assert cultural and political differences. Cantonese rock music, videos, movies, and television programs, all heavily influenced by Hong Kong, are now popular throughout China. Whereas comedians used to make fun of southern ways and accents, southerners now scorn northerners for their lack of sophistication and business acumen. As any Mandarin-speaking Beijing resident will tell you, bargaining for vegetables or cellular telephones in Guangzhou or Shanghai markets is becoming more difficult for them due to growing pride in local languages: nonnative speakers always pay a higher price. Rising self-awareness among the Cantonese is paralleled by the reassertion of identity among the *Hakka*, the southern Fujianese *Min*, the *Swatow*, and a host of other generally ignored peoples now empowered by economic success and embittered by age-old restraints from the north.

Interestingly, most of these southern groups traditionally regarded themselves not as Han, but as Tang people, descendants of the great Tang dynasty (618–907 A.D.) and its southern bases (Moser 1985). Most Chinatowns in North America, Europe, and Southeast Asia are inhabited by descendants of Chinese immigrants from the mainly Tang areas of southern China and built around Tang Person Streets (*tang ren jie*). The next decade may see the resurgence of Tang nationalism in southern China in opposition to northern Han nationalism, especially as economic wealth in the south eclipses that of the north. There is also a newfound interest in the ancient southern *Chu* kingdom as a key to modern southern success. Some southern scholars have departed from the traditional Chinese view of history and begun to argue that, by the sixth century B.C., the bronze culture of the *Chu* spread north and influenced the development of Chinese civilization, rather than this culture originating in the north and spreading southward. Many southerners now see *Chu* as essential to Chinese culture, to be distinguished from the less important northern dynasties—with implications for the nation's economic and geopolitical future. Museums to the glory of *Chu* have been established throughout southern China. There is also a growing belief that northerners and southerners had separate racial origins based on different histories and contrasting physiogenetic types. These ideas are influenced by highly speculative nineteenth-century notions of race and Social Darwinism (see Mair 1999). There has also been an outpouring of interest in *Hakka* origins, language, and culture on Taiwan, which may be spreading to the mainland. The *Hakka*, or "guest people," are thought to have moved southward in successive migrations from northern China as early as the Eastern Jin (317–420 A.D.), or the late Song dynasty (960–1279 A.D.) according to many *Hakka* (who claim to be Song people as well as Tang people). The *Hakka* have the same language and many of the same cultural practices as the *She* minority, but never sought minority status themselves—perhaps because of a desire to overcome their long-term stigmatization by Cantonese and other southerners as "uncivilized barbarians" (Blake 1981). This low status may stem from the unique *Hakka* language (which is unintelligible to other southerners), the isolated and walled *Hakka* living compounds, or the refusal of *Hakka* women during the imperial period to bind their feet. Nevertheless, the popular press in China is beginning more frequently to note the widely perceived *Hakka* origins of important political figures (including Deng Xiaoping, Mao Zedong, Sun Yat-sen, former Party General Secretary Hu Yaobang, and former President Ye Jianying). People often praise Zhou Enlai by stressing his Jiangnan linkages and Lee Kuan Yew as a prominent *Hakka* statesman. Even Chiang Kai-shek is lauded as a southerner who knew how to get money out of the United States.

INTERNET CAFES, DISCOS, AND DEMOCRATIZATION?

China's very economic vitality has the potential to fuel ethnic and linguistic division, rather than further integrating the country as most would suppose. As southern and coastal areas get richer, much of central, northern, and northwestern China is unlikely to keep up, increasing competition and contributing to age-old resentments across ethnic, linguistic, and cultural lines (see Wang et al. 2000). Southern ethnic economic ties link wealthy Cantonese, Shanghainese, and Fujianese (also the majority people in Taiwan) more closely to their relatives abroad than to their political overlords in Beijing. Already provincial governments in Canton and elsewhere not only resist paying taxes to Beijing, but also restrict the transshipment of goods coming from outside across provincial—often the same as cultural—lines. Travelers in China have seen an extraordinary expansion of toll roads, indicating greater interest in local control. Dislocations from rapid economic growth may also fuel ethnic divisions. Huge migrations of "floating populations," estimated to total over 150 million nationally, now move across China seeking employment in wealthier areas, often engendering stigmatized identities and stereotypical fears of "outsiders" (*waidi ren*) within China. Crime, housing shortages, and lowered wages are now attributed most to these people from Anhui, Hunan, or Gansu who are taking jobs from locals, complaints similar to those in West Germany about the influx of Easterners after reunification. Reports that 70 percent of those convicted of crimes in Beijing were "outsiders" have fueled criticisms of China's increasingly open internal migration policy (Fei Guo 1999). Eric Harwit has noted that, in parallel with this fragmenting, the "digital divide" in China is closing, and the rapid expansion of Internet usage (up to 27 percent of all households are online in Beijing) has fostered wider communication and dissemination of news and information.[8]

The result of all these changes is that China is becoming increasingly decentered. This is a fearsome prospect for those holding the reins in Beijing and, perhaps, was a factor in the decision to crack down on the June 1989 demonstrations in Tiananmen Square. At that time central authorities had begun to lose control of a country they feared could quickly unravel. That such fears have not eased is shown by the increased calls for national unity during National Day celebrations and by the efforts to reduce corruption. Worker and peasant unrest reported throughout China cut across and may at times exacerbate cultural and ethnolinguistic differences between the haves and the have-nots, who in today's China are often and increasingly divided by ethnicity.

Recent studies of democracy and democratization in China suggest that, at least at the village level, legitimate local elections are leading to a rising civil society and increasing pluralization (see Brook and Frolic 1997: 12). Nevertheless, few see this process advancing to the level of actually posing a serious threat to the rule of the Communist Party (see Hu 2000). Most scholars locate China's increasing civil society, not in the political domain, but in those spaces created by the market economy that the state has difficulty controlling, such as the dance halls and discos (Schell 1989), the karaoke bars, massage parlors, and private businesses (Liu Xin 2001), and the free marketplace (Anagnost 1997).

Interestingly, scholars of Taiwan democratization were equally skeptical of the democratic process ever dislodging the KMT, the wealthiest and most entrenched Chinese political party in history (Rigger 1999: 23). Comparisons between China and Taiwan suggest that democratization will never happen as a result of encouragement from the top, as it would only dislodge those in power, but only as an uncontrollable coalition of marginal groups (Dickson 1997: 82). Bruce Dickson (1997: 26ff) coherently argues that the Leninist system, though theoretically open to participatory governance, is inherently resistant to pluralist democratic processes due to the role of the Communist Party leadership as the permanent leader of the proletariat. Nevertheless, it was the Leninist system that created a system of recognizing and legitimating separate nationalities, which many scholars suggest was the Soviet Union's ultimate undoing (see d'Encausse 1993: 31–47).

In the Taiwan case, Shelley Rigger (1999: 80–93) has argued forcefully for the role of marginal coalition politics in the rise of the Democratic Progressive Party (DPP), which Chen Shui-bian masterfully united to unseat the ruling KMT. The successful mobilization of women, temple organizations, Taiwanese nationalists, environmentalists, Aboriginals, and disenfranchised workers helped to unseat a well-organized political machine (see also Chang in this volume). Rigger pays scant attention to the role of the minority Aboriginal peoples (*yuanzhu min*) in this process of "Taiwanization." Though small in number (about 2 percent of the total population), they were a significant emblem of Taiwanese separate identity from mainland China, and enlisting their support was a pivotal symbolic move on the part of the DPP. Might not China's indigenous minority groups (numbering about 9 percent) also play a role in China's future democratization? Certainly, many of them are pushing at the seams of Chinese rule, and some, like the *Uyghurs* and Tibetans, are receiving increasing international support. Only time will tell if they play an increasing role in Chinese affairs. Meanwhile, the challenge for China's leadership is to ensure that minority nationalities and Han ethnicities— mobilized by the regime's own legitimation strategies, including economic liberalization—do not become dangerously marginalized.

CONCLUSION: NATIONAL DISUNITY?

While ethnic separatism on it own will never be a serious threat to a strong China, a China weakened by internal strife, inflation, uneven economic growth, or struggles for succession could become further divided along cultural and linguistic lines. China's separatists such as they are could never mount such a coordinated attack as was seen on September 11, 2001, in the United States. China's more closed society lacks the openness that has allowed terrorists to move so freely in the West. China's threats will most likely come from civil unrest and, perhaps, internal ethnic unrest from within the so-called Han majority. We should recall that it was a southerner, educated abroad, who led the revolution that ended China's last dynasty; and, when that empire fell, competing warlords—often supported by foreign powers— fought for local turf occupied by culturally distinct peoples. Moreover, the

Taiping Rebellion that nearly brought down the Qing dynasty also had its origins in the southern border region of Guangxi among so-called marginal *Yao* and *Hakka* peoples. These events are being remembered as the generally well-hidden and overlooked "Others" within Chinese society begin to reassert their own identities, in addition to the official nationalities. At the same time, China's leaders are moving away from the homogenizing policies that alienated minority and non-northern groups. Recent moves to allow and even encourage the expression of cultural difference, while preserving political unity, indicate a growing awareness of the need to accommodate cultural diversity. Further evidence of this trend was the 1997 incorporation of Hong Kong, a city that operates on cultural and social assumptions very different from those of Beijing and that was granted an unprecedented degree of autonomy within China.

The construction of Chinese national identity has always been tentative. In June 1989, while China's future hung in the balance, there was significant concern over which armies—those based in Sichuan, Hunan, Canton, or Beijing, each with its own local concerns—would support Deng's crackdown. The military has since been reshuffled and somewhat downsized, attempting to uproot any local attachments and professionalize the command structure (Lilley and Shambaugh 1999: 28). However, this only underlines the growing importance of regional and local ties. China, as of now, is a unified country militarily and, perhaps, politically. As a result of Hu Jintao's and Jiang Zemin's continuance of the Deng Xiaoping reforms, it is increasingly less unified economically. Yet how can China continue to withstand the forces of globalization and nationalism without a government legitimated through popular elections, transparency in the political process, adherence to the rule of law, and good governance?

In November 2000, an ambassador from one of the Muslim states friendliest to China remarked privately to this writer that, by the end of the next decade, China would be divided into nine republics. Historians debate whether a foreign threat has been the only thing that has held China together. Now that the encirclement doctrine, upon which Nixon and Kissinger built the Sino–American alliance, is no longer valid, and containment has been replaced by improving U.S.–China relations based on "engagement," China faces its only enemies from within. Certainly, the events of September 11, 2001, and China's participation in the war on terrorism have helped to reign further in China's separatist groups and further secure its borders (see Gladney, forthcoming).

Senator Daniel Patrick Moynihan predicted that there will be fifty new countries in fifty years. The trend began with the Soviet Union in 1991 and has continued throughout much of Africa and Asia, particularly Indonesia. Why should China be immune from such global fragmentation? Ethnic strife did not dismantle the former Soviet Union; but it did come apart along boundaries defined in large part by ethnic and national difference. The Chinese press reported more than 5,000 organized social protests in 1998 alone, with many more in 1999, culminating in the widespread Falungong uprising and crackdown. Many of these protests have been organized by labor groups and peasant associations, but increasingly ethnic and religious groups have begun to speak out. Some provincial governments continue to assert their autonomy. In addition to the reassertion of the identities of generally well hidden and overlooked "Others" amongst the Han and of the "official" nationalities on China's borders, increasing Taiwanese nationalism has caused great consternation in Beijing, an "internal" ethnic nationalism that few Chinese nationalists can understand.

The rising politics of difference are of concern not only in Lhasa and Urumqi, but in Canton and Shanghai as well. The "Kosovo effect" may very well turn into the "Chechnya effect," where ethnic groups, especially Muslims in general (not just the *Uyghur*), become stereotyped as internal threats and as separatists, and *cleansing* is launched as an "internal" affair. China also may link *Uyghur* separatist actions to the issue of Tibet and Taiwan, leading to broader international ramifications from any crackdown. The problem for China, however, is that many of its internal threats may not come from official nationalities, who are more easily singled out by race or language. China's Chechnya, like Indonesia's Aceh, may very well come from within the Han majority from those who mobilize ethnic differences to seek economic and political advantage. The admission of China into the WTO will mean even further enrichment of the largely coastal and urban developed areas over the more rural central provinces and peripheral minority areas, exacerbating underlying tensions and cultural fault lines. The next decade promises to be as momentous for China as the last decade was for the United States, Europe, and Russia.

NOTES

1. See the statements by Zainuddin, spokesman for the Indonesian Islamic Defenders Front: "Israelis are not welcome in Indonesia because their illegal colonization has killed thousands of Muslim people. . . . We are ready to go to war, a holy war, to defend Islam. . . . The Israelis are colonialists, and we are against what they have done to the Palestinians, therefore they should have been barred from coming to Indonesia" (Calvin Sims, "Islamic Radicals in Indonesia Vow Vengeance on Israelis," *New York Times*, 15 October 2000). For Xinjiang as an "internal colony of China," see Gladney (1998b: 47).

2. Shambaugh (2000) dismisses the ethnic issue as minor and completely unlike the troubles encountered by the former Soviet Union.

3. See the critical report by Amnesty International (1999).

4. The best "*Uyghur* nationalist" retelling of this unbroken descent from Karakhorum is at Eastern Turkestani Union in Europe (c. 1996). For a recent review and critique, including historical evidence for the multiethnic background of the contemporary *Uyghur*, see Gladney (1999: 812–34). For a discussion of the recent archeological evidence derived from DNA dating of the desiccated corpses of Xinjiang, see Mair (1999: 1–40).

5. Ian Johnson, "China Arrests Noted Businesswoman in Crackdown in Muslim Region," *Wall Street Journal*, 18 August 1999.

6. China State Council (1999).

7. The China Institute for Contemporary International Relations (CICIR), under the State Council, has initiated a "Nationality Studies Project" in order to examine security implications of China's minority problems (see China Institute for Contemporary International Affairs 1999).

8. For a critical discussion of China's "digital divide" and the often surprising accessibility of many Internet sites, see Harwit (2003).

REFERENCES

Amnesty International. 1999. *People's Republic of China: Gross Violations of Human Rights in the Xinjiang Uyghur Autonomous Region*. London, 21 April.

Anagnost, Ann S. 1997. *National Past-Times: Narrative, Representation, and Power in Modern China*. Durham, N.C.: Duke University Press.

Blake, Fred C. 1981. *Ethnic Groups and Social Change in a Chinese Market Town*. Honolulu: University of Hawaii Press.

Brook, Timothy, and B. Michael Frolic. 2000. "Introduction: The Ambiguous Challenge of Civil Society." In *Civil Society in China*, eds. Timothy Brook and B. Michael Frolic. Armonk, N.Y.: M.E. Sharpe.

Chao, Yuen Ren. 1976. *Aspects of Chinese Sociolinguistics*. Stanford, Calif.: Stanford University Press.

China Institute for Contemporary International Relations. 1999. Nationality Studies Project. Chu Shulong interview, 14 November.

China State Council. 1999. *National Minorities Policy and its Practice in China*. Beijing: China State Council, October.

Dickson, Bruce. 1997. *Democratization in China and Taiwan: The Adaptability of Leninist Parties*. New York and London: Clarendon Press.

Dikotter, Frank. 1992. *The Discourse of Race in Modern China*. Stanford, Calif.: Stanford University Press.

Duara, Prasenjit. 1995. *Rescuing History from the Nation*. Chicago: University of Chicago Press.

Eastern Turkestan Union in Europe. c. 1996. "Brief History of the Uyghurs." Alachua Freenet, available at www.geocities.com/CapitolHill/1730/buh.html. Accessed 11 June 2003.

Encausse, Hélène Carrère d'. 1993. *The End of the Soviet Empire: The Triumph of the Nations*. trans. Franklin Philip. New York: Basic Books.

Fei, Xiaotong. 1981. "Ethnic Identification in China." In *Toward a People's Anthropology*, ed. Fei Xiaotong. Beijing: New World Press.

———. 1989. *"Zhonghua minzu de duoyuan jiti juge"* ("Plurality and unity in the configuration of the Chinese nationality"). *Beijing Daxue Xuebao* 4: 1–19.

Gladney, Dru C. 1994a. "Representing Nationality in China: Refiguring Majority/Minority Identities." *The Journal of Asian Studies* 53, no. 1: 92–123.

———. 1994b. "Sino–Middle Eastern Perspectives and Relations since the Gulf War: Views from Below." *The International Journal of Middle Eastern Studies* 29, no.4: 677–91.

———. 1996. *Muslim Chinese: Ethnic Nationalism in the People's Republic.* 1991. Cambridge, Mass.: Harvard University Press.

———, ed. 1998a. *Making Majorities: Constituting the Nation in Japan, Korea, China, Malaysia, Fiji, Turkey, and the United States.* Stanford, Calif.: Stanford University Press.

———. 1998b. "Internal Colonialism and the Uyghur Nationality: Chinese Nationalism and its Subaltern Subjects." *CEMOTI: Cahiers d'études sur la Méditerranée Orientale et le Monde Turco-Iranien,* no. 25: 47–64.

———. 1999. "Ethnogenesis and Ethnic Identity in China: Considering the Uygurs and Kazakhs." In *The Bronze Age and Early Iron Age People of Eastern Central Asia*: vol. 2, ed. Victor Mair. Washington, D.C.: Institute for the Study of Man.

———. Forthcoming. *Dislocating China: Muslims, Minorities, and other Sub-Altern Subjects.* Chicago: University of Chicago Press.

Guo, Fei. 1999. "Beijing's Policies Towards Ethnic Minority/Rural Migrant Villages." Paper presented at the conference on Contemporary Migration and Ethnicity in China. Institute of Nationality Studies, Chinese Academy of Social Sciences. Beijing, 7–8 October.

Harwit, Eric. 2003. "The Digital Divide of China's Internet Use." Paper presented at the Association for Asian Studies annual meeting. New York, 28 March.

Honig, Emily. 1992. *Creating Chinese Ethnicity.* New Haven, Conn.: Yale University Press.

Hu, Shao-hua. 2000. *Explaining Chinese Democratization.* New York: Praeger Publishers.

Lilley, James R., and David L. Shambaugh, eds. 1999. *China's Military Faces the Future.* Armonk, N.Y.: M.E. Sharpe.

Litzinger, Ralph A. 2000. *Other Chinas: The Yao and the Politics of National Belonging.* Durham, N.C.: Duke University Press.

Liu, Xin. 2001. *The Otherness of Self: A Genealogy of the Self in Contemporary China.* Ann Arbor: University of Michigan Press.

Mackerras, Colin. 1994. *China's Minorities: Integration and Modernization in the Twentieth Century.* Hong Kong: Oxford University Press.

Mair, Victor, ed. 1999."Introduction." In *The Bronze Age and Early Iron Age People of Eastern Central Asia*: vol. 2. Washington, D.C.: Institute for the Study of Man.

Moser, Leo J. 1985. *The Chinese Mosaic: The Peoples and Provinces of China.* Boulder, Colo.: Westview Press.

Norman, Jerry. 1988. *Chinese.* Cambridge: Cambridge University Press.

Rigger, Shelley. 1999. *Politics in Taiwan: Voting for Democracy.* London and New York: Routledge Press.

Schein, Louisa. 2000. *Minority Rules: The Miao and the Feminine in China's Cultural Politics.* Durham, N.C.: Duke University Press.

Schell, Orville. 1988. *Discos and Democracy: China in the Throes of Reform*. New York: Anchor Books.

Shambaugh, David, ed. 2000. *Is China Unstable? Assessing the Factors*. Armonk, N.Y.: M.E. Sharpe.

Wang, Shaoguang, Hu Angang, and Kang Xiaoguang. 2000. *The Political Economy of Uneven Development: The Case of China*. Armonk, N.Y.: M.E. Sharpe.

Zhang, Tianlu. 1999. "Xiandai Zhongguo shaoshu minzu renkou zhuangkuang" ("Analysis of the contemporary China minority nationality population situation"). Paper presented at the conference on Contemporary Migration and Ethnicity in China. Institute of Nationality Studies, Chinese Academy of Social Sciences. Beijing, 7–8 October.

8

Democratic Transition and Cultural Diversity: Buddhist Organizations and Identity Construction in Taiwan

André Laliberté

Many observers have heaped praise on the people and government of the Republic of China (ROC) because, first, of this country's relatively quiet political transition from authoritarian rule to democracy, and, second, the absence of major social inequalities accompanying its economic growth (Rubinstein 1999; Chao and Myers 1998; Hood 1997). The inhabitants of Taiwan increasingly recognize themselves as citizens by virtue of their shared destiny rather than ethnicity. This represents another dimension of the "Taiwan miracle" that deserves attention (Hughes 1997). Previous governments have imposed an unfair political structure on the island, subordinating a majority of the population to an immigrant minority and thereby creating a potentially volatile ethnic cleavage. However, the subordinated groups have not for the most part used the opportunities offered by the opening of the political process to push for changes that could be detrimental to the welfare of the hitherto dominant group. In other words, during its political transition from authoritarian rule to democracy, Taiwan has not faced the deadly cycle of ethnic conflicts observed in other societies going through political transition. This relatively peaceful and inclusive political transition appears all the more remarkable because some other societies with ethnic cleavages in Asia, as discussed elsewhere in this book, are fragmenting under the pressures of democratization processes. In particular, while societies with a diversity of religious communities, such as India, Indonesia, and Sri Lanka, are experiencing serious communal conflicts that may jeopardize their democratization, Taiwan's diversity has yet to be highly divisive.

While there are a number of reasons for this, relatively little attention has been paid to the role of Buddhist, Daoist, Christian, and other religious institutions in Taiwan in nurturing comparatively harmonious interethnic relations.

153

Buddhist institutions, which represent a particularly large part of the population, are a rather interesting puzzle in this regard. Despite a leadership that accommodated the old regime during the period of martial law, and despite a closer identification with China than Taiwan, Buddhist organizations have received *increasing* support from native Taiwanese since the lifting of martial law. What explains this turn of events, and what have been its implications for ethnic identities and relations? This chapter argues that, in their transnationalization strategies and their emphasis on lay participation, Buddhist organizations have helped bridge the divisions between native Taiwanese and more recent immigrants from China and, thus, helped cultivate an ethnically inclusive understanding of citizenship. Moreover, their refusal to get involved in a confrontational style of politics that could be based on ethnic divisions, helped in promoting an ethnically neutral civic citizenship, an objective consistent with the ideals of the secular, ethnically inclusive state that is foundational to civic nationalism. These strategies, in turn, position them to play an increasingly important role in the island's evolving politics of identity. In other words, while the long history of Buddhism in Taiwan and the cultural similarities between native Taiwanese and more recent Chinese immigrants are important, these factors alone cannot account for the contribution of Buddhist groups to the fostering of principles of citizenship consistent with civic nationalism. To explore this issue, the chapter first clarifies the nature of ethnic identity claims in Taiwan, continues with a description of their evolution in Taiwan during democratization, then briefly documents the stand of Buddhist organizations with respect to these claims, and finally looks at how the international networks of the latter have affected their perspectives on identity.

DEMOCRACY AND ETHNIC IDENTITY CLAIMS

This chapter asserts that Taiwan is a consolidated democracy. However, as others have expressed reservations about the extent of this consolidation (Solinger 2001; Chu et al. 2001), it is important to clarify this terminology. The ROC stands apart from other Asian democracies, such as Indonesia or Malaysia, where transition toward democracy has either coincided with civil unrest (Acharya 1999), or has been stopped on its rails by the refusal of the ruling elite to accept dissidence from within the ruling party (Case 2001). The fact that the Nationalist Party (KMT—Kuomintang) and the People First Party (PFP, or *Qinmindang*) can still use their combined strength in the legislature to constrain the Democratic Progressive Party (DPP, or *Minjindang*) presidency and limit the exercise of power by the executive until the 2004 legislative elections, is not grounds for arguing that the consolidation is incomplete. Borrowing from the distinction between consolidated and formal democracy used by Ichimura and Morley (1999: 25), this chapter proposes that, since the election of the opposition candidate Chen Shui-bian to the ROC presidency in 2000, Taiwan qualifies as a consolidated democracy. To extrapolate from the two authors just quoted—who did not believe Taiwan had reached that stage when they wrote in 1999—ROC institutions demonstrated during that landmark election their responsiveness to popular preferences and their capacity to sustain themselves while doing so. Of more relevance here, however, is the widely recognized political reality that ethnic violence does not threaten the future of Taiwanese democracy.

This terminological discussion must also clarify how the chapter uses the concept of nationalism and understands the ethnic identity claims that inform it. As Chang Maukuei has already discussed, the "creole nationalism" identified by Benedict Anderson (1991) does not capture the subtleties of Taiwanese nationalism. However, creole nationalism after World War II would provide the inspiration for postcolonial movements of national liberation. Civic nationalism, based on abstract notions of citizenship and promoting related universalizing values, may appear suited to multicultural societies such as Taiwan, where the values of ethnic communities differ, if not clash. However, it is never clear how much these "abstract values" are themselves culturally specific. The difference between civic and ethnic nationalism, or ethnonationalism (Smith 1991), also does not entirely capture the subtleties of identity politics in Taiwan. No less a modern phenomenon than civic nationalism (Hobsbawm 1990), state leaders subscribing to ethnonationalism are bent on creating a cohesive nation out of different regional identities. To achieve their objectives, they must rely on essentialist definitions of nation based on a shared language or history (Smith 1991). KMT leaders have promoted a nationalism based on Chinese identity and many opposition politicians have promoted a rival nationalism based on Taiwanese identity. In both cases, the watertight categories of ethnic and civic nationalism do not coincide with the respective Chinese and Taiwanese nationalist claims. The KMT variant of nationalism has always included nonethnic Chinese Mongolia and Tibet, and the nationalism of the opposition DPP since 1987 has included nonethnic Chinese Taiwanese Aboriginal people as well as the descendants of Chinese immigrants.

Yet, politicians from both sides have encouraged demands articulated on the basis of ethnic cleavages to mobilize their respective constituencies. Resort to such identity claims, some critics from postcolonial societies argue, responds to the need for the stronger bonds offered by a national identity closely related to one's own culture, which the abstract values of civic nationalism fail to provide (Madan 1987). Others take issue with civic nationalism on the ground that the "nation-building" efforts of postcolonial states in ethnically diverse societies are bound to fail in the face of resilient cleavages between groups with conflicting interests (Connor 1972). Ethnic "nation-building" in postcolonial states, however, represents a daunting task, especially in religiously and linguistically diverse societies such as Indonesia, where colonial rule often represents the only source of collective memory shared by all citizens. Ethnic nation-building, as non-Hindu Indians are discovering with a Hindu nationalist government, is a dangerous path.

This chapter's argument is premised on the view that the choice between ethnic or civic nationalism is a matter of volition: it is not preordained by specific ethnic cleavages, as the latter are noticeably unstable (Barth 1995; Horowitz 2000). It refutes the essentialist position that non-Western societies are unable to nurture their own brand of civic nationalism and argues that, within postcolonial societies, local institutions can nurture such a trend.

In light of this discussion, it is important to clarify what this chapter means by citizenship and its relationship with civic nationalism. It is also important to distinguish between the minimal *direct* contribution of Buddhist organizations to building civic nationalism in Taiwan and their significant *indirect* contribution to this goal through the building of ethnically inclusive citizenship norms and practices, which some might call an inclusive civic consciousness. The definition of citizenship proposed here goes beyond a narrowly legal understanding of citizenship as determined largely by governments and legislatures. Civil society actors, including religious organizations, can have an important impact both on the nature of citizenship and on who gets to enjoy it. As Henders (2003: 1) has written elsewhere, drawing from Wong (2002):

> citizenship is not only legal status with related rights and duties, but also the recognition of identity and meaningful participation in multiple political communities, civil societies, and public spheres. Therefore, citizenship . . . is not synonymous with nationality and is not conferred only by the state through its laws and regulations. Substate and suprastate public authorities and *nongovernmental actors* also play important roles in determining who enjoys citizenship in all its dimensions, as do *civil society and economic actors*" [my emphasis].

The example discussed in this chapter thus suggests that ethnically inclusive citizenship and civic nationalism are important and potentially mutually reinforcing components of an ethnically inclusive democracy.

DEMOCRATIZATION AND
ETHNIC IDENTITY CLAIMS IN TAIWAN

The current situation of Taiwan must be seen in the context of the history experienced by most postcolonial Asian states whose leaders, aware of the cultural diversity within their polities, have welded together elements of ethnic and civic nationalism in their effort to establish their authority. The results to this day are mixed in many Asian states. Despite more than four decades of efforts to establish a secular and nondenominational Indian state, the current government rules the country as a result of its appeal to nationalist sentiments based on a communal Hindu identity (Hansen 1999). As Jacques Bertrand argues in the present volume, despite years of cultivating the interfaith principle of *Pancasila*, the Indonesian government appears unable to prevent the fragmentation of the country along ethnic including religious fault lines. Throughout East Asia, the glue of civic nationalism appears even weaker since state institutions articulate definitions of national identity based on *jus sanguinis*, the concept that citizenship is not a function of one's residence in a country, but of one's "ethnic" origins, defined by ancestry. Emblematic of this approach is former Japanese Prime Minister Nakasone's assumption in 1986 that Japan has only "one people" (*minzoku*), a form of conventional wisdom that is only rarely challenged, as John Lie suggests in an earlier chapter (see also Lie 2001).

Although the contemporary states of China, Japan, Vietnam, and the two Koreas can claim historical continuity with ancient polities that are at least as ancient as the states that would later evolve into the French Republic or the constitutional monarchies of England and Spain, the emergence of national consciousness represents an entirely different matter. For instance, Prasenjit Duara (1994) and Frank Dikotter (1992) have demonstrated, in their studies of Chinese national identity during the late Qing and the early Republican periods, that this notion of national consciousness defined by a shared historical memory and ethnicity is a modern phenomenon. Moreover, this ethnic nationalism creates some intractable problems for the government of contemporary China. Although all inhabitants of the People's Republic are citizens of China (*Zhongguoren*), they also belong to one of the officially recognized fifty-six "nationalities" (*minzu*) of China, the most important of which, in number and political power, is the "Chinese" (*Hanzu*). Notwithstanding the fact that the notion of "Chinese citizenship" is problematic to the people self-identified as Tibetans, *Uyghurs*, Mongols, and the like, Dru Gladney's chapter reminds us that the homogeneity of the *Hanzu* itself needs to be questioned.

This diversity within the Han population, denied in the People's Republic at the official level, was similarly not recognized in Taiwan until several decades after the island fell under KMT rule. The historical circumstances there, however, have given ethnic identity a political salience that differs from what is observed in mainland China. Ethnic identity claims in Taiwan have changed according to the island's political circumstances, and ethnic cleavages have not always overlapped with political divisions. Hence, the most "visible" cleavage on the island, which distinguishes Aboriginal and Han people, does not represent the most politically volatile division today.

Out of a population of more than 21 million people in 1995, only 1.5 percent are known as the *Yuanzhumin* (Aboriginal people). Although their ethnic identity claims have been an important element of the democratization process in Taiwan, the most dangerous threats to democratic consolidation have come from ethnic claims *within* the Han majority. Before 1945, ethnic cleavages among Han people were defined primarily by the differences between the population whose ancestors originated primarily from the province of Fujian and those who identified themselves as *Hakka* (Shepherd 1999: 128–29). Whatever the extent of these ethnic divisions, they would be superseded by another cleavage within the Han people, when Japanese rule ended at the end of World War II. To this day, the divide between the postwar Han immigrants from mainland China and the Han already resident in Taiwan remains the main ethnic fault line.

By 28 February 1947, two years after China assumed control of Taiwan, KMT misrule and corruption had already led to resentment from the islanders. The government responded to an uprising by islanders by massacring many local elites (Phillips 1999; Kerr 1966). This tragedy created a legacy of divisions that would only deepen after the defeat of the KMT on the continent in 1949, when a massive influx of refugees and immigrants moved from mainland China to the island. The Han people living in Taiwan before this exodus came to define themselves as *Benshengren* (the people of this province), and they designated the other Chinese coming from the continent as *Waishengren* (the people from outside the province). Individuals identified with the latter group have always rejected this designation and prefer to call themselves *Zhongguoren* (citizens of China), a designation that in turn, many of the *Benshengren* do not accept for themselves. Some of them prefer to call themselves *Bendiren* (the people of this land), to emphasize that they are not living in a Chinese province, or they downplay the existence of other ethnic cleavages (such as between Taiwanese Aborigines and Taiwanese of Chinese ancestry or, within the latter group, between *Hokkien* and *Hakka*). These contested markers of identity speak volumes about the complexity of identity in Taiwan and its links to the question of loyalty to a broader Chinese nation or, instead, to a distinct and separate Taiwanese nation. Furthermore, mutually exclusive *Waishengren* and *Benshengren* identities belong increasingly to the margins of Taiwanese society: over the years, surveys have shown that a majority of the islanders identify themselves as both Chinese and Taiwanese, although to different degrees.

The identity fostered by the government from 1945 until the lifting of martial law did not encourage such a development. Over the years, the governments of Chiang Kai-shek and his son Chiang Ching-kuo tried to instill a Chinese national identity in Taiwan through the use of Mandarin (*Guoyu*—the national language) as the language of instruction. They also put an emphasis on mainland China rather than local knowledge in the curriculum for high school teaching in history, geography, and sociology. Until the end of martial law, the media could not use *Taiyu* (also known as *Hokkien*—or Fujienese—for native speakers, *Hoklo* for *Hakka* Chinese, or *Minnanhua* for Mandarin speakers) nor *Hakka* (*Kejiahua* for Mandarin speakers). Academic research on the events of February 28 was taboo. Finally, and most importantly, *Waishengren*, who represented less than 15 percent of the Taiwanese population, controlled a majority of the seats in the Legislative Yuan until 1987. They also held more than half of the KMT Central Committee and government positions and constituted 84 percent of generals (Tien 1989: 36–39). From the 1970s, however, this domination by a minority did not go unchallenged: nonparty politicians of the *Dangwai* (literally, outside the Party) have opposed the KMT. Aware that KMT policies were untenable in the long run, Chiang Ching-kuo started to address some of the grievances of *Benshengren* by including a growing number of native Taiwanese in the ruling party structure and, then, in 1986, legalizing the DPP, an opposition party identified with the promotion of *Benshengren* interests (Tien 1989).

After four decades, the policy of assimilating all Taiwanese into a pan-Chinese community had failed. That policy was undermined even more significantly during the Lee Teng-hui regime, when reform-minded members of the KMT sought to broaden its support and enhance its legitimacy by adopting a two-pronged strategy combining a more assertive diplomacy with a domestic policy of reconciliation. The various foreign policies adopted by Lee shrewdly combined the anticommunist leanings of the *Waishengren* with the aspiration for Taiwanese self-determination hitherto identified with *Benshengren* grievances. The latter stressed the fact that the ROC in Taiwan was already a sovereign state that was not under the jurisdiction of the PRC. Meanwhile, Lee's policy of reconciliation—dramatized in his public atonement for the February 28 tragedy mentioned earlier—sought to downplay the political relevance of ethnic cleavages within Taiwan. The discourse used by Lee had shifted from references to "China" as the political community designated by the ROC, to references to "Taiwan" as the relevant polity for everyone living on the island. This strategy aimed to construct a Taiwanese identity defined by the nature of the island's political system, not by ethnicity (Wachman 1994). It has worked to a certain extent: as noted earlier, recent surveys have demonstrated that most inhabitants of the ROC, independent of their place of origins, see themselves as both "Chinese" and "Taiwanese" to varying degrees and refuse to lock themselves into a one-dimensional ethnic identity (Rigger 1999–2000). This is not to say that Taiwanese politicians never use ethnicity for electoral gains. Lee Teng-hui himself, since quitting government, has encouraged the formation of a new political party, the Taiwan Solidarity Union (TSU, or *Taiwan tuanjie lianmeng dang*) that emphasizes the interests of *Benshengren*. But while appeals to ethnic identity may attract some segments of the electorate, an inclusive civic nationalism generally prevails in Taiwan under President Chen Shui-bian.

The alienation felt by most citizens on the island toward the political up-heavals in the PRC, as well as the circulation of elites between Taiwan and Western countries (a majority of the members of successive KMT cabinets held American Ph.D. degrees), have certainly played no small part in this civic nationalism. Among other factors that have reinforced the emergence of civic nationalism in Taiwan, however, the internationalization of religious institu-tions has received scant attention. This is not surprising because the notion that religious institutions can contribute positively to the creation of civic na-tionalism does not appear intuitively plausible in the West, where religious identity is most often associated with premodern developments such as the religious wars of the sixteenth century or more recent communal conflicts in Northern Ireland and the Balkans. In many postcolonial societies, religious identities are also associated with narrow identity claims. It is only lately that scholarship on Asian politics has started to question these assumptions. Re-cent studies have regarded the political assertiveness of transnational reli-gious organizations as the expression of alternative visions of authority in the context of states whose legitimacy is threatened by the adverse effects of globalization (Keyes 1994; Rudolph et al. 1997). Many transnational religious traditions originating abroad, such as Buddhism, Christianity, and Islam, as well as transnational "Chinese" new religious movements, such as the Way of Unity (*Yiguandao*), the Heavenly Virtue religion (*Tiendejiao*), and Falun-gong, prosper in Taiwan to the point where they cannot be considered main-land or foreign religions. A few of them have asserted alternative visions of authority: the Presbyterian Church has long promoted the self-determination of Taiwan against KMT-sponsored Chinese nationalism (Rubinstein 1991), as well as self-determination for Aboriginal people (Stainton 1999). Many others remained quiet during the martial law period, their silence seemingly en-couraging the officially approved nationalism. The most important of these traditions, Buddhism, represents an interesting case study: despite a leader-ship coming for the most part from China, millions of *Benshengren* identify with its institutions. This suggests that Buddhist leaders have successfully de-veloped a discourse that transcends ethnic cleavages and therefore provides some of the foundations for the cultivation of civic nationalism.

BUDDHIST INSTITUTIONS
AND CIVIC NATIONALISM IN TAIWAN

Religious organizations in Taiwan can hardly be described as in "retreat from quick modern globalization" (White 1999: 115). Many of them enthusiasti-cally participate in the process. This eagerness, in turn, relates to the broader political context unfolding on the island in the last decades. Namely, while the ROC government in Taiwan under Chiang Kai-shek derived much of its legitimacy from American strategic support in the late 1970s and some success in international markets, the governments of Chiang Ching-kuo, Lee Teng-hui, and Chen Shui-bian have had to fight for international recognition without American diplomatic recognition. In its effort to increase shares in global markets and maintain—if not improve—an eroding position in international organizations, ROC governments have been engaged since 1989 in a series of diplomatic efforts aimed at promoting Taiwan's image abroad. Within that context, ROC governments have increasingly welcomed transnational religions on the island and encouraged attempts by local religious organizations to expand abroad. This is especially so if they present internationally an image of the island as a society that is tolerant, pluralist, and open to multicultural international trends. Conversely, in the domestic context, the leaders of many Taiwanese religious organizations have realized that projecting inclusiveness is more likely to generate state support and broaden popular appeal.

Christian churches (Rubinstein 1991; Stainton 1999) and other foreign religions such as Ba'haism embraced by minorities on the island are likely candidates to support civic nationalism in Taiwan. Too close an identification with ethnic nationalism, whether *Waishengren* or *Benshengren*, is more likely to limit the reach of their proselytizing efforts. Some of the "Chinese" religions and cults born in Taiwan are less familiar to outsiders, but often count more adherents than the Christian churches. They have also transcended barriers of ethnicity in their political activities. One interesting case remains the *Yiguandao* sect. This syncretic religion originating in China— and wrongly associated in the past with secret societies—seeks to reconcile the common principles of Chinese traditions and foreign religions (Jordan and Overmyer 1986; Bosco 1994). Its origins on the mainland, however, did not prevent its adherents from helping reformist politicians identified with the Taiwanization of the KMT to win local elections. The behavior of the *Yiguandao* was not entirely disinterested: the government legalized the sect after the candidates it supported won a majority in the legislature (Lin 1994). Yet, this religious institution nonetheless did not let ethnicity stand in the way of supporting politicians more sensitive to its goals. After 2000, the new ROC President Chen Shui-bian seemed to recognize this by expressing his gratitude to the *Yiguandao* for its achievements.

The attitude of Buddhist institutions toward those who opposed martial law and supported democratization, however, has been a different matter. In particular, the mainland Chinese origins of several prominent monks has precluded the ecclesiastical orders from supporting political parties and social movements emphasizing Taiwanese self-determination, thereby confirming the widespread perception by many Taiwanese that Buddhism is a religion unrelated to local realities (Jiang 1996: 454). It was only after the economic take-off of Taiwan that the expanding ranks of the laity made Buddhism more popular and the religion started to reflect more faithfully the cultural identity of the island. This is remarkable, considering that for decades the spiritual leaders propagating the faith were largely *Waishengren* who never hid their allegiance to China and headed organizations propagating teachings rooted in the continent.

The increases of membership in large Buddhist organizations such as the *Foguangshan* Monastic Order and the *Ciji* Foundation (the two largest and most important Buddhist organizations on the island), and the ordination and promotion of an increasing number of *Benshengren* in the *Sangha*, have paralleled the Taiwanization of the KMT. As a result of these trends, Buddhism represented in 1995 the faith with the largest number of adherents in Taiwan at 22.8 percent of the total population (ROC 1997: 466). This relative importance of Buddhism among religions in Taiwan, and the favorable political conditions that have prevailed since the legalization of opposition parties in 1989, have provided Buddhist organizations in Taiwan with the opportunity for political involvement. The numerous associations (*hui*), foundations (*jijinhui*), societies (*xiehui*), and research institutes (*xuehui*) associated with Buddhism in Taiwan possess considerable resources and influence in society through networks of schools and universities, hospitals and clinics, as well as charity organizations (Kang and Jiang 1995). However, they seldom directly intervene in politics. There are no associations comparable to the Japanese *Soka Gakkai* (Society for the Creation of Value) and its political branch, the Buddhist political party *Komeito* (the Party for Clean Politics) (Metraux 1994: 49–56).

In contrast to the Presbyterian Church, Buddhist organizations never joined the civic organizations on the island that pressured the authorities to respect human rights during the decades of martial law. Even when their corporate interests were challenged by state actions, most of these organizations were not very assertive. During the more liberal climate of the 1990s, they were involved only sporadically in the political process, sometimes withdrawing entirely from public debates. Deeper involvement in politics occurred twice. The *Foguangshan* briefly attempted to mobilize people for a more ethical government; Xingyun, the founder of *Foguangshan*, went as far as supporting an independent candidate for the 1996 presidential election, the *Waishengren* lay Buddhist Chen Lü'an (a former Minister of National Defense, who had resigned as head of the Control Yuan and left the KMT before announcing his candidacy). Meanwhile, the activist nun Zhao Hui has campaigned for animal rights and against the construction of a nuclear plant. These actions indicate that Taiwanese Buddhists as individuals are not always apolitical and that some of them do not uncritically support the ruling party. Most Buddhist organizations in Taiwan, however, avoid open confrontation with the government or even encourage abstention from political participation altogether. This avoidance of formal politics extends to refusing to endorse any politician, even a respected lay Buddhist, as was the case when the nun Zhengyan, leader of *Ciji,* refused to support Chen Lü'an in 1996. These organizations not only refused to sponsor political opposition, but also avoided giving the impression that they too openly sanctioned the government. In sum, even though Buddhists are numerous and organized enough to be politically assertive, most of their leaders have behaved cautiously.

Taiwanese Buddhists lack an alternative program on domestic issues on which they could build a party distinguishing them from the KMT, the DPP, the PFP, or the TSU. This is made all the more difficult because the leaders of Buddhist organizations do not agree among themselves on issues concerning the welfare of Buddhists. This emerged clearly in 1995–1996, when Chen Lü'an ran for the ROC presidency, but failed to gain the endorsement of many prominent Buddhist organizations in the country. These divisions surfaced again when the Buddhist Association of the Republic of China (BAROC) proposed a law on Buddhism in 1996 against the wishes of most Buddhist organizations in Taiwan. One of the very few issues on which members of the *Sangha* seem to agree, however, is on their need to remain impartial in the central debate of ROC politics between partisans of Taiwanese independence and supporters of reunification with China, and to avoid reference to the ethnic dimension of Taiwan politics. Notably, this is true of *Foguangshan* and the *Ciji* Foundation (Chen 1994).

In this light, the goal of the monk Xingyun to "propagate the Dharma" (*hongyang Fofa*) has not directly nurtured civic nationalism, but did foster identities and norms conducive to bridging differences of ethnicity and diverging visions of Taiwan's status. This is critical for ethnically inclusive citizenship. *Foguangshan* reaches out to the largest possible constituency in Taiwan and abroad, in contrast with the ethnically narrow base of the KMT until the 1980s. Xingyun was aware of the limited pool of talent available among the *Waishengren* to sustain his plans for the expansion of *Foguangshan* and has adopted over the years many practical measures to recruit, train, and promote *Benshengren* disciples into the hierarchy. As a result, a majority of the thirteen permanent members of the *Foguangshan* monastic order's Committee for Religious Affairs, the highest authority in the organization, are natives of small localities in Taiwan (Fu 1997). Realizing that sustaining the growth of *Foguangshan* and maintaining links with society outside of the monastery also require support from lay Buddhists, Xingyun decided in 1990 to give them an institutional framework by founding the Buddha Light International Association (BLIA), which also reached out to *Benshengren.* Hence, Wu Boxiong, who was elected in January 1998 as the president of the most important section of the BLIA, the ROC headquarters, was a popular KMT politician with a Taiwanese *Hakka* background (Guoji Foguanghui 2003). The distribution of temples affiliated with *Foguangshan* throughout the island also reflects the objective of Xingyun to reach out to a cross-section of Taiwanese society, sometimes as a response to demands from specific communities (Jones 1999: 188). The same can be said of the attempt by high-ranking members, such as Cihui, to proselytize in *Minnanhua*, the native language of most Taiwanese *Benshengren*, even before the lifting of martial law. This was a time when the government still forbade the teaching of *Minnanhua* in schools (Fu 1997). Although these activities stopped short of actively promoting civic nationalism through direct political participation, they helped overcome ethnic barriers. In fact, throughout his career Xingyun has followed the ideals of the monk Taixu, a major figure in early twentieth-century Chinese Buddhism known for his liberal views (Jiang 1993). This appears to have helped him recruit and attract people who may not have been otherwise predisposed to join a Buddhist organization led by a *Waishengren*.

The other major Taiwanese Buddhist organization in Taiwan, the *Ciji* Foundation, is also led by a charismatic figure who indirectly claims to follow the teachings of Taixu. Zhengyan, who is often referred to as the "Mother Teresa of Taiwan," delivers her lectures in *Minnanhua* and is herself a *Benshengren*. This has led to speculation that *Ciji* supports *Benshengren* ethnic nationalism. Her refusal to support the *Waishengren* candidate Chen Lü'an during the 1996 presidential election further gave credence to that view. This interpretation, however, does not hold. Some *Waishengren* Buddhist leaders did not support Chen, while many of the *Benshengren* members of *Foguangshan* were enthusiastic about his candidacy. The reluctance of Zhengyan to support Chen may have had the same rationale that many of her followers have expressed: they believed that Chen Lü'an, despite his knowledge of Buddhist philosophy, could not help the country. The refusal of Zhengyan to support a lay Buddhist candidate or *Benshengren* candidates in other elections simply reflects an apolitical attitude that she has consistently adopted, despite the numerous attempts by politicians to obtain her support over the years.[1] This discourse on compassion expressed by members of *Ciji* nurtures values of tolerance and inclusiveness that help undermine the appeal of ethnic nationalism. However, the aloofness from politics advocated by Zhengyan, represents a drift toward apoliticism that cannot directly strengthen an ethnically inclusive democracy—one of the "precepts" of *Ciji* even forbids political participation. Nevertheless, it is consistent with the maintenance of a *secular* ethnically inclusive state, which some regard as a cornerstone of democracy in ethnically plural societies (e.g., Rankin and Goonewardena in this volume).

Moreover, although *Ciji* encourages individuals to feel responsible for the welfare of fellow human beings and cultivates other norms associated with ethnically inclusive citizenship, it does not directly advocate the formal dimensions of citizenship foundational to civic nationalism. While *Ciji*'s activities go further than the schemes of volunteer work generally encouraged by the government, they are never used as opportunities to assess, evaluate, or criticize government policy and always remain within the bounds of state-approved grassroots actions (Feng 1993: 146). In performing their charitable activities and remaining aloof from politics, members of Ciji differ significantly from organizations like the Presbyterian Church, which have reached the conclusion that the advocacy of political reform is the logical consequence of their soteriology (Wang 1991). This difference is apparent in the tone adopted by Zhengyan with respect to the many issues addressed by the Presbyterian Church over the years. For example, Zhengyan has always been very evasive on the issue of Taiwanese self-determination. She has never taken a stand on this issue on the basis of either civic or ethnic nationalism, merely saying that she is primarily concerned with "national security."

However, the apolitical behavior of *Ciji*, in some ways conservative in its support of the status quo, does not mean a complete and radical disengagement from this-worldly matters, for its actions may positively affect aspects of citizenship critical to building civic nationalism in Taiwan. In particular, the organization's ethnically inclusive civic consciousness is consistent with the tolerance central to civic nationalism. This principle has been followed in the close contacts that high-ranking members of the organization have nurtured over the years with politicians of all parties and all ethnic backgrounds. Zhengyan has made efforts to cultivate good relations with political leaders as diverse as the *Hakka* Taiwanese Wu Boxiong, both BLIA leader and a KMT high-ranking member, other *Benshengren* politicians such as Xu Xinliang, a former DPP leader, Lin Yanggang and Lee Teng-hui, longtime KMT rivals, and numerous *Waishengren* KMT leaders, from Chiang Ching-kuo to Song Chu-yu.[2] The arrival to power of Chen Shui-bian has not modified the attitude of the organization and its leader. The inclusiveness and the avoidance of controversy even extend to the domain of religious affairs. In the area of legislation on religion, for instance, *Ciji* has refused to intervene in the debates promoted by the BAROC for a law on religions and on Buddhism. By not entering the fray, *Ciji* could certainly not be suspected of encouraging communal divisions.

In sum, Buddhist institutions in Taiwan nurture civic nationalism in a manner that is much less visible and direct than the actions adopted by the Presbyterian Church and many popular organizations. However, the values of compassion and selflessness to which many adherents of these organizations subscribe clearly compel them to look beyond the narrow confines of family, clan, and ethnicity. In addition, the leaders of the two largest organizations have recruited new members and volunteers and promoted individuals within their own organizations on criteria other than their ethnic origins. Furthermore, the important Buddhist organizations in Taiwan are national in scope: they do not limit their activities to one ethnic area within the island. Finally, the participation in public affairs advocated by the theology of "this-worldly Buddhism" (*Renjian Fojiao*)— adopted by Xingyun, Zhengyan, and most other popular Buddhist leaders on the island—is usually couched in universalistic terms: it emphasizes a socially activist orientation and encourages Buddhist devotees to care about their fellow human beings, regardless of whether they belong to the *Sangha* or not (Zhao 1998) and regardless of their family's ethnic origins or their stance on the status of Taiwan.

This involvement in charity and social work, however, does not directly translate into political participation: in this last respect, members of Buddhist organizations in Taiwan often evoke their adherence to the principle of a "separation between politics and religion" (*zhengjiao fenli*). Because their inclusive values and their observance of principles such as the separation between politics and religion mirrors elements of liberal democratic values normally associated with Western societies, this raises the question of the extent to which processes of normative globalization can explain the code of conduct adopted by Buddhist organizations in Taiwan.

GLOBALIZATION AND TAIWANESE BUDDHIST INSTITUTIONS

Many analysts see the revival of religion and local ethnic identities in contemporary societies as a dramatic symptom of the decline of the state in the face of the global expansion of the market economy (Robertson 1991). The acceleration of globalization, characterized by the growing influence of market forces and the increasing difficulty states have in shielding themselves from adverse financial flows and the relocation of production processes, arguably complicates the process of nation-building. It can have adverse effects on the emergence of civic nationalism, especially in societies where civic national identity itself is not well defined. Many observers of East Asian societies see the resurgence of alternative forms of ritual as a popular form of resistance to states that have failed to entrench the values of civic nationalism in a context of state weakening under globalization. Although the ultimate significance of phenomena such as the revival of shamanism in South Korea (Kim 1994) or the emergence of Falungong in China (Zheng 2000) remains unclear, the impact of globalization on ethnic identity claims or religious revivalism cannot be denied. These processes of religious and local identity revival, however, need not always adversely affect societies, as the Taiwanese case demonstrates.

This tension between the modern state and alternative visions of authority represented by religion and ethnicity should have had all the more impact on Taiwan, given that the processes of globalization affect the ROC in unique ways: its status as a political pariah in international forums coincides with an intense participation in the global economy. However, the misfortunes of the ROC government after the U.S. diplomatic de-recognition of Taipei in 1979 has been a blessing in disguise for religious organizations in Taiwan. Since the crisis, the government has relied increasingly on the informal diplomacy of civic organizations and religious institutions for international recognition and participation. Other determinants, such as the integration of Taiwan into the global economy, have also influenced the development of its religious institutions (Weller 2000). This integration has both favored the internationalization of Taiwanese religious institutions and attracted foreign institutions to the island. Both types of organizations integrate the island into international society through networks that transcend the links provided by formal international organizations. The internationalization of the Taiwanese economy has served the Taiwanese organizations very well, providing them with many opportunities for expansion. In particular, many Taiwanese faiths pursue their transnational activities through expatriate and overseas Chinese communities, which provide the ROC with an important interface with the global economy and political community. This trend is not limited to Christian denominations originating from North America. *Yiguandao* membership has spread throughout Asia, to the Americas, Western Europe, Australia, and South Africa.[3] Even a small sect such as the Lord of Heaven has branched out to Los Angeles.[4]

The scope of the international links from which some religious institutions in Taiwan benefit explains in good part why globalization has affected their capacity to shape the processes of democratization and the nurturing of civic nationalism on the island. Taiwanese Christians, in particular, have transnational links through churches, which give them a distinct advantage over Chinese religions. Don Baker (1997) has argued that the highly activist attitude of Christian organizations, relative to that of other ROC religious organizations, can be attributed to the fact that Taiwanese Christians belong to international denominations based predominantly in the United States. Because successive ROC governments have depended on the U.S. government for their security, they have been reluctant to clamp down too harshly on Christian organizations because that could have alienated American public opinion and jeopardized their main source of foreign support. As a result, Christian pastors and priests in Taiwan have been able to be more outspoken in their criticism of governments than were adherents of religions that did not have a significant international presence. In other words, different religious denominations have reacted differently to state policies toward religion, depending on their transnational linkages. In particular, the greater the internationalization of a religious organization, the more likely it was to become politically assertive.

Yet, Buddhist institutions such as *Foguangshan* have also benefited in the last two decades from the deepening inclusion of Taiwan in the global economy and, ironically, from its exclusion from interstate institutions. Barely three years after its founding, sources from the BLIA satellite organization boasted that its membership had reached about one million devotees (Fu 1996: 377), ranking it as the world's fourth largest nongovernmental organization after the Rotary Club, Lion's International, and Kiwanis (Fu 1996: 279). The headquarters of the BLIA are in the California-based temple of Xilai, and the organization now has a hundred branches in 30 countries, with 342 subchapters in Taiwan alone (Guoji Foguanghui Zhonghua Zonghui 1995: 45). As the head of this organization, Xingyun has embarked on a mission of global ecumenism with a high degree of visibility. He has encouraged a rapprochement between the Mahayana, Theravada, and Tibetan Buddhist traditions, been instrumental in restoring the ordination of women in countries belonging to the Hinayana tradition (Tsai 1997), and been active in interreligious dialogue with Christians and Muslims. The numerous encounters between Xingyun and his counterparts in South Korea, Thailand, Sri Lanka, and India project an image of Taiwan as a progressive and inclusive country. For that reason, and in light of the diminishing international presence of the ROC, they are welcomed by the KMT and the DPP alike, who are anxious to generate sympathy abroad for Taiwan. There is no question that the religious activities of Xingyun serve the interests of the ROC government, as they often offer an opportunity to score points in the competition for legitimacy between the PRC and ROC governments. The religious meetings between Xingyun and the Dalai Lama, for instance, naturally invite comparison between Taiwanese religious pluralism and the lack of flexibility displayed by Chinese authorities toward the exiled Tibetan leader. The former encounters nurture a spirit of tolerance among communities with different cultural backgrounds, an attitude that fosters civic nationalism.

The behavior of *Ciji*, however, also demonstrates that an attitude of tolerance does not suffice to nurture civic nationalism and illustrates the weaknesses of Buddhist organizations as actors capable of furthering that development. *Ciji*, in ways that parallel *Foguangshan*, has also used the climate of political democratization in the 1990s and the opening of Taiwan to the global economy to expand its charity work outside of the ROC. In that process, the prestige of the ROC has also greatly benefited. Like Xingyun, Zhengyan ignores boundaries of identity and community. The charitable activities of her organization reach out to people regardless of their background, even though it has been sometimes in response to specific requests by the ROC government. In 1992, for example, at the request of the Mongolian and Tibetan Affairs Commission (*Mengzang Weiyuanhui*) (MTAC), *Ciji* sent a fact-finding mission and provided relief to victims of a deluge in Nepal. In 1994, *Ciji* volunteers helped ethnic Chinese refugees in North Thailand in response to a demand by the cabinet-level Overseas Chinese Affairs Commission.[5] In order to perform their charitable missions and fulfill their goal of offering "great love" (*da ai*) to perfect strangers, however, *Ciji* volunteers must sometimes keep a low profile and avoid participation in public life, for fear of drawing attention to their acts. In particular, the provision of relief to the victims of natural disaster in mainland China, which makes perfect sense from the perspective of the humanitarian values embraced by *Ciji* members, does not appeal to many Taiwanese, who are resentful of the threat of war wielded by the PRC government. Although *Ciji* volunteers may be right to think of their activities transcending barriers of ethnicity and nationality, their successes sometimes depend on the avoidance of publicity. Some degree of the latter, however, is necessary for the wider promotion of civic nationalism.

CONCLUSION

The impact of religious organizations on the emergence of civic nationalism and democratic consolidation is a complex issue. In the case discussed here, the lay volunteers working for Buddhist organizations in Taiwan may adopt a resolutely activist approach when facing the problem of human misery. However, with the exception of a few individuals, their behavior has not extended to formal political participation except, perhaps, as voters. This pragmatism sits well with a conservative temper that shuns criticism of the authorities and slows down, if not hampers, democratization. On the other hand, these organizations appear to have favorably influenced democratic consolidation in indirect ways. Until recently, Taiwanese society has been derided abroad as the "island of greed" because of its cutthroat capitalism, which has long retarded the development of civic consciousness, making democratic consolidation all the more problematic. The deeds performed by Buddhist organizations in Taiwan have gone a long way to overcoming these failings. The genuinely unselfish concern of their members for the wider society nurtures throughout Taiwan the emergence of a citizenry that look beyond the boundaries of family, clan, local community, and ethnicity. In that sense, these institutions quietly nurture civic nationalism: for the moment, by recruiting members and reaching out to people on the basis of their needs without consideration for their ethnic identity, they constitute a school for tolerance and, as such, have helped create a social climate supportive of a relatively peaceful transition toward an inclusive democracy. The privileged location of Taiwan in the global economy, and the unique strategic and diplomatic context of the ROC, both affect these organizations by providing them with unique opportunities for expansion that are not always available to religious organizations in many other Asian societies. It remains to be seen if it is these opportunities, in the final analysis, that make the necessity of inclusiveness a virtue.

NOTES

The author would like to thank Susan Henders and the anonymous reviewers for their helpful suggestions. They are not responsible for omissions and mistakes

1. *Zhongguo Shibao*, 28 November 1995.
2. *Shangye Zhoukan*, 26 September 1999.
3. See the organization's website, available at www.1-kuan-tao.org.tw/index_1.html.
4. See its official website, available at www.tienti.org/teaching/detail.html#F.
5. *Zhongyang*, 3 September 1996.

REFERENCES

Acharya, Amitav. 1999. "Southeast Asia's Democratic Moment." *Asian Survey* 29, no. 3 (May/June): 418–32.

Anderson, Benedict R. O'G. 1991. *Imagined Communities*. London: Verso.

Baker, Don. 1997. "World Religions and National States: Competing Claims in East Asia." In *Transnational Religion and Failed States*, eds. Susanne Hoeber Rudolph and James P. Piscatori. Boulder, Colo.: Westview Press.

Barth, Fredric. 1995. "Les groupes ethniques et leurs frontières." In *Théories de l'ethnicité (Theories of ethnicity)*, eds. Philippe Poutignat and Jocelyne Streiff-Fenart. Paris: PUF.

Bosco, Joseph. 1994. "Yiguan Dao: 'Heterodoxy' and Popular Religion in Taiwan." In *The Other Taiwan: 1945 to the Present*, ed. Murray Rubinstein. Armonk, N.Y.: M.E. Sharpe.

Case, William. 2001. "Malaysia's Resilient Pseudodemocracy." *Journal of Democracy* 12, no. 1 (January): 43–57.

Chao, Linda, and Ramon H. Myers. 1998. *The First Chinese Democracy: Political Life in the Republic of China on Taiwan*. Baltimore: John Hopkins University Press.

Chen, Zailai. 1994. *Zongjiao yu Guanli* (Religion and administration). Research Report for the Management Science Research Institute. Hsinchu, Taiwan: Chiaotung University. Manuscript.

Chu, Yun-han, Larry Diamond, and Doh Chull Shin. 2001. "Halting Progress in Korea and Taiwan." *Journal of Democracy* 12, no. 1 (January): 122–36.

Connor, Walker. 1972. "Nation-building or Nation-destroying?" *World Politics* 24, no. 3 (April): 319–55.

Dikotter, Frank. 1992. *The Discourse of Race in Modern China*. Stanford, Calif.: Stanford University Press.

Duara, Prasenjit. 1995. *Rescuing History from the Nation: Questioning Narratives of Modern China*. Chicago: University of Chicago Press.

Feng, Wenrao. 1993. Zhiyuan fuli fuwu zuzhi xingcheng ji yunzuo zhi tantao: yi Ciji Gongdehui wei lie (An inquiry into the formation and the achievements of voluntary welfare provider organizations: using Tzu Chi as an example). M.A. thesis, National Taiwan Chungcheng University, Chiayi County.

Fu, Chi-ying. 1996. *Handing Down the Light: The Biography of Venerable Master Hsing Yun.* Trans. Amy Lui-ma. Hacienda Heights, Calif.: Hsi Lai University Press.

Fu, Zhiying. 1997. *Xinhuo: Foguangshan chengxianqihou de gushi (Xinhuo: the story of foguangshan founders' spiritual heirs).* Taipei: Tianxia Wenhua Chuban.

Guoji Foguanghui (Buddha Light International Association). 2003. "Zhonghua zonghui huizhang" ("A word from the ROC chapter's chairman"). Available at www.blia.org.tw/usual/director%20general.htm. Accessed 11 June 2003.

Guoji Foguanghui Zhonghua Zonghui (Buddha's Light International Association, ROC). 1995. *Yijiujiuwu nian tekan (1995 Special edition)* Taipei: Guoji Foguanghui Zhonghua Zonghui.

Hansen, Thomas Blom. 1999. *The Saffron Wave: Democracy and Hindu Nationalism in Modern India.* Princeton, N.J.: Princeton University Press.

Held, David, Anthony McGrew, David Goldblatt, and Jonathan Perraton. 1999. *Global Transformations: Politics, Economics, and Culture.* Cambridge, U.K.: Polity Press.

Henders, Susan J. 2003. "Is there an Emergent Right to Transnational Citizenship? The Production of International Migrants, Minorities, and Indigenous Peoples in International Legal Discourse." Paper presented to the YCAR/CERLAC Workshop on The Politics of Transnational Ties. York University, 7–8 March.

Hobsbawm, Eric J. 1990. *Nations and Nationalism since 1870: Programme, Myth, Reality.* Cambridge: Canto.

Hood, Steven J. 1997. *The Kuomintang and the Democratization of Taiwan.* Boulder, Colo.: Westview Press.

Horowitz, Donald. 2000. *Ethnic Groups in Conflict.* Berkeley: University of California Press.

Hughes, Christopher. 1997. *Taiwan and Chinese Nationalism: National Identity and Status in International Society.* London: Routledge.

Ichimura, Shinichi, and James W. Morley. 1999. "The Variety of Asia-Pacific Experience." In *Driven by Growth: Political Change in the Asia-Pacific Region,* ed. James W. Morley. Armonk, N.Y.: M.E. Sharpe.

Jiang, Canteng. 1983. *Taixu Dashi Qianzhuan (A biographical sketch of Taixu's early teachings).* Taipei: Xinwenfu.

———. 1996. *Taiwan Fojiao bainianshi zhi yanjiu, 1895–1995 (Research on a century of Buddhism in Taiwan, 1895–1995).* Taipei: Nantian.

———. 1997. *Taiwan Dangdai Fojiao (Buddhism in contemporary Taiwan).* Taipei: Nantian.

Jones, Charles B. 1996. Buddhism in Taiwan: A Historical Survey. Ph.D. diss., University of Virginia.

Jones, Charles Brewer. 1999. *Buddhism in Taiwan: Religion and the State, 1660–1990.* Honolulu: University of Hawaii Press.

Jordan, David K., and Daniel L. Overmyer. 1986. *The Flying Phoenix: Aspects of Chinese Sectarianism in Taiwan.* Taipei: Caves.

Kang, Le and Jian Huimei. 1995. *Xinyang yu shehui (Belief and society).* Panchiao, Taiwan: Taipei County Cultural Center Publishing.

Kerr, George. 1966. *Formosa Betrayed*. London: Eyre and Spottiswoode.

Keyes, Charles F., Laurel Kendall, and Helen Hardacre, eds. 1994. *Asian Visions of Authority*. Honolulu: University of Hawaii Press.

Kim, Kwang-ok. 1994. "Rituals of Resistance: The Manipulation of Shamanism in Contemporary Korea." In *Asian Visions of Authority: Religion and the Modern States of East and Southeast Asia*, eds. Charles F. Keyes, Laurel Kendall, and Helen Hardacre. Honolulu: University of Hawaii Press.

Lie, John. 2001. *Multiethnic Japan*. Cambridge, Mass.: Harvard University Press.

Lin, Benxuan. 1994. *Taiwan de Zhengjiao Chongtu* (*The conflict between politics and religion in Taiwan*). Banqiao, Taiwan: Daoxiang Chubanshe.

Madan, T. N. 1987. "Secularism in its Place." *Journal of Asian Studies* 46, no. 4 (November): 747–59.

Metraux, Daniel A. 1994. *The Soka Gakkai Revolution*. Lanham, Md.: University Press of America.

Phillips, Steven. 1999. "Between Assimilation and Independence: Taiwanese Political Aspirations under Nationalist Chinese Rule, 1945–1948." In *Taiwan: A New History*, ed. Murray A. Rubinstein. Armonk, N.Y.: M.E. Sharpe.

ROC. Republic of China, Government Information Office. 1997. *Republic of China Yearbook, 1997*. Taipei: GIO.

Rigger, Shelley. 1999–2000. "Social Science and National Identity: A Critique." *Pacific Affairs: Taiwan Strait-Special Issue* 72, no. 4 (Winter): 537–52.

Robertson, Roland. 1991. "Globalization, Modernization, and Postmodernization: The Ambiguous Position of Religion." In *Religion and Global Order*, eds. Roland Robertson and William R. Garrett. New York: Paragon House.

Rubinstein, Murray. 1991. *The Protestant Community on Modern Taiwan: Mission, Seminary, and Church*. Armonk, N.Y.: M.E. Sharpe.

———, ed. 1999. *Taiwan: A New History*. Armonk, N.Y.: M.E. Sharpe.

Rudolph, Susanne Hoeber, and James P. Piscatori, eds. 1997. *Transnational Religion and Failed States*. Boulder, Colo.: Westview Press.

Shepherd, John R. 1999. "The Island Frontier of the Ch'ing, 1684–1780." In *Taiwan: A New History*, ed. Murray A. Rubinstein. Armonk, N.Y.: M.E. Sharpe.

Smith, Anthony D. 1991. *National Identity*. London: Penguin.

Solinger, Dorothy. 2001. "Ending One-Party Dominance: Korea, Taiwan, Mexico." *Journal of Democracy* 12, no. 1 (January): 30–42.

Stainton, Michael. 1999. "Aboriginal Self-Government: Taiwan's Uncompleted Agenda." In *Taiwan: A New History*, ed. Murray A. Rubinstein. Armonk, N.Y.: M.E. Sharpe.

Tsai, Wen-ting. 1997. "Sa ti daoshang duo nu'er" ("Daughters of the Buddha"). *Sinorama* 22, no. 12 (December): 82–106.

Tien, Hung-mao. 1989. *The Great Transition: Political and Social Change in the Republic of China*. Taipei: SMC Publishing.

Wachman, Alan M. 1994. "Competing Identities in Taiwan." In *The Other Taiwan: 1945 to the Present*, ed. Murray A. Rubinstein. Armonk, N.Y.: M.E. Sharpe.

Wang, Hongying. 1999. "Hong Kong and Globalization." *Asian Perspective* 23, no. 4: 143–65.

Wang, Shunmin. 1991. "Zongjiao fuli sixiang yu fuli fuwu zhi tanjiu—yi Ciji Gongdehui, Taiwan Jidu Changlaohui wei lie" ("Religious thought on welfare and the provision of welfare: an enquiry using the Buddhist Compassion Relief Tzu Chi foundation and the Presbyterian church as examples"). Taichung, Taiwan: Tunghai (Donghai) University. Unpublished manuscript.

Weller, Robert P. 2000. "Markets, Margins, and the Growth of Religious Diversity: Taiwan in Comparative Perspective." Paper presented at Third International Conference on Sinology, Academia Sinica. Nankang, Taiwan: Academia Sinica, 29 June–1 July.

White III, Lynn T. 1999. "Globalization and Taiwan." *Asian Perspectives* 23, no. 4: 97–141.

Wong, Lloyd L. 2002. "Transnationalism, Diaspora Communities, and Changing Identities: Implications for Canadian Citizenship." In *Street Protests and Fantasy Parks: Globalization, Culture, and the State*, eds. David R. Cameron and Janice Gross Stein. Vancouver: University of British Columbia Press.

Zhao, Hui Shi. 1998. *"Renjian Fojiao" shilianchang (Examining "this-worldly Buddhism")*. Taipei: Fajie Chubanshe.

Zheng, Zhiming. 2000. "Falungong de xinyang beijing yu zhengjiao chongtu" ("The background of the falungong belief system and the conflict between politics and religion"). Paper presented at Third International Conference on Sinology, Academia Sinica. Nankang, Taiwan: Academia Sinica, 29 June–1 July.

III

REFLECTING ON SOUTHEAST ASIA

9

Democratization and Religious and Nationalist Conflict in Post-Suharto Indonesia

Jacques Bertrand

This book poses an important comparative question: Why does democratization sometimes produce ethnic, including religious, conflict?[1] In the Third Wave of democratization that spread across the world from the mid-1970s to the 1990s, ethnic conflict accompanied regime change in many countries with ethnically diverse populations. Earlier studies on democratization had virtually ignored its effects on ethnic communities because of the relatively homogeneous nature of societies they were studying, particularly in Latin America and Southern Europe (Schmitter et al. 1986; Mainwaring et al. 1992). After the collapse of the Soviet Union, the cases of ethnic instability after a democratic opening began to multiply, thereby warranting a revision of analyses of democratization to assess systematically its impact on ethnic diversity and the propensity for conflict.[2] East and Southeast Asia were "latecomers" in this wave of democratization as well as outliers. Authoritarianism was more resilient and, where democratization did occur, it often produced illiberal forms of democracy, as Susan Henders noted in chapter 1. Yet, with very diverse societies across the region, the analysis of ethnic conflict and its relationship to democratization is particularly salient.

I approach this question in the following way. First, for analytical purposes I adopt a procedural definition of democratization distinctive from the broader conceptualization adopted by various other contributors to this volume. I further consider only the phase of democratic transition, from the opening of an authoritarian regime to the establishment of a democratic government through free and fair elections with de jure sovereignty over executive, legislative, and judicial power.[3] Second, I analyze the period of democratic transition and assess whether it has been associated with an increase in ethnic conflict. If so, how can we explain the effects of democratic transition on the eruption of these conflicts? Finally, I attempt to draw some comparative generalizations in light of the above analysis.

Based on the analysis of Indonesia, this chapter confirms that democratic transition is associated with heightened conflict. Yet, this observation requires further explanation because heightened conflict does not occur in all cases. In the Indonesian case, I argue that two preconditions were particularly important. Firstly, prior tensions in relations between two ethnic groups were fostered by policies adopted during the authoritarian phase and were also contained through authoritarian means. If a rapid democratic transition occurs, this condition is likely to produce conflict. Conflict between Muslims and Christians in Ambon illustrates this condition, in that prior tensions were present well before the transition and these tensions were exacerbated by policies of the Suharto regime. Similarly, the ethnonationalist movements in East Timor, Aceh, and Irian Jaya (or Papua) were developed well before the democratic opening, but were contained by the tight noose of Suharto's armed forces. The weakening of repressive power that accompanied Suharto's fall opened up a space for the ethnonationalist movements to reemerge in full force. They were intensified as well by past policies of the Suharto regime. Therefore, democratization did not cause ethnic conflict, but released forces hitherto repressed.

The second precondition is the absence of a nation with clearly defined terms of inclusion for certain ethnic minorities. At the time of independence, the Indonesian nation was defined in broad, inclusive terms. During the New Order period, however, some groups became increasingly worried that inclusion in the Indonesian nation threatened their identities. In the case of Christians in Maluku, this translated into a *perceived* threat that it increasingly meant inclusion in a Muslim Indonesian nation, while Muslim Ambonese had perceived a threat to their own identity under regional Christian dominance until the early 1990s. For Acehnese, East Timorese, and Papuans in Irian Jaya, inclusion in the Indonesian nation came to mean exploitation and abuse from the state, and even a denial of cultural expression in the case of Papuans. The East Timorese and Papuans in particular were never given the choice of inclusion in the Indonesian nation, even at a time when they had already developed a sense of separate nationhood, albeit a weak one.

These two factors, the legacy of authoritarian policies and the terms of inclusion in the nation, were conducive to ethnic conflict during the democratic transition. They heightened group fears of being reduced to powerless minorities or of seeing their group identities erode or even disappear. Rather than being an opportunity to develop common democratic values with other groups, democratic transition was seen instead as a moment of weakness in the state and, therefore, either a source of insecurity or an opportunity for mobilization. The next section situates the democratic transition in relation to the broader place of ethnic minorities in Indonesia. Subsequent sections examine two cases of ethnic conflict: religious conflict in Maluku and eth-nonationalist movements in Aceh, East Timor, and Papua.

ETHNIC MINORITIES AND DEMOCRACY IN INDONESIA

The nature of the relationship of ethnic identities to the Indonesian nation laid the basis for conflicts to erupt in the 1990s prior to democratization. Ethnic conflict in different periods of Indonesia's postindependence history has reflected unresolved questions of inclusion and exclusion in the Indonesian nation. Furthermore, these conflicts were almost all resolved through repressive means. When the democratic transition occurred in the late 1990s, these two issues converged: new democratic institutions, combined with heightened uncertainties about inclusion, allowing groups to mobilize and ethnicized conflict to occur.

The Indonesian nation reflected a modified civic nationalism. It was founded on the principles of the self-determination of nations and the ideals of nation-state building. For the founding fathers of the nation, the maintenance of boundaries inherited from the former Dutch East Indies was insufficient to ensure national unity. A new nation, based on common principles and values, had to be built to establish the foundations of the new nation-state.[4]

The draft Constitution of 1945 and *Pancasila* ideology were the written forms that spelled out the core elements of this nationalism.[5] After a brief attempt to use a decentralized, federalist model, a unitary state was deemed essential to building a single, Indonesian nation and integrate the diverse parts of an otherwise culturally plural archipelago. Indonesian leaders enshrined this principle in the formation of a republic, with a powerful executive and layers of provincial, regional, and local bureaucracy whose powers were devolved from the center.

Pancasila, a state ideology formulated by Sukarno on the principle of religious tolerance, upheld the civic values of modern nationalism while recognizing the distinctiveness of the Indonesian archipelago. Four of its principles appealed to modern values the nation was meant to enhance, such as nationalism; internationalism or humanitarianism; representative government; and social justice and prosperity. Its most important principle, belief in one God, was primarily aimed at appeasing those Muslims who wanted the establishment of an Islamic state. As David Brown has discussed in this volume, the principle was sufficiently ambiguous to enshrine religious tolerance and recognition that all religious groups could freely practice their respective religions, while conceding that the nation would not be purely secular.[6]

Indonesia had a brief period of liberal democracy shortly after its independence. When the Dutch finally relinquished their claim to the archipelago in

1949, the Republic of Indonesia consolidated its authority. A unitary state model was adopted in 1950 and a Constituent Assembly was created to negotiate a new constitution that could be ratified democratically. Free and fair elections were scheduled for 1955 because the existing parliament was a result of negotiation between the parties rather than popular vote. While the 1955 elections were run successfully, the Constituent Assembly failed to reach a sufficiently large consensus on the basic principles for a new constitution. In the wake of this crisis, President Sukarno suspended the Assembly and the parliament and replaced the regime of liberal democracy with that of Guided Democracy in the late 1950s.[7]

Two conflicts contributed to the fall of the democratic regime. The first was the question of Islam. The *Darul Islam* movement emerged as the most significant resistance to the new Republic. Formed in West Java, it spread to Aceh, parts of Sumatra, and Sulawesi. It lasted for more than a decade before it was defeated by the Indonesian National Army (TNI).[8] Alongside violent resistance, political channels were also used to advance the idea of the Islamic state, especially through the *Masjumi* party. During the 1950s, political Islam clashed with the nationalist *Pancasila* ideology and communism. Proponents of each ideology were well represented in the party structure and competed strongly for their alternative visions for the Indonesian state. No democratic process was ever followed to reach agreement on a constitution and ideological basis for the state.

The second conflict involved regional rebellions against the central state. Elites in South Sulawesi, West Sumatra, and other regions rebelled against the centralization of political and economic power by the Indonesian government. They were also critical of the increasing dominance of the Javanese in the Republic and the "Javanization" of the polity.

Guided Democracy ended these conflicts through repressive means. With support from the Indonesian military, President Sukarno suspended the Constituent Assembly and the parliament. He imposed a return to the 1945 Constitution as well as the state ideology of *Pancasila*. *Masjumi* was banned in 1960, and the Indonesian military was able to defeat the *Darul Islam* in 1962. The question of the Islamic state was muted through force, and regional rebellions were also curtailed. Regional military commands and governments lost even more autonomy as a strong center was seen as the primary means to prevent future regionalist rebellions and threats to national unity.

These threats were directly related to relations between ethnic groups and the state. Most ethnic groups had espoused the nationalist vision of an "Indonesian" nation in which groups shared certain values and experience. Because most had participated in the revolution, they also saw themselves as constituents and nation-builders. Only when the Javanese appeared to dominate central political institutions did some groups choose to rebel. The question of Islam, however, was much more profound because it struck at the heart of the definition of the Indonesian nation. Muslim groups with distinctive languages and cultures in many cases adopted the Islamic vision of Indonesian nationalism, and this tension would remain. More secular Muslims, but especially non-Muslims, and Christians in particular, felt included within the Indonesian nation only if it was based on *Pancasila.*

Under Guided Democracy, Sukarno did a balancing act between the military, Islamists, and Communists. The military supported his nationalist vision. Islamists were curtailed but Sukarno also sought to gain the support of some major Islamic organizations. The Communist Party proposed yet another vision of the Indonesian nation.[9]

The confrontation between the military and the Communist Party came to a climax in September 1965. As the Communist Party gained momentum in the countryside and increasingly resorted to extra-legal actions to gain advantage, groups in the military feared a Communist uprising. On 30 September 1965, six top generals of the Indonesian military were assassinated. In reaction to these events, General Suharto seized control over the country and established the dominance of the military. His regime led a purge of Communist sympathizers that resulted in the death of hundreds of thousands of people.[10] Over the next eight months, Sukarno's power was drastically reduced until he was forced formally to relinquish power to Suharto, who succeeded him as President.

Suharto solidified the authoritarian regime and established his New Order. He raised the specter of Communism to justify the need for more political control and use of the military. He reaffirmed that *Pancasila* would remain the basis of the Indonesian nation and that the 1945 Constitution would also continue. He moved against Islamic groups identified as potential threats to the nation based on *Pancasila. Pancasila* was eventually imposed as the sole ideology of all sociopolitical organizations. Furthermore, Suharto significantly weakened political parties in the mid-1970s by forcing their amalgamation into three political parties, including the government party, Golkar. Military personnel occupied a large number of positions at all levels of government and the bureaucracy was streamlined to reinforce central control and ensure order even in remote areas of the country. Elections were held regularly, but structural measures as well as intimidation and vote manipulation maintained the dominance of Golkar. The media were censured and the freedoms of expression and association were curtailed. This regime lasted for more than thirty years.[11]

Indonesia's democratic transition began in May 1998. Before then, there was little sign that a transition was under way. Although the Suharto government was weakening, Suharto himself intended to stay in power and preserve the characteristics of the New Order regime. It was only after months of instability, partially triggered by the Asian financial crisis that hit Indonesia in the summer of 1997, that signs emerged of the end of the regime. Only with the fall of Suharto in May 1998, after days of intense rioting, could one argue that the regime had the potential to change. Under intense domestic and international pressure, B. J. Habibie, Suharto's successor, saw little choice but to reform the political system lest he be faced with the same fate as his mentor.

Legislative elections were held in June 1999 and presidential elections in October of the same year. In both instances, the opposition was victorious. There were no restrictions on voters or on the participation of political parties. From only three political parties allowed during most of the New Order period, forty-eight parties competed in the June 7, 1999 election. Opposition leader Megawati Sukarnoputri's Indonesian Democratic Party for the Struggle won the greatest number of seats in the legislature, and Muslim leader Abdurrahman Wahid was elected president in October. Wahid as the leader of the *Nahdlatul Ulama*, Indonesia's largest Islamic organization, had been a critic of the Suharto regime and promoted democratic reforms for several years. Golkar, formerly the government's unbeatable party machine, obtained second place, but was unable to secure sufficient allies among other parties to ensure the election of Habibie as president. Habibie bowed to the wishes of the electorate and ensured a rapid, smooth transition of power to Wahid.

Indonesia's transition was, in many ways, rapid. Although many signs of a *fin de régime* were apparent from the mid-1990s onward, no one believed that Suharto would lose power so suddenly and so rapidly. That a democratically elected government emerged in slightly more than a year after Suharto's fall was a very fast change in a country where the political system had seen few changes in the previous thirty years. As a result, while elections were held, few institutions were actually changed. The constitution and the basic apparatus of legislative, executive, and judicial institutions remained. More importantly, although the crisis had severely weakened the armed forces, they only reluctantly accepted reduced influence in the polity. Despite a change of government through democratic elections, the military retained seats in Indonesia's supreme legislative body, the People Consultative Assembly (*Majelis Permusyawaratan Rakyat* or MPR) as well as a few seats in Indonesia's parliament (*Dewan Perwakilan Rakyat* or DPR). Therefore, de jure, Indonesia's democratic transition remained incomplete well after the election of President Wahid.

This precipitated and incomplete transition created uncertainty that exacerbated two types of ethnic conflicts. The institutions of the New Order regime remained intact during the early phase of transition. As a result, the basic principles of the unitary state and the *Pancasila* ideology were also retained, despite the fact that these principles had been imposed through authoritarian means and had remained so through more than thirty years of New Order rule. Equally important, the New Order had used military, bureaucratic, and political means of enforcing its own vision of these national-ist principles and their embodiment of the "Indonesian" nation.

The first effect of transition was a revival of the issue of the Islamic state. In the latter years of the New Order regime, Suharto had manipulated Islamic groups and given them more voice in the regime. This had led to specula-tion that the agenda of an Islamic state could be revived. Democratization al-lowed some Islamic groups to openly suggest a more Islamic dimension to the Indonesian nation, especially because *Pancasila* had lost its appeal dur-ing the New Order years. In this context, tensions between Christians and Muslims rose steadily.

The second effect of the transition was an intensification of ethnonation-alist movements. While most ethnic groups had adhered to the notion of a single, united Indonesian nation, even under authoritarian rule, those groups that were included on different terms did not share such a vision. The East Timorese and Papuans had been integrated long after the Revolution through nondemocratic means and then subjected to authoritarian rule. The Acehnese, whose participation in the *Darul Islam* rebellion had been crushed, never regained the Indonesian nationalist orientation of their early participation in the anticolonial Revolution. Instead, they developed a re-gionalist identity that became increasingly strong in response to the repres-sive policies of the New Order regime in Aceh.

Democratization brought these tensions to the surface more openly. Furthermore, it created new uncertainty about the future status of these ethnic groups. Would Christians become marginalized under an increas-ingly Islamic state? Would Muslims lose the gains they had made during the last years of the New Order regime? Would a new, centralized regime emerge that might continue to curtail demands in East Timor, Irian Jaya, and Aceh? The process of democratization did not create these conflicts, but intensified insecurities as its rapid nature created heightened uncer-tainties about the future.

MUSLIM–CHRISTIAN RELATIONS IN MALUKU AND THE ROLE OF ISLAM IN THE INDONESIAN STATE[12]

The democratic transition unveiled a tense relationship between Christians and Muslims in Maluku. The two groups lived peacefully together for several decades as long as their respective representation in the state and access to state resources appeared fair. While Muslims had long been disadvantaged in the region, there were steady improvements in their situation in the decades following independence. Christians, overwhelmingly dominant in the political institutions of the region, saw their relative representation de-cline, but maintained some significant strongholds. Serious conflict was avoided as long as both groups thought they had sufficient means of protecting their interests and their survival. This balance was threatened when the New Order regime changed its policies and began to favor Muslims in the early 1990s. These changes created rising tensions between the two religious groups, but no conflict erupted. Democratic transition destroyed this carefully controlled balance by removing the tight military and political control in the region, and by heightening uncertainties about the future.

The relationship between Christians and Muslims in the region was influenced by larger events that determined the role of Islam in the Indonesian state. During the independence war against the Dutch from 1945–1949, the newly established Republic fought to consolidate support from regions that were organized by the Dutch under a federal structure. The colonial government withdrew in 1949, when the Republic began to form an independent federation of the United States of Indonesia. This federation, however, was short-lived and dissolved rapidly. Most states agreed peacefully to be integrated into the Republic of Indonesia. Once it was clear that the federation was collapsing, a few regions resisted the integrationist movement. In particular, there were attempts in the South Moluccas to form an independent state in protest against the absorption of the federal state into the Republic. Christian Ambonese had been particularly favored during Dutch colonial times, as they served in the colonial bureaucracy and in the Dutch colonial military. There were fears that Christian minorities would find themselves powerless in an overwhelmingly Muslim Indonesian republic, especially in Maluku because of previous Christian support for the colonial regime. The Republic of Southern Maluku movement (RMS) was defeated by the TNI in 1950, and the region joined the Republic. Although a significant proportion of Christians had actually supported the Indonesian Republic, the central government would continue to doubt the region's loyalty.[13]

Nevertheless, in the Sukarno years Ambonese Christians retained some regional dominance. Their control of bureaucratic positions in Ambon and the region continued after independence, in part because Muslims had been insufficiently educated during colonial times to compete in the new Republic. They were also protected by the favorable position at the national level of Christians included in the various governments formed during the liberal democratic period as well as under Guided Democracy. Sukarno's decision to ban *Masjumi*, curtail the issue of the Islamic state, and reinforce *Pancasila* was favorable to Christians while dampening the ability of Muslims to use Islam for political mobilization nationally or regionally.

After consolidating his hold over the military and government apparatus, Suharto moved against Islamic groups that were inclined to revive Islamic issues. By the mid-1970s, Muslim political parties were forced to amalgamate under the banner of the Development Unity Party (PPP), while non-Muslims were regrouped with the former Nationalist Party under the Democratic

Party of Indonesia (PDI). Golkar became the main party machine for accessing resources and power, while the two other parties were structurally reduced to political channels with no chances of gaining real electoral success. Many Islamic leaders joined Golkar, and Islamic political activists shifted away from an oppositional strategy to one based on working within government-established boundaries. When in 1984 the government imposed *Pancasila* as the sole ideology underlying all sociopolitical organizations, Wahid, as the leader of the *Nahdlatul Ulama*, supported the government's regulation along with other prominent Muslim leaders. Within Islamic groups such as *Muhammadiyah* and the *Dewan Dakwah Islamiyah Indonesia* there was more disgruntlement. Despite complaints about government policies, it appeared nevertheless that political Islam would no longer become a threat to the nationalist vision of the state, as expressed in *Pancasila*.[14]

It was in this context that Christians continued to enjoy favor under the Suharto regime. The regime was backed by the military, a strongly secular institution in which Christians were well represented. Furthermore, Christians, who had benefited from better education during Dutch colonial rule still dominated high positions in the bureaucracy. Economists who were recruited to solve Indonesia's deep economic problems, for example, were predominantly Christian. In areas where Christians were numerous, such as in Maluku and in other parts of Eastern Indonesia, they tended to be overrepresented in the government bureaucracy because of patrimonial links and advantages in education. They supported the regime's emphasis on *Pancasila* as a guarantee against Muslim forces that had espoused the idea of an Islamic state in the past.[15]

In the early 1990s, Suharto changed his patrimonial approach by attempting to co-opt the Islamic intellectual elite that had risen throughout the first few decades of his rule. After the repression of the early New Order, many Islamic leaders had gradually penetrated Golkar and the government machinery while increasing their influence in society. Islamic groups gained new access to power without threatening the basic principles of the Indonesian nation. Suharto then supported the creation of the Association of Muslim Intellectuals of Indonesia (ICMI), which rapidly became a powerful channel for Muslim groups to advance their interests. Within a few years, ICMI members obtained positions in high levels of government, including a large representation in the 1993 cabinet. At the same time, the Indonesian armed forces top command was replaced by officers more closely identified with Islam, while Christian and more secular officers were sidelined.[16]

The growth of ICMI and the "greening" of the armed forces did not constitute a departure from the fundamental principles of the Indonesian nation. The armed forces remained committed to the unity of the Indonesian state. ICMI entered the government, and its members continued to support

Pancasila and the Constitution of 1945 from their positions as cabinet members. Only a few ICMI leaders, notably Amien Rais, the leader of *Muhammadiyah* (one of the largest Islamic organizations), began to question the government. They demanded more democracy and more openness in the political system, while increasingly criticizing Suharto's leadership. They claimed more representation for the Muslim majority and denounced the corruption surrounding Suharto and his business partners, his family, and Christian-Chinese businessmen. However, they neither demanded an Islamic state nor questioned the fundamental principles of *Pancasila*.

Nevertheless, Suharto's support for ICMI and the rapid "greening" of the New Order's institutions was to have a destabilizing impact in Maluku. Religious violence exploded in Maluku in January 1999 and claimed more than 5,000 victims in the following three years. For decades, Indonesians had praised the tolerance between religious communities and harmonious relations that *Pancasila* had helped maintain. Maluku experienced a sense of heightened insecurity, a legacy of Suharto's recently intensified patrimonial use of Islamic groups. Although relations between Muslims and Christians were more tense in Maluku than elsewhere because of the equal numbers of both communities, the conflict reflected a deeply unresolved issue of the proper place of religion in Indonesian politics. The renewal of Islam created a sense of mounting fear among non-Muslims. Meanwhile Muslims saw an opportunity to redress past restrictions on their access to political control in the region. Despite the fact that the region was mainly controlled by the military (directly and through retired military officers as governors and regency heads), much of the civil service in Maluku and Ambon was dominated by Christians. The democratic transition created uncertainty about the future of Indonesia, the role of Islam in the state, and the relative representation of Christians and Muslims, fueling already tense relations in the region.

Some of the religious violence that subsequently occurred in Maluku can be explained by local and regional factors. As mentioned, the proportion of Christians and Muslims was almost equal. Competition between both groups for government positions or for access to government resources was stronger than in other regions. Also, migration from predominantly Muslim areas of Indonesia had gradually changed the proportion of both communities, threatening the advantageous position of Christians in certain areas, such as Ambon city. This factor has been especially threatening to Christians because migrants often displaced local Ambonese in commercial sectors, where they developed some strength. Jealousies began to emerge as Muslim entrepreneurs from Southeast Sulawesi and other parts of Indonesia gained greater market share at the expense of Ambonese Christians. With an increased intensity of migration in the 1980s and 1990s, these tensions had become stronger by the time the Suharto regime fell in May 1998.

Beyond these local factors, however, the crisis in Maluku took place during a changing political context that revealed the uneasy relationship between Christians and Muslims in Indonesia generally. Religion was a stronger characteristic of group identities than other forms of ethnicity. The New Order regime's policies intensified these identities and made them more relevant politically, especially during the 1990s. As a result, tensions were high between Muslims and Christians during that decade, intensified due to local factors, and reached crisis levels in Maluku.

Even prior to the transition, therefore, policies favorable to Muslims tipped the uneasy balance in Maluku. In the early and mid-1990s, the governor became an active promoter of Muslim interests in the region. By attempting to improve Muslim access to positions in government, he pushed the agenda far enough to threaten some of the last Christian strongholds. Within a few years, almost all top positions in the provincial bureaucracy were given to Muslims. Controversial attempts to nominate Muslims as mayor of Ambon and head of Pattimura University only intensified the tensions.

The resignation of President Suharto and the transitional government of President Habibie created even greater uncertainties. Muslims could see their position threatened and a return of Christian dominance in the region, while Christians were worried that the religious tolerance embedded in the principles of *Pancasila* might be lost, thereby also weakening their ability to justify their political control. Group tensions erupted into open violence only eight months after Suharto's resignation.

The first violent outburst occurred in Ambon in January 1999. At first, the violence pitted Muslim migrants against local Ambonese Christians, but the violence then spread to include Ambonese Muslims too. Within days, several villages across Ambon and neighboring islands were hit by violence and hundreds of people were killed. Within the next few months, the conflict spread to other regions of Maluku. Clashes occurred in the South Moluccas and then spread to North Maluku on Halmahera island. Casualties continued to accumulate. The city of Ambon, where conflict erupted periodically, became a virtual war zone. Thousands of people fled the region, especially migrants from Southeast Sulawesi (Buton).

The armed forces were incapable of ending the violence. In fact, many soldiers were drawn into the conflict. Muslim and Christian soldiers began to take sides with their respective religious communities, thereby intensifying the conflict as both sides accused each other of benefiting from armed forces support.

The conflict also raised emotions in the rest of the country. Demonstrators in Jakarta demanded a *jihad* in Maluku. While religious leaders were able to quell the first wave of calls to support Muslim brethren being killed in Maluku, they were unable to prevent a Muslim organization from training and arming a *jihad* force for Maluku, as the conflict continued for several months. In May 2000, "Laskar *Jihad*" volunteers went to Maluku, despite stated attempts by the armed forces and the government to prevent them. More than 2,000 men were reported to have gone to Maluku, and the conflict began to intensify after their arrival.

While many factors explain the violence and its intensity, two were particularly important in determining the conditions leading to violence. Firstly, as noted earlier, the question of the Islamic state had never been resolved democratically and, therefore, remained a source of uncertainty that was exaggerated in locations such as Maluku. Secondly, the political system of patrimonial control and use of repressive forces to quell dissent hid the tensions that were brewing in Maluku. There were no guarantees of political control and, therefore, of advancement of the interests of each community, without tightly knit relations with the regional sources of patronage (through the governor and military) and links to Jakarta. The growth of ICMI was particularly destabilizing because it changed the balance of favors in the region in a rapid and dramatic way. This heightened the Christians' sense of threat, while Muslims saw their situation as a justifiable redress for past neglect. The democratic transition triggered violence because it altered established patrimonial relationships and loosened repressive controls, while heightening the uncertainty surrounding the question of Islam and the guarantees that the interests of both Christians and Muslims would be protected.

EAST TIMOR, IRIAN JAYA, AND ACEH

Democratization was also accompanied by violence in East Timor, Irian Jaya, and Aceh. In these three regions, however, open conflict had occurred during authoritarian rule and was mainly intensified following the fall of Suharto. Conflicts pitted secessionist movements against the centralist Indonesian government. Attempts to advance the secessionist cause in the three regions during the Suharto era were met with brutal repression by the Indonesian armed forces. Nevertheless, the movements continued to develop. The democratic transition created an opportunity for regional elites to challenge the central state at a moment of weakness. Instead of viewing the advent of democracy as a progressive evolution in Indonesian politics that would allow them to accept their integration, these elites increased the intensity with which they mobilized support for independence. The violence was greatest in Aceh and East Timor, but less intense in Irian Jaya.

All three regions rejected the terms of inclusion that had defined the relationship of their respective region to Indonesia. For the Acehnese, who had joined the struggle for independence and been part of Indonesia from its beginnings, participation in the Indonesian state had become increasingly associated with abusive exploitation of the region's resources by the central government and, more importantly, state violence against the people. For the East Timorese and the Papuans, the initial integration into Indonesia was itself contested because it had been done through force rather than popular consultation. In neither case did a popular movement emerge in support of Indonesian nationalism or the integration into the republic at the time of Indonesia's independence in 1945. The increase in mobilization against the Indonesian state, therefore, also represented a contestation of inclusion in the Indonesian nation.

As David Wurfel discusses in his chapter, East Timor was invaded by the Indonesian armed forces in 1975, only a few days after its official declaration of independence. At its beginning, Indonesian support for prointegrationist parties in East Timor was done through political campaigning, but it rapidly took a military turn. By December 1975, the Indonesians launched a full-scale invasion. The war was meant to be short and with few casualties, but the Indonesians met a fierce resistance by the Revolutionary Front for an Independent East Timor (FRETILIN). As a result, the military campaign was intense and prolonged. It is estimated that the invasion and its effects caused the death of about 200,000 people. From the Indonesian military's perspective, the invasion was justifiable to prevent the installation of a pro-Communist government at its doorstep and the potential secessionist influence it could have over other regions, notably Aceh and Irian Jaya. From the mid-1980s, the guerilla movement moved away from military resistance and began an intensive diplomatic campaign in association with overseas nongovernmental organizations. It received much attention after the 1991 Dili massacre, as Wurfel notes. From that moment onward, an increasing number of states began to pressure the Indonesians to find a diplomatic solution to the question of East Timor, as only very few countries had actually recognized Indonesia's integration of the territory. For most East Timorese, the integration was neither legitimate nor accepted.[17]

After the fall of Suharto, the East Timorese were the first group to mobilize. Demonstrations were held in East Timor and in Jakarta, demanding a resolution of the conflict with Jakarta.[18] East Timorese representatives stepped up their diplomatic efforts internationally once authoritarian rule appeared to be diminishing. Faced with difficulties in consolidating his powers, Habibie came to rely on the military's ability and willingness to quell dissent. However, the military was overstretched, and East Timor was a thorn in Indonesia's relationship with foreign donors.

In a surprise move aimed at creating allies abroad and solidifying his leadership at home, Habibie offered a special autonomy package for East Timor with the possibility of independence if it was rejected. At first, he announced in June 1998 that Indonesia was prepared to offer wide-ranging autonomy to the territory. Faced with mass protests demanding a referendum, a resurgence of violence by armed groups in the province, and little enthusiasm for the offer from the East Timorese leadership, Habibie proposed on 27 January 1999 that, if wide-ranging autonomy was rejected, East Timor would be given its independence.[19] He eventually agreed to a referendum on this question to be held in August 1999.

Violence escalated in the months leading up to the referendum. While Habibie favored a diplomatic solution to the East Timor question, the armed forces were infiltrating East Timor and arming paramilitary groups to create a civil war aimed at disrupting the referendum and ensuring that East Timor would remain in the Republic. A small United Nations mission, the United Nations Transitional Administration for East Timor (UNTAET), was dispatched to support the organization of the referendum, but did not have the mandate to prevent the mounting violence in the territory.[20]

The referendum was held on 30 August in relative peace, but the announcement of the results unleashed an unprecedented wave of violence against the civilian population. With 97 percent of registered voters participating, 78.5 percent rejected Indonesia's autonomy proposal and therefore supported independence.[21] Hours after the results were announced on 4 September, proautonomy militias descended on villages, burning, looting, and displacing the local population. Within a few days, 200,000 refugees fled to the mountains and to the neighboring province of West Timor, while the militias engaged in vast destruction. Supported by elements of Indonesia's armed forces, and apparently with the tacit approval of high levels of the military command, the militias undertook to either maintain Timor through violence or, at least, to punish the Timorese for opting for independence.[22]

The transition to independence occurred swiftly. Even though Habibie was blamed widely for losing East Timor, the MPR approved the transfer of authority to a temporary UN body that would oversee the gradual transfer of power to an independent East Timorese government. East Timor gained its full independence in May 2002.

Thus, a little over one year after the fall of Suharto, East Timor had left Indonesia. As twenty-five years of resistance to integration into the Republic made clear, the Indonesian invasion in 1975 was never accepted by the Timorese. Assimilationist and repressive policies of the Indonesian government did nothing to increase their loyalty to the Indonesian state. Democratic transition did not create their resistance, but was an opportunity to intensify diplomatic efforts and make greater demands for independence.

Irian Jaya shares a history similar to East Timor.[23] The main difference is its earlier inclusion in the Dutch East Indies. It did not join the Republic, however, during the struggle for independence in the late 1940s. It was integrated in the late 1960s, when the Dutch agreed to depart the country under United Nations pressure and the imminent intention of Indonesians to invade the territory. Indonesia was given control of the territory for a transitional period before the Papuans could be consulted on their future. An "Act of Free

Choice" was conducted by the Indonesian government in 1969, which saw unanimous support by handpicked representatives for integration into the Republic of Indonesia. Although the consultation was accepted by the United Nations, the process was not democratic and was widely criticized by Papuans and many foreigners. For most Papuans, thereafter, the integration to Indonesia was accomplished without their democratic consent.

Resistance to Indonesia took the form of a guerilla movement. As in East Timor and Aceh, where FRETILIN and the Free Aceh Movement fought for independence, the Free Papua Movement (*Organisasi Papua Merdeka* or OPM) led a violent campaign for independence. In comparison to guerilla movements in the other two regions, however, the OPM was weaker and less capable of challenging the Indonesian armed forces. It faced tremendous geographic challenges, given the difficulties of the mountainous terrain. It was also a very divided movement with little capacity to rally mass support across the province. It mainly engaged in short skirmishes from its position across the border in Papua-New Guinea. In a few instances during the 1980s and 1990s, it captured hostages who were held for several days.

Aside from the OPM's activities, occasional protests occurred, mainly in Timika, close to the vast mining operations of the U.S.-based company Freeport. The Indonesian government under Suharto gave mining rights to Freeport, which mined the area for more than twenty years with little benefit to the surrounding population. Most skilled workers were brought from other areas of Indonesia and few revenues were retained in the region. This resulted in occasional attacks on Freeport facilities and skirmishes with local authorities.[24]

Irian Jaya avoided a violent escalation in the wake of democratization, but there was a resurgence of ethnonationalist demands. The transition allowed a group of Papuans to demand a referendum for independence, especially following President Habibie's opening toward East Timor. However, the OPM remained marginal and divided in the first few months after the transition to democracy. Instead, local elites pursued peaceful means of promoting independence. A first demonstration occurred on 29 May 1998 in Jakarta and was organized by Papuan students who denounced past human rights abuses in Jayapura. In July, thousands of people demonstrated in major cities throughout Irian Jaya to demand a referendum on independence.[25] They sang the Papuan anthem and raised the Papuan flag in defiance of the Indonesian Republic. Students demanded the demilitarization of Irian Jaya, a referendum on independence, and a revision of the process leading to the "Act of Free Choice."

The government's response was mixed. On the one hand, the armed forces moved against demonstrations that raised the Papuan flag. At the same time, a dialogue was begun. Papuan groups reiterated their demands for "freedom" (*merdeka*), as reaffirmed in a meeting of 700 delegates at a conference in Jayapura that included representatives from student, youth, and *adat* (traditional) groups.[26] In February 1999, a group of 100 representatives from Irian Jaya met with President Habibie to discuss the future of the province. The delegates bluntly stated that Papuans wanted their independence. A shocked Habibie reasserted that independence was impossible and ended the dialogue.[27]

The Habibie government's policy was not consistent. It supported a referendum in East Timor, but it opposed this option for Aceh and Irian Jaya, despite the similarity of their demands. Habibie explained the government's position by stating that East Timor was historically different, but could not adequately explain to Papuans why they also could not also constitute a category on their own. Instead, the government insisted that its new laws on autonomy and fiscal decentralization would be sufficient to ensure that provinces could pursue their interests. The government proposed a division of Irian Jaya into three provinces, supposedly to increase the amount of resources retained in the province and the capacity of local governments to govern this vast area with difficult terrain and communications.[28] The implementation of this division was short lived, as Papuans protested and accused the government of attempting to divide them to prevent further separatist tendencies.[29] The Wahid government restored the unity of the province.

Democratic transition also opened up the opportunity for Papuan elites to demand a referendum. With the state unable to contain rising incidents of violence across the archipelago, and with the precedent of East Timor, Papuans could more forcefully demand a referendum on independence. They saw little reason to remain in Indonesia and work through a new democratic political regime. Instead, the support for secession was strengthened by the fall of the authoritarian regime.

The conflict in Aceh was born out of the initial conception of the Indonesian nation. Although Acehnese supported the revolution of 1945 and were active supporters of the new Republic, there were numerous occasions when the central government, under a unitary state model, was able to undermine Acehnese interests. Acehnese supported protest movements such as the *Darul Islam* and regional rebellions in the late 1950s because of an inability to prevent centralization from Jakarta. Investments in the region bypassed local interests during the Suharto era, leading to the emergence of the Free Aceh Movement (*Gerakan Aceh Merdeka* or GAM) in the 1970s. At first, the movement was widely seen as a direct result of investments in the oil and gas sectors with revenues accruing to Jakarta. Few benefits trickled down to the local population, and so the movement was seen as resistance to foreign investors and their Jakarta collaborators. As the armed forces responded with violence, the movement increasingly became a rejection of Indonesia and its violent policies against the Acehnese. The resurgence of the movement in the late 1980s was met with brutal repression and thousands of deaths over the following decade. A fundamental mistrust of the Indonesian state settled in during those years.[30]

For a decade, Aceh was under tight military security, designated as a "Military Operation Zone" (*Daerah Operasi Militer* or DOM). After having killed hundreds of people in a brutal "shock therapy" in the early 1990s to stomp out GAM supporters, the armed forces maintained a strong presence in Aceh and continued to use violence against suspected separatists. Hundreds more people were killed. Reports of torture and intimidation were widespread. The Acehnese had lived under a climate of fear that curtailed open support for independence.[31]

Now, the events in East Timor showed the post-Suharto central government's weakness and had a direct effect on political mobilization in Aceh. While demonstrations and lobbying were intensifying in East Timor, similar demands began to rise in Aceh. After demanding a withdrawal of the Indonesian armed forces from the province, groups of civilians began to demand a referendum on independence. Previously the Acehnese ethnonationalist movement was mainly represented by GAM. After the fall of Suharto, however, the core ethnonationalists included also groups of students, intellectuals, and other nonarmed groups.

Pressures mounted to put an end to the DOM regime in both Aceh and Irian Jaya. Acehnese began to speak openly of the atrocities committed by the armed forces during the DOM years. As evidence began to surface, the National Human Rights Commission announced in June 1998 that it would investigate reports of thousands killed or tortured between 1989 and 1998. It also pressured the government to lift the DOM status in Aceh.[32] In August 1998, General Wiranto announced an end to the DOM and the withdrawal of combat troops from the area.

Despite the official lifting of the DOM, soldiers continued to operate in the region, and the number of casualties began to escalate. As the elections for the new national Parliament approached in June 1999, the GAM began operating openly, and units of the armed forces responded with increasing violence. Government buildings and schools were burned to the ground. Sporadic attacks and killings took place regularly. In May 1999, a truckload of soldiers shot down forty civilian protesters in Krueng Geukeueh, North Aceh, and footage of the killings was broadcast on national television. A similar shooting in July, in which a local religious leader, Teungku Bantaqiah, and several of his students were shot by soldiers in West Aceh, raised a similar chorus of protest against the armed forces. In its defense, the armed forces argued that the victims were GAM supporters and had been carrying weapons at the meeting. Military personnel continued to operate under former practices of weeding out perceived GAM supporters and eliminating them through violent means. More than 300 people were killed between the lifting of DOM in August 1998 and October 1999.[33]

As violence escalated, several student and nongovernmental organizations held demonstrations requesting trials for past abuses as well as a referendum on self-determination. The Center for Information on the Aceh Referendum (*Sentra Informasi Referendum Aceh* or SIRA), an umbrella organization created to advance the referendum cause, escalated its campaign.[34] On 8 November 1999, shortly after Wahid was sworn in as president, SIRA organized a mass rally in Banda Aceh in favor of a referendum. An estimated 500,000 people massed in the streets of Banda Aceh, showing strong support for the referendum as well as the strength of SIRA.[35] The mobilization in favor of an independence referendum continued in subsequent months despite various offers for special autonomy from the Habibie and Wahid governments and promises to implement Islamic law and to address Acehnese demands.[36] From students and nongovernmental organizations to members of the GAM, a large number of activists and local elites seized the opportunity of state weakness while it lasted.

IMPLICATIONS FOR THE STUDY OF DEMOCRATIZATION AND ETHNIC CONFLICT

This analysis suggests that democratic transitions tend to produce ethnic conflict when faced with specific conditions. Firstly, a rapid and incomplete transition is particularly destabilizing because extrajudicial forces remain operative and may fuel resentment against the state, such as in Aceh, Irian Jaya, and East Timor. The militias in East Timor, supported by the Indonesian armed forces, are the most obvious illustration of this issue. The inconsistency between the armed forces response to GAM and attempts by the government to find a negotiated settlement in Aceh also fueled the conflict. This finding suggests that prior efforts to reduce ethnic tensions before transition begins may have stabilizing effects.[37] This is consistent with studies of democratization and ethnic conflict, such as Snyder (2000), which see democracy as fostering peaceful relations between ethnic groups over time, but the immediate context of democratization as being conducive to instability.

Secondly, ethnic conflict tends to occur during democratic transition because authoritarian means of control are weakened or removed. There is no reason why ethnic groups will necessarily conflict at the time of the democratic transition. However, if tensions and grievances were created during the authoritarian period, then the removal of authoritarian controls can heighten insecurity and increase the probability that groups will resort to violence to protect their respective interests. These interests could include protecting patronage resources rooted in the authoritarian past, as much as defending the group against a perceived threat to its identity. In Maluku, elements of both were present, while in East Timor, Aceh, and Irian Jaya the threat to identity was much more important. In both cases, grievances were fueled by policies of the authoritarian period: the manipulation of religion and resulting regional shifts in the balance of patrimonial access for Christians and Muslims in Maluku; the use of violence to quell secessionist demands in East Timor, Aceh, and Irian Jaya; as well as aggressive policies to maintain national unity that made the three regions more resentful of the state.

This finding differs from arguments in the literature that place too much emphasis on the role of elites. In such arguments, ethnic conflict or ethnonationalist resurgence under democratic transition are considered to be mainly a product of elite interests and manipulation.[38] Elites are only successful at mobilizing political support for independence, however, when prior grievances are present and sufficiently widespread. Furthermore, group identities are created and politicized prior to the democratic transition, as opposed to being created during the transition itself. The Indonesian case suggests that it is the removal of authoritarian means of control that reveals the underlying tensions and their expression in ethnonationalist movements, as shown in Aceh, Irian Jaya, and East Timor.

Finally, the terms of including ethnic groups in the nation can be important sources of conflict during democratic transition. Indonesia's original conception of the Indonesian nation was portrayed in civic terms, with the modification that the state was not secular. Under *Pancasila*, the state had an obligation to foster religiosity without favoring any religion in particular. But the uncertainty surrounding the question of the Islamic state and the future of *Pancasila* from the 1990s heightened tensions between Christians and Muslims. This contributed to the conflict in Maluku after the democratic opening. Also, military actions against separatism in Aceh, Irian Jaya, and East Timor revealed the forced unity of the Indonesian state and nation. By denying special recognition to these groups, the Indonesian state was consistent with its civic orientation, although enforced it through authoritarian means. This denial was even more significant for East Timor and Irian Jaya, which had been integrated by nondemocratic means. A narrow conception of the Indonesian nation, with little space to accommodate the diversity of its component groups, tempted the state to use authoritarian force in the name of "national unity."

The Indonesian case also creates problems for the analytical dichotomy between ethnic and civic nationalism. In a sense, the civic orientation of Indonesian nationalism was consistent with policies aimed at reducing group differences and enforcing equal treatment across the archipelago. However, the New Order regime did not avoid the use of military force in achieving these goals in Aceh, Irian Jaya, and East Timor. Furthermore, the Indonesian state could not portray itself as secular and civic without creating much discontent among Muslims. Yet, it did not espouse an ethnic nationalism based on Islam. At the same time, a pure civic nationalist orientation would likely not have been accepted. This shows the complex forms that nationalism must take to accommodate ethnic and religious diversity. During democratic transitions as well as under authoritarian rule, national models are subject to a creative, negotiated process. The outcome in Indonesia lies precariously somewhere between ethnic and civic types. It is precisely in the process of finding this "mid-range" conception of the nation that the sources of stability and inclusive democracy probably lie.[39]

NOTES

1. I agree with Horowitz (1985), who includes religious identities in his definition of ethnic identities.

2. For a good example of a book that revisits this question in a broad comparative framework, see Snyder (2000).

3. I adopt the definitions of democratic transition and consolidation of Linz and Stepan (1996), essentially characterizing it as a period between the initial opening of an authoritarian regime and a fully consolidated democracy. Elections are considered insufficient for the completion of transition. Instead, they argue that transition can be considered complete when a free and fair election produces a government with actual power to produce policies and with de jure sovereignty over executive, legislative, and judicial power. Democracy is consolidated when it becomes the "only game in town," i.e., it is fully internalized and routinized. In chapter 5, Rankin and Goodewardena contest this definition. In my view, a procedural definition helps to disentangle factors that may be conducive to ethnic conflict, but does not make any statement (or value judgment) about "ideal" forms of democracy and the diverse ways communities can develop democratic institutions that differ from the liberal norm.

4. On Indonesian nationalism, see Kahin (1952).

5. I am simplifying the complexity of this period for analytical purposes. In fact, the Constitution of 1945 was adopted in haste in the dying days of the Japanese occupation. It was a poorly written draft with many loopholes. A federal system was adopted in 1949 with a draft constitution that lasted seven months, following an agreement between the Netherlands and the Republic of Indonesia (see Kahin 1952: 446–51). Shortly thereafter, another constitution (1950) laid the basis of the liberal democratic system under a unitary state, which was in force throughout the 1950s (see Feith 1962).

6. On *Pancasila* and its original formulation, see Kahin (1952: 123–27).

7. For an analysis of the period of liberal democracy, see Feith (1962).

8. On the *Darul Islam*, see van Dijk (1981).

9. On Guided Democracy, see Lev (1996).

10. Exact figures are unknown. Estimates vary from 100,000 to over 1,000,000 (see Cribb 1990). On the 1965 events, see Harold Crouch (1998). On the 1965 coup, see Anderson and McVey (1971); Schwarz (1994: 18–23).

11. On the early years of Suharto's New Order and particularly the role of the military, see McDonald (1980); Jenkins (1984). On various periods of the New Order and

the role of Suharto, see Liddle (1996). See Bertrand (1996) for a discussion of a brief period of openness in the New Order and early signs that Suharto was attempting to build a power-base for Habibie to succeed him.

12. This section is based on Bertrand (2002) unless otherwise specified.

13. On the South Moluccas Movement (*Republik Maluku Selatan* or RMS), see Richard Chauvel (1990, 1985).

14. See Robert W. Hefner (2000); see also Aminudin (1999: 176–79).

15. On the disproportionate role of Christians, see Crouch (1988: 242–43, 271–72); Jenkins (1984: 21). On the role of patrimonialism and leadership in the New Order system, see Liddle (1985). For its application in the realm of religion, see Hefner (2000: 153, 171–74).

16. On ICMI, see especially Hefner (2000: 128–56).

17. On the East Timor issue, see Schwarz. The figure of 200,000 deaths resulting from the invasion (directly and indirectly) is taken from Taylor (1999).

18. See "East Timor Rises Again," *The Economist*, 20 June 1998. Student demonstrations also held in Dili demanded a referendum on independence (see "Demo Mengusung mayat," *Gatra*, 27 June 1998).

19. Between July and December 1998, protests and violence escalated. Even United Nations' Special Envoy for East Timor, Jamsheed Marker, had to flee Dili after being attacked by a mob of 50,000 people asking for a referendum (see *Tempo* 27, no. 13, 29 Dec. 1998–4 Jan. 1999). On the offer of independence, see *Tempo* (27 no. 18, 1–8 Feb. 1999).

20. Early reports raised suspicions that armed prointegration militias were being supplied with weapons by supporters in the Indonesian armed forces. For example, see statements by Clemento Dos Reis Amaral, General Secretary of the Indonesian Human Rights Commission, in "Tembakan Peringatan dari Dili," *Gatra*, 6 February 1999 and *Tempo* 27, no. 19, 9–15 Feb. 1999. Reports of escalating violence and the suspected links of the militias to the armed forces were made quite forcefully by East Timorese representatives at a round table in Ottawa in February 1999, attended by the author (Canadian Centre for Foreign Policy Development, 1999). A systematic campaign by the military and prointegration militias, called *Operasi Sapu Jagad*, was reported by Tapol (see "Indonesia's Dirty war in East Timor," *Tapol Bulletin*, 7 June 1999). Reports of elements of the Indonesian armed forces' involvement in the violence was confirmed by the Indonesian and United Nations inquiries on human rights violations in East Timor, following the August 1999 referendum (see International Commission of Inquiry on East Timor 2000; Commission to Investigate Human Rights Violations in East Timor 2000).

21. "East Timorese Choose Independence," *Associated Press*, 3 September 1999.

22. The Indonesian Human Rights Commission named high-level officers suspected of involvement in the violence following the referendum (see Commission to Investigate Human Rights Violations in East Timor 2000).

23. *Gatra*, 11 July 1998. The province was named West Irian during the period of decolonization by the Dutch and the integration to Indonesia, then renamed Irian Jaya. Papuan nationalists prefer the name West Papua to designate the territory and some accept Papua as a better designation than Irian Jaya. The name was officially changed to Papua in 2001.

24. Violent clashes were most severe during days of rioting in 1996 (see U.S. State Department 1997).

25. *Forum Keadilan* 7, no. 8, 27 July 1998; *Gatra*, 18 July 1998.

26. *Forum Keadilan* 7, no. 10, 24 August 1998.

27. *Gatra*, 6 March 1999; *Forum Keadilan* 7, no. 25, 22 March 1999; *Tempo* 28, no. 22, 2–8 March 1999.

28. See *Gatra*, 8 May 1999.

29. *Gatra*, 9 October 1999; *Forum Keadilan* 7, no. 29, 24 October 1999.

30. On the Free Aceh Movement and its causes, see Morris (1985, 1983) and Kell (1995).

31. For an analysis of the "shock therapy" of the early 1990s, see Kell (1995). There are no recognized estimates of the number of people killed in Aceh between 1989 and 1998. Al-Chaidar et al. (1999) give an estimate of 1,834 people killed or missing.

32. *Jakarta Post*, June 5 1998.

33. Early incidents occurred as soon as December 1998, when around twenty people were killed in various incidents involving suspected GAM members and armed forces units (see *Tempo* 27, no. 16, 19–25 Jan. 1999). On the Krueng Geukeueh violence, see *Tempo* 28, no. 10, 11–17 May 1999. On the killing of Teungku Bantaqiah, see *Tempo* 29, no. 22, 2–8 August 1999.

34. Calls for a referendum on independence occurred shortly after Habibie's offer to East Timor, in a congress held in Banda Aceh (see *Tempo* 27, no. 20, 14–22 Feb. 1999).

35. *Gatra*, 20 November 1999; *Forum Keadilan* no. 33, 21 November 1999; "Alarms in Aceh," *Far Eastern Economic Review*, November 18, 1999.

36. Autonomy laws were passed for all regions of Indonesia, but deemed insufficient to satisfy the Acehnese. Under the initiative of pro-Indonesia Acehnese, including the governor Syamsuddin Mahmud, a draft special autonomy law was proposed under the Habibie government and supported by President Wahid after his election. During the Habibie presidency, an initiative was taken to allow the immediate implementation of Islamic law, although this measure was not fully implemented (see *Tempo* 28, no. 36, 8–14 Nov. 1999). On the offer of Islamic law, see *Tempo* 28, no. 24, 16–22 August 1999.

37. Sisk (1995).

38. See Snyder's (2000) arguments about the strong role of elites in creating nationalist movements at the time of democratic transition. At least the Indonesian case offers a different account of the role of elites.

39. For arguments favoring the dichotomy between ethnic and civic nationalism, see Greenfeld (1992).

REFERENCES

Al-Chaidar, Sayed Mudhahar Ahmad, and Yarmen Dinamika. 1999. *Aceh Bersimbah Darah: Mengungkap Penerapan Status Daerah Operasi Militer (DOM) Di Aceh, 1989–1998 (Aceh drenched in blood: revealing the application of the status of military operation area in Aceh, 1989–1998)*. Jakarta: Pustaka Al-Kautsar.

Aminudin. 1999. *Kekuatan Islam Dan Pergulatan Kekuasaan Di Indonesia: Sebelum Dan Sesudah Runtuhnya Rezim Suharto (Islamic forces and the struggle for power in indonesia before and after the fall of Suharto's regime*). Yogyakarta, Indonesia: Pustaka Pelajar.

Anderson, Benedict R. O'G., and Ruth McVey. 1981. *A Preliminary Analysis of the October 1, 1965 Coup in Indonesia*. Ithaca, N.Y.: Southeast Asia Program, Cornell University. Interim Report Series, Modern Indonesia Project.

Bertrand, Jacques. 1996. "False Starts, Succession Crises, and Regime Transition: Flirting with Openness in Indonesia." *Pacific Affairs* 69, no. 3 (Fall): 319–40.

———. 1999. *East Timor Roundtable Report*. Canadian Center for Foreign Policy Development (22 February).

———. 2002. "Legacies of the Authoritarian Past: Religious Violence in Indonesia's Moluccan Islands." *Pacific Affairs* 75, no. 1 (Spring): 57–86.

Chauvel, Richard. 1985. "Ambon: Not a Revolution But a Counter-Revolution." In *Regional Dynamics of the Indonesian Revolution: Unity From Diversity*, ed. Audrey R. Kahin. Honolulu: University of Hawaii Press.

———. 1990. *Nationalists, Soldiers, and Separatists*. Leiden: KITLV Press.

Canadian Center for Foreign Policy Development. 1999. *East Timor Roundtable Report*, 22 February 1999.

Commission to Investigate Human Rights Violations in East Timor (KPP-HAM). 2000. *Executive Summary Report on the Investigation of Human Rights Violations in East Timor*. Indonesian Human Rights Commission, Jakarta (31 January).

Cribb, Robert. 1990. *The Indonesian Killings, 1965–66: Studies From Java and Bali*. Clayton: Center of Southeast Asian Studies, Monash University.

Crouch, Harold. 1988. *The Army and Politics in Indonesia*. 2d ed. (1978). Reprint, Ithaca, N.Y.: Cornell University Press.

Feith, Herbert. 1962. *The Decline of Constitutional Democracy in Indonesia*. Ithaca, N.Y.: Cornell University Press.

Greenfeld, Liah. 1992. *Nationalism: Five Roads to Modernity*. Cambridge, Mass.: Harvard University Press.

Hefner, Robert W. 2000. *Civil Islam: Muslims and Democratization in Indonesia*. Princeton, N.J.: Princeton University Press.

Horowitz, Donald. 1985. *Ethnic Groups in Conflict*. Berkeley: University of California Press.

International Commission of Inquiry on East Timor. 2000. *United Nations Report of the International Commission of Inquiry on East Timor to the Secretary-General*. New York: United Nations (January).

Jenkins, David. 1984. *Suharto and His Generals: Indonesian Military Politics, 1975–1983*. Ithaca, N.Y.: Cornell Modern Indonesia Project, Cornell University Press.

Kahin, George McT. 1952. *Nationalism and Revolution in Indonesia*. Ithaca, N.Y.: Cornell University Press.

Kell, Tim. 1995. *The Roots of Acehnese Rebellion, 1989–1992*. Ithaca, N.Y.: Cornell Modern Indonesia Project.

Lev, Daniel S. 1966. *The Transition to Guided Democracy: Indonesian Politics, 1957–1959*. Ithaca, N.Y.: Modern Indonesia Project, Southeast Asia Program, Dept. of Asian Studies, Cornell University.

Liddle, R. William. 1985. "Soeharto's Indonesia: Personal Rule and Political Institutions." *Pacific Affairs* 58, no.1: 68–90.

————. 1996. *Leadership and Culture in Indonesian Politics.* Sydney: Asian Studies Association of Australia in association with Allen and Unwin.

Linz, Juan J., and Alfred Stepan. 1996. *Problems of Democratic Transition and Consolidation: Southern Europe, South America, and Post-Communist Europe.* Baltimore, Md.: Johns Hopkins University Press.

Mainwaring, Scott, Guillermo O'Donnell, and J. Samuel Valenzuela, eds. 1992. *Issues in Democratic Consolidation: The New South American Democracies in Comparative Perspective.* Notre Dame, Ind.: University of Notre Dame Press.

Marx, Anthony W. 1997. "Apartheid's End: South Africa's Transition From Racial Domination." *Ethnic and Racial Studies* 20, no. 3 (July): 474–96.

McDonald, Hamish. 1980. *Suharto's Indonesia.* Blackburn: Fountain Books.

Morris, Eric E. 1983. Islam and Politics in Aceh: A Study of Center-Periphery Relations in Indonesia. Ph.D. diss., Cornell University.

————. 1985. "Aceh: Social Revolution and the Islamic Vision." In *Regional Dynamics of the Indonesian Revolution: Unity From Diversity,* ed. Audrey R. Kahin. Honolulu: University of Hawaii Press.

Schmitter, Philippe C., Guillermo O'Donnell, and Laurence Whitehead, eds. 1986. *Transitions From Authoritarian Rule: Tentative Conclusions about Uncertain Democracies.* Baltimore, Md.: Johns Hopkins University Press.

Sisk, Timothy D. 1995. *Democratization in South Africa: The Elusive Social Contract.* Princeton, N.J.: Princeton University Press.

Snyder, Jack L. 2000. *From Voting to Violence: Democratization and Nationalist Conflict.* New York: W.W. Norton.

Schwarz, Adam. 1994. *A Nation in Waiting: Indonesia in the 1990s.* Boulder, Colo.: Westview Press.

Taylor, John G. 1999. *East Timor: The Price of Freedom. Politics in Contemporary Asia.* London and New York: Zed Books.

U.S. Department of State. 1997. "Indonesia Report on Human Rights Practices for 1996." Bureau of Democracy, Human Rights and Labor. (January 30).

van Dijk, C. 1981. *Rebellion Under the Banner of Islam: The Darul Islam in Indonesia.* The Hague: Martinus Nijhoff.

10

Democracy, Nationalism, and Ethnic Identity: The Philippines and East Timor Compared

David Wurfel

It is our purpose here to compare two countries in Southeast Asia so disparate in size and recent history that they are rarely regarded as comparable. Yet we will also find surprising similarities, which will help us explore the connections between ethnic and religious makeup, national identity, and democracy. For the Philippines the question is: What has made possible the modest success with democracy despite a multiethnic society? For East Timor we are curious about the degree to which similarities with the Philippines are likely to produce similar political outcomes. This chapter asserts, using these two examples, that ethnic conflict occurs in authoritarian, democratizing, and democratic polities, and that democracy is compatible with interethnic harmony in some circumstances. It identifies as crucial variables shaping the strength and ethnic inclusiveness of national identity under democratic and democratizing regimes: "balanced diversity," the strength of the national identity to emerge during colonialism, and postcolonial religious, political, social, and economic institutions that cross ethnic lines.

The differences between the Philippines, today a state of about 80 million people, and East Timor, with less than one million, are obvious. The geographic contrast is as great as the demographic: the Philippines has more than 300,000 square kilometers and East Timor fewer than 15,000. East Timor is only half of one of the smaller islands in the Indonesian chain, while there are more than 7,000 islands in the Philippine archipelago.

Historically the Filipinos were the first people in Southeast Asia to throw off colonialism—if in the first instance only temporarily—and the Timorese were the last. The level of development in the two countries is also sharply different. Whereas literacy in the Philippines is reported at more than 90 percent, in East Timor it is probably less than 30 percent. The per capita GDP in the Philippines is more than five times that of East Timor, where unemployment, at least in the towns, has hovered at about 80 percent for the first few years since Indonesian withdrawal. Whereas agriculture in the Philippines contributes less than one quarter of the GDP, for East Timor it is the overwhelming majority (World Bank 1998: 181). Altogether, East Timor's society is more traditional than that of the Philippines.

National identity has also emerged in East Timor much more rapidly than it did in the Philippines. The process began in the Philippines in the 1870s and is still evolving today; ever since Rizal the intelligentsia have had an important role in "imagining" the nation. In East Timor, however, talk of an East Timor "nation" only started in the 1970s, as some of the educated elite began to return from abroad. From the time of the Indonesian invasion, however, nation formation was dramatic and intense and involved the local elite in only a relatively minor role, unlike cases cited by Anderson (1991). The sense of national identity was born of the shared suffering by all the people; one-third of them perished. For those who were not fighting the Indonesians in the jungles, the daily insults and oppression meted out by the Indonesian overlords—who consistently called the local residents, not by their ethnic categories, but "East Timorese"—consolidated that identity. These differences, demographic, geographic, economic, and historical, are not insignificant when trying to understand the respective polities.

Yet the similarities between these two very unequal entities, while less well known, may be more important for a political comparison. The first and longest colonial regime in both was Iberian. Thus—though the causal link in East Timor is actually quite complex—both are today dominantly Catholic countries; the figure of 85 percent of the population is most often used in both places. Much more recently in East Timor, Christianity displaced, or at least overlaid, animist beliefs and practices. It helped form a relatively cohesive multiethnic elite. Though the historical role of the church has been quite different in the two during the twentieth century, as we shall note later, the religious affinity has been recognized by both sides in the last few years, leading to closer civil society contacts between East Timor and the Philippines than East Timor has with any other Southeast Asian country. Moreover, Catholicism played an important role in the democratization of both.

The avoidance of violence in interethnic relations—with the exception of Moro-Christian conflict and the much more limited fighting in the Cordilleras (Northern Luzon mountains)[1]—was also, of course, a result of the fact that the Filipino elite was first heavily Hispanicized, then even more intensely Americanized, just as the East Timorese were brought together by the Portuguese and Indonesian colonial impact. Common educational experiences, first Catholic then later also secular, contributed powerfully to elite cohesion, also a prerequisite of democracy.

The two societies are also heavily influenced by the values and relationships of patrimonialism, though the intrusion of bureaucracy and the rule of law today has been sufficient to earn the overall societal label of "neo-patrimonial" for the Philippines, and now probably also for East Timor (Wurfel 1988: 153) (the differences of degree within that category will be explored later). Patronage networks interlace ethnic identity and tend to dilute it by abetting a tendency to factionalism, as Brown also points out in this volume. Some intraethnic factions discover beneficial alliances with other factions outside the ethnic group. In both countries local patrons have needed to bargain with larger patrons elsewhere. On the eve of independence, both peoples chose democracy, which strengthened the bargaining position of clients and local patrons vis-à-vis central patrons. So democracy in both societies has been and will be infused with patron–client networks, a sign of an incomplete democracy. It survives in conditions of great inequality, where the poor and weak find little or no protection in the rule of law or from the actions of an honest and independent bureaucracy. For the weak client, patronage serves as the substitute source of security, but itself constitutes an obstacle to progressive change.

It is also probable that the culture of bargaining in the Philippines, which was essential for the maintenance of patronage networks based on calculations of mutual benefit, contributed to the avoidance of violence in interethnic relations. For instance, it had been agreed that the members of the pre-1935 Senate would be elected by regions—some of which were ethnically homogenous—to ensure adequate representation for each. Party tickets for president and vice president were balanced between north and south. After 1946 in elections for the Senate from a national constituency, representation of each region on the ticket was the first principle for both major parties. Patronage networks encourage interethnic and interlinguistic bargaining in East Timor as well.

What is probably the most important similarity to note in the context of this book is the fact that in neither society is there a "majority culture" defined in ethnic terms. The Philippines is the only country in Southeast Asia having prolonged experience with democracy—albeit with the Marcos interruption—that also has a multiplicity of ethnic groups. There are more than eighty-seven distinguishable languages. This very multiplicity, and the fact that no one group has more than 25 percent of the population, has been crucial in the ability of Filipinos to develop a supraethnic national identity. East Timor, despite its small size, has more than fifteen distinct ethnolinguistic groups, representing two different language families, Austronesian and Papuan. Four languages cover most of the territory, but data on the number of speakers do not seem to be available (Wurm and Hattori 1981: Map 40).

Some analysts have argued that statewide ethnoreligious homogeneity is essential for democratic stability (earlier it was said to be essential even for nationhood). It has certainly facilitated nation-building in Thailand and contributed to the rapid growth of Thai democracy in the last generation. But if the "ethnic arithmetic" is diverse and balanced—what we might call "balanced diversity," with no one group assuming the right to control—a supraethnic national identity can and does emerge. The consequences for democracy may even be more beneficial than in the case of ethnic homogeneity because a culture of interethnic, then intergroup, bargaining is encouraged.

Also helpful for national unity in the Philippines was the fact that the largest ethnic group was not located around the capital. This is in contrast with Indonesia, where the Javanese, while little more than 40 percent of the population, were at the center and thus believed that they had the right to dominate—and had done so in earlier historical periods. They constituted the "majority culture," even without a numerical majority. In fact, the Javanese have been nearly as confident about their destiny to rule as have the ethnic Burmese in Burma (Myanmar), who constitute around 70 percent of the population.

In early 1947, Aung San, the widely trusted national leader of Burma, had made a deal with the ethnic minorities (Tin Maung Maung Than 1997: 172).[2] It was actually a rather awkward deal, with "self-governing" states for some minorities and not others. When Aung San was assassinated, just prior to the January 1948 independence, the glue of trust dissolved, and ethnic rebellions soon broke out. Minorities have been repressed by the military for decades in the name of "national unity." The ethnic Burmese have remained unwilling to relinquish tight control over minority peoples; they also believe it is their right to impose their language and religion. This is a major obstacle to democracy even within the "majority culture."

Another configuration of "ethnic arithmetic" is found in Malaysia, where "Malays" (broadly defined) constitute a narrow majority, followed by the Chinese and the Indians. Any tendency of the Malays to exercise unwanted control over the immigrant groups, which are geographically scattered, is slowed by the economic importance of the Chinese; without their capital and entrepreneurial skills the economy would founder. So a consociational policy has been followed, with the ethnic elites working out mutually acceptable political arrangements. Within Southeast Asia only Malaysia has an ethnic mix that would make this possible. And it does not always work; sometimes Malay rule has been oppressive, as Judith Nagata's chapter discusses. But it has certainly avoided the tragedy of interethnic warfare experienced by Burma or Sri Lanka. In the latter case the minority Tamils are for the most part geographically isolated and do not have the economic clout of the Malaysian Chinese.

MOROS

To be sure, the Philippines has had to deal with an ethnic rebellion in the Muslim portions of Mindanao and in Sulu off and on for thirty years. However, these struggles have had little impact on the nature of the central regime, which has been both authoritarian and democratic in this period. Muslims were on the geographical, cultural, and thus political periphery of the state, demonstrating that democratization can take place alongside ethnonationalist rebellion in such circumstances. The Moros (a term first used by Spaniards), a religious minority encompassing three major ethnic groups as well as smaller ones, had never been fully subdued by the Spaniards. Only in the American period did they begin to be integrated into the national society. By the 1950s many in the Moro elite were fully participant in patronage politics, even at the national level, but this was disrupted by the declaration of martial law in 1973. In the meantime Muslim religious education had grown remarkably (McKenna 1998). From the Moro viewpoint, there was a "majority Filipino culture"—a Catholic one, though ethnically diverse—and it was a real threat. The rebellion continues to simmer because the economic and cultural threat is still formidable, because rebels get some external support, and because the military, ever since the Marcos era, is arrogant, abusive, and ineffective—all at once—creating more enemies than it subdues (Wurfel 1985). The Manila elite cannot reach a consensus either on basic policy reforms to undermine the rebellion or on a massive military campaign to crush it (as if that were possible). Conciliatory gestures by President Macapagal-Arroyo, though encouraging, have been inconsistent and thus probably not adequate.

A comparison between the Moro struggle for independence and that in East Timor is instructive. Even though it diverges somewhat from the theme of this chapter, this comparison demonstrates that ethnonationalist rebellion can and does occur under authoritarian and democratizing, as well as democratic, regimes and the regime type alone cannot explain its incidence. The first lesson is that massive and ruthless military might cannot subdue a nationalist rebellion (President Estrada never had at his command the military capacity that Suharto did, but still imagined in 2000 that he could "crush" the rebels). Neither can an assimilationist policy succeed. In East Timor its imposition merely caused a strengthening of Catholicism as a reaction and pushed church leaders as well as guerilla fighters to embody nationalist goals. In Mindanao and Sulu the threat of assimilation stimulated a Muslim revival—now heavily fundamentalist.

In both the East Timorese and Moro resistances the fear of cultural genocide, made credible by a policy of assimilation from the center, was a major factor motivating continued struggle. In Mindanao and Sulu a policy of assimilation alternated from time to time with offers of, and feeble attempts to

implement, autonomy both by authoritarian and democratizing governments. Other than the elites and their clients who cooperated in the "autonomy charade," there was little or no benefit to Moros. The failure of real autonomy merely reinvigorated the demand for Moro independence, as under
the present leadership of the MILF (Moro Islamic Liberation Front). In East
Timor when the offer of autonomy finally came in 1999, it was too late; Timorese could not trust the Indonesian government. Though the nationalist
leadership in East Timor had earlier considered the possibility of autonomy
during a transitional period, by 1999 they had been given the hope of an internationally supervised referendum on self-determination and, thus, the
possibility of independence. Autonomy was much less attractive.

There were two other important differences between the two areas, firstly
in the "ethnic arithmetic." In East Timor there were more than fourteen different linguistic groups, none large enough to claim hegemony and each
splintered by the sway of more than one *liurai*, a chieftain or "king." The
half-island-wide nationalist leadership was not riven on ethnic lines. In Mindanao and Sulu, while the Muslim population was also divided by a variety
of languages, major and minor, three linguistic groups were sufficiently
large, politically well-organized, and historically self-conscious to imagine
that they could lead all Moros. In fact, the factions within each Moro nationalist grouping and differences between each organization were most often
explainable in terms of Tausug, Maranao, and Maguindanao rivalries. This
facilitated manipulation of Moro elites from Manila. The ethnic boundary between Moros and Christians was, nevertheless, very important, reinforced by
religious identity.

Secondly, the demographic realities in the two areas were quite different.
Indonesian migration to East Timor was overwhelmingly urban, to take up
jobs in commerce and government. It was also fairly recent, mostly since the
1980s. For most Indonesians within East Timor, "home" was another
province. Thus the political strength of ordinary Indonesian *colons*—to use
an Algerian term—was not itself a major obstacle to genuine autonomy (in
fact, most of them fled before the referendum in August 1999). Indonesian
nationalist pride, especially within the military, was a more important reason, as were the economic interests of the Jakarta elite. All reinforced the fear
of Indonesian breakup if the Timorese "lynch pin" were removed.

The migration of Christian Filipinos to Moro areas, however, had been going on for nearly a century. It occurred both as a direct result of government
policy and without any government assistance, simply because of land
hunger in other regions of the Philippines. A very large portion of the migration was by farmers taking over Moro land, most often illegally. The
largest Muslim province before the war, Cotabato, had a non-Muslim majority already by 1948. The province of Lanao, which had a two-to-one Muslim
majority in 1948, was split in two in the 1950s, with one of the resulting

provinces becoming overwhelmingly Christian (Gowing 1980). In the 1960s and 1970s more and more previously Muslim municipalities elected Christian mayors. Thus, little by little the area where Moro independence or autonomy could be fairly or effectively asserted was shrinking. Muslim fear of demographic and, thus, cultural genocide intensified, just as successive Manila governments, authoritarian, democratizing, and democratic alike, have found it more and more difficult to gain national political support for genuine Moro autonomy. The resistance of Christian Filipinos in Mindanao to Moro independence grew even stronger. The ingredients of a stalemate were evident, and factors that could break it are not at all evident.

In sum, religion has played an important role in both areas in forming national identity, though the cultural and historical depth of Muslim identity in Mindanao and Sulu was deeper than in Catholic East Timor. And, because military repression of East Timor was much more severe, the Indonesian government did not have the options for manipulating local elites that Manila did. The outcome of the struggle in East Timor was also significantly influenced by the quality of international pressure, a reaction partly to the severity of the repression. In the Philippines, on the other hand, while a few Muslim countries aided the rebels, the effectiveness of the Organization of the Islamic Conference in exerting pressure on the Philippine government was limited by the fact that Indonesia, the largest and closest Muslim country, was reluctant to see too much international intervention on behalf of separatist rebels for fear that it would set a precedent for Aceh.

The similarities between the Philippines and East Timor that we have highlighted—the presence of "balanced diversity" instead of a majority (nonreligious) ethnic culture; the emergence of elite cohesion fostered by common educational experiences and Catholicism; and the prevalence of patronage networks fostering a culture of bargaining across ethnic lines—all help prevent ethnic conflict, at least of a nonreligious nature. They thus provide some grounding for democracy. Timor is at a much earlier stage of modernization, which carries its own problems. Nevertheless, on balance, East Timor would seem to be launching its ship of state with more favorable conditions for democratic stability than those in Indonesia today. Timorese conditions are in some ways more similar to those in the Philippines a century ago.

Having introduced the major similarities and differences between the two countries, and the general conclusions that might be drawn from them, let us next describe in more detail the parallel developments in the two polities during two periods: (1) colonialism, Iberian in the first stage, and either American or Indonesian in the second; and then (2) independence and the preparation for it. This will preface a fuller elaboration of the impact of these developments on democratization in the Philippines and prospects for it in East Timor, particularly in light of ethnic diversity.

THE COLONIAL ERA

The Philippines

While both Spain and Portugal ruled their Southeast Asian colonies for more than 300 years, Spanish rule was much more direct. In its origins it was also more church-centered. Thus though native animism was the belief system of the great majority of East Timorese until the mid-twentieth century, that stage had already been passed by the eighteenth century in the Philippines, where the church expended tremendous effort to proselytize and then participate in colonial rule. Catholicism thus played an early role in the formation of Filipino national identity.

On the other hand, the manipulation of traditional elites was the mechanism for Portuguese dominance until after 1912, when the colonial government crushed an extensive rebellion, which those elites had mounted. In the Philippines such indirect rule ended in most areas in the seventeenth century. Traditional elites there had either been eliminated or co-opted into a system of direct Spanish administration. Already by the 1870s the wealthier and more ambitious families in the new multiethnic elite (especially Chinese *mestizos*) were sending their sons to Manila and to Europe, especially Spain, for higher education.

The result of these differences was that nationalism, first voiced as a desire for equality with Spaniards, burst forth in the Philippines in the 1880s clothed in sophisticated European language, nearly one hundred years before the same development in East Timor. While the early nationalist movement was disproportionately Tagalog, in the vicinity of Manila where the political and economic impact of Spanish rule was the greatest, by 1898 it also had its adherents among the elites of most major ethnic groups. So, when the Revolution was launched near Manila, there were also some uprisings in other provinces (Constantino 1975: 212ff).[3] Where it could be linked to agrarian unrest, the nationalist movement also had a mass base, an element repeated in East Timor in 1975.

The Revolution in Cebu has been carefully chronicled by Resil Mojares (1999). He found that, as in Luzon, the war against Spaniards, then Americans, was fought for diverse reasons by various segments of society. Foot soldiers were often more motivated by religious imagery or social discontent than by nationalist aspirations. But the fact remains that the uprising in Cebu in April 1898 was instigated by the *Katipunan*—which had triggered the first uprising near Manila—and organized by agents from Luzon. Until his capture in 1901, the leading Cebu rebel acted in the name of the Philippine Republic headed in Luzon by Emilio Aguinaldo, within the framework of his policies and, when possible, under his command. Those who fought for independence had their commitment strengthened by Spanish brutality in

1898 and by bloody American repression later. Ethnic tensions did sometimes erupt between Tagalogs in Luzon and those Cebuanos who joined in the struggle. However, given the paucity of their common experiences before 1898 and the difficulties of communications between them at the time, what is more notable is the degree of their cooperation in the nationalist cause.

Yet the Filipino elite, whether in Luzon or Cebu, which briefly rallied to the anticolonial cause when revolutionary chances seemed good, was quickly co-opted by the Americans when the nationalist army was routed. After 1902 American rule offered social stability and local self-government, amidst talk of eventual independence. Local elites were soon given full control over municipal government. By 1907 the election of representatives to a national legislature under the banner of specifically nationalist parties—within the context of patronage politics—helped to create a moderate, accommodationist nationalism. Teaching about Jose Rizal was promoted in the American-run public schools, where English became the language of instruction.

Pardo de Tavera, a leading member of the elite who quite successfully survived the transition from Spanish to American colonialism, commented in 1928, "Each day tribal differences are being erased; and by means of facilities in communication, by our system of education . . . and principally by the extension of the Spanish language and now of the English, we have seen how local differences have passed away . . . how the idea of nation is gaining ground" (Abueva 1998: 169).

When a new constitution was framed in 1935 for the Philippine Commonwealth, Tagalog was voted "the national language," even though the working language of government, education, and business remained English. Fortunately for nation-building, that "national language" was not pushed hard enough to produce a strong hostile reaction from non-Tagalog regions. Its usage expanded because Manila was the center of commerce and of journalism. Even more important was the fact that the Tagalog movie industry dominated the Philippine screen. It was already becoming a lingua franca before the enforcement of the use of Tagalog in public schools after independence.

The common experience of American administration (which greatly expanded education), the nationalist rhetoric of politicians—in full flight at election time, helping to keep alive, at least dimly, memory of the Revolution—and, third, the constant growth of interisland trade permitted the gradual strengthening of a Filipino national identity in the American period. However, because most Filipinos did not regard themselves as anti-American, especially after fighting alongside Americans against the Japanese, by the time of formal independence in 1946 many Asian neighbors

regarded Filipino nationalism as "weak." In fact, many Filipinos were themselves conscious of this perception. Said one writer, "Unlike the Indonesians
and the Vietnamese, we Filipinos did not regain our independence on the
battlefield, which would have given us a strong sense of nationhood. Instead
our independence was restored almost on a silver platter. . . ." (quoted in
Abueva 1998: 227).

East Timor

In comparison, the period of anticolonial nationalism in East Timor was
brief—a few years under the Portuguese and twenty-four years against Indonesia—and intense. However, the beginnings of Timorese nationalism
were not so different from those in the Philippines and overlay ethnic divisions every bit as numerous. There was no university in Dili, so by the 1960s
the sons of the elite began to go abroad, often to Portugal. Those who went
to Portuguese colonies in Africa, either exiled or by choice, got a particularly
strong dose of anticolonial nationalism, with a large portion of socialism
mixed in (Joliffe 1978: 56ff). However, the vigilance of the Portuguese political police was such that when they returned home nothing could be said or
written publicly about their nationalist aspirations.

Nevertheless, when the dictatorship was overthrown in Portugal in
April 1974, so much nationalist political activity boiled to the surface so
quickly that it was obvious that the underground had been active. Three
major political parties were formed: the *União Democrática Timorense*
(UDT) in early May 1974 and, less than two weeks later, the Social Democratic Union (known as FRETILIN). Both supported independence. Some
of the founders of both parties were in the 2001 Dili cabinet. The third
party was the Indonesian-backed APODETI (*Associação Popular
Democrática Timorense*), already committed to integration with Indonesia. Most leaders of both UDT and FRETILIN were Catholics. However,
while the anti-Communist UDT retained close links with the Church hierarchy, the younger FRETILIN leaders were at odds with the Church as an
arm of the Portuguese administration, even though several had trained for
the priesthood (Joliffe 1978: 70). Similarly, as Rizal and the leaders of the
1898 Revolution had opposed the Spanish church in the Philippines. Notably, then, East Timorese parties expressed ideological rather than ethnic
divisions.

The newly progressive Portuguese government launched a decolonializa-
tion process, which was well under way by the end of 1974. At the same time
FRETILIN organized agricultural cooperatives and literacy programs using
Tetum (the most widely used indigenous language in villages around the
country). Agreement was reached on formation of a transitional government
in October 1975. Under increasing threat from Indonesia, UDT and FRETILIN

formed a coalition to work toward independence. Early 1975 was a time of hope (Joliffe 1978: 109).

But friction between UDT and FRETILIN was growing, sometimes triggering street fights. "Communist" charges against FRETILIN by UDT and the church multiplied—with Indonesian backup, even inspiration. In May UDT withdrew from the coalition. Then, in August, after some of their officers had visited Jakarta, they launched a coup against the Portuguese colonial regime. Many of FRETILIN's local leaders were killed. Some Portuguese troops sided with UDT. But within days FRETILIN regained strength and by August 19 launched a counter-coup, also gaining the support of elements in the colonial army. By September they were in control of almost all the half-island. The Portuguese civil servants fled, and FRETILIN took over the administration.

In the next three months, though faced by increasing Indonesian threats and incursions, FRETILIN won widespread support from the population and continued to build agricultural cooperatives and village schools. There was a functioning administration in some ways comparable to parts of the Philippines in 1898. But the Indonesian invasion of border areas and, finally, the November 27 capture of Atabae, on the road to Dili, was a turning point. In order to try to get the international attention that it had found so difficult to secure, the FRETILIN regime declared independence the next day. On December 8 the long-feared event happened: the Indonesian army launched a full-scale attack, including the dropping of paratroopers on Dili (Taylor 1999: 62–65). The major powers looked the other way. After bitter fighting with heavy casualties, colonialism was reimposed, though it took years for the Indonesian National Army (TNI) to control most of the countryside.

In 1974–1975 the role of an educated elite "imagining East Timor" had been quite important. The dominant party helped spread its national vision to the countryside with a mass literacy program. Through the Dili media and by policy decisions, FRETILIN leaders were also able to disseminate their concept of economic nationalism, which was clearly distinct from the policies of the UDT. But in the subsequent twenty-four years of Indonesian military oppression, it was the common experience of that oppression, and the people's reaction thereto, that formed a nation in a crucible of fire. Elite images, despite moving rhetoric, were insignificant in comparison to the fact that virtually every citizen had had a family member killed by the TNI. Even the limited good done by the Indonesian occupation, especially the expansion of the school system, deepened the formation of a nation. Though the introduction of *Bahasa Indonesia* gave Timorese another common language, its forcible imposition, along with the doctrine of *Pancasila*, intensified student opposition to the occupying power.

Using time-honored, scorched-earth tactics, the Indonesian military burned villages and crops and relocated farmers to virtual concentration camps along roads, trying to destroy traditional social structures that might form the basis of opposition. One third of the population died. By a cruel twist of fate this Indonesian brutality was largely responsible for creating a nation out of a mélange of linguistic and tribal groups, a process barely begun by the nationalist elite in 1975. Mass movements of population, whether under TNI orders or under FRETILIN leadership escaping the TNI by going deeper into the mountains, contributed immensely to the formation of a national identity, atop surviving traditional values and social networks. The tactical necessity for the guerillas to find a means of communication among their units that was generally unintelligible to the TNI also contributed to the process. For that means was Tetum, used in the mountains by the guerillas and in the towns more and more by the Catholic Church.

A segment of the elite that made a substantial shift toward assisting nation formation in this period was the church hierarchy. As we noted, the church had been widely viewed, even by devout Catholics, as an arm of Portuguese colonialism. In fact, in 1975 the Portuguese bishop was taking a stronger stand against FRETILIN than some of the progressive military officers representing Lisbon. But even the conservative Dom José Joaquim Ribeiro could not tolerate the slaughter of innocent civilians going on around him, so in 1977 requested retirement (Taylor 1999: 152ff). His assistant, Martinho da Costa Lopes, was named to replace him. Costa Lopes, formerly a member of the National Assembly in Lisbon, was the first Timorese—though obviously a fully assimilated one—to hold this position. Receiving regular reports from his priests in the countryside gave him a good understanding about the course of the war. At first he tried dialog with the Indonesian commanders. When this failed he turned to public criticism.

Costa Lopes became sufficiently successful as a spokesman for the Timorese people that Indonesian pressure on the Vatican brought the bishop's forced "early retirement" in 1983 (see Lennox 2000). He was replaced by a young Timorese priest, Carlos Belo, who had spent thirteen years in Portugal and Rome. Many of the Timorese clergy, presuming he would be an Indonesian tool, boycotted his inauguration. But the Indonesian military was soon disappointed. Within five months of arriving Bishop Belo protested vehemently against Indonesian violence. His ongoing reports on the details of TNI massacres produced a sympathetic response from the Portuguese hierarchy, but alienated the Indonesian Catholic leadership. In February 1989 Belo wrote to the UN Secretary General calling for a referendum on independence. Meanwhile priests were frequently beaten and churches entered by the military to arrest parishioners. Major Prabowo, President Suharto's son-in-law and an officer active in East Timor, warned, "The church . . . threatens East Timor's integration with Indonesia. The people must turn against it" (Taylor 1999: 157). But the Indonesian tactics were clearly counterproductive.

As John Taylor (1999) points out, "[The Church's] opposition to the forcible Indonesian annexation marked the culmination of the process of growing institutional rejection" throughout East Timorese society. He notes that, "the differentiated social structure of the pre-invasion period," marked by cleavages between urban and rural, rich and poor, assimilated and indigenous, and distinct linguistic groups, "converged politically and ideologically because of the military occupation." The Church benefited from its nation-building role: the percentage of East Timorese who were Church members more than doubled in the years of Indonesian occupation. Prabowo was right, but, as a result of his regime's policies, the people turned even more toward the Catholic Church. Ironically, there was a period in the 1980s when the Indonesians had decided, "If you can't lick 'em, join 'em," and built, at government expense, a number of large new churches, hoping to win over the priesthood. It was to no avail. TNI slaughter of innocent civilians in the countryside continued.

Though FRETILIN and the church were fierce competitors in 1975, divided by charges of "communist" on one side and "colonialist" on the other, the struggle against the Indonesian occupation brought them together, just as it healed the bitter rift between FRETILIN and its political rival, UDT. Such reconciliations did not happen automatically, however, but were in part a product of enlightened leadership with an inclusive view of the nation, especially that of the charismatic Xanana Gusmao. By 1981 he had become president of both FRETILIN and its guerilla arm, FALANTIL. Soon afterward he took the lead in the creation of a broader nationalist coalition, *Conselho Nacional de Resistência Revolucionária* (CNRR), which brought segments of UDT under its umbrella. FALANTIL too was widened to include UDT elements.

Though he had made overtures to the church even earlier, in May 1986, after Bishop Belo had already displayed his nationalist mettle, Gusmao wrote a long letter to East Timorese Catholic youth, revealing considerable movement since the heady days of FRETILIN Marxism in the late 1970s. Said Gusmao (2000: 123ff), himself an ex-seminarian, "The Church in East Timor . . . has been the moral support in the struggle of our people, a precious helping hand that has eased the pain of our people during their resistance to the vile and cowardly Indonesian aggression. . . . " He added, "A Church like this is a church of and for the people!" He also noted the similarity in the role of the church in bringing the overthrow of Ferdinand Marcos in the Philippines. But he concluded with another important point, helping to maintain unity along another dimension: "FRETILIN is a movement of liberation in which a militancy of Christians, as well as non-Christians, co-exists."

Clearly to a much greater degree than in the Philippines, it was the nationalist struggle itself, against terrible odds, that formed an East Timorese nation. Benedict Anderson admitted that his emphasis, in earlier writing on nationalism, on the confluence of the spread of capitalism and printing was not appropriate for East Timor (Anderson 1993). But he could not bring himself to see the overwhelming importance of the experience of struggle in shaping identities.

THE POSTCOLONIAL ERA

The Philippines

There are those who doubt if colonialism has really passed in either country. In the Philippines, as long as the presence of U.S. military bases dominated the country's external relations, a type of neocolonialism persisted (neocolonial attitudes helped facilitate the renewed U.S. military role after September 11, 2001). Though the American economic presence is still powerful, it is balanced by the cooperative/competitive role of Japan (Wurfel 1988: 197–201). The American cultural hangover from which Filipinos have not yet recovered is now the primary, and still very noticeable, colonial residue.

A number of nationalizing tendencies continued, for example, the spread of Tagalog, or Filipino, even to the point of being used in university classes and state addresses as well as pervading the media. Consciousness of national identity was intensified by the campaign against U.S. bases in the 1980s, culminating in the Senate's rejection in 1991 of a treaty extending their tenure. Most important to remember is that there has been no revival of ethnic identity among the various Christianized linguistic groups since the transition to independence, or since the restoration of democracy in 1986. This is a tribute to the cultural cohesion of the elite and a political system that did not impose a "majority culture," except in the view of the Moros.

To be sure, Muslim unrest in the south spread under authoritarian rule in the 1970s, as already noted. However, it has not been extinguished since the fall of Marcos. Even though a series of negotiations with the Moro National Liberation Front finally produced a second ceasefire in the early 1990s (the first, only temporary, was in 1976) and the co-optation of its leaders, true autonomy was not granted. Thus a new, more militant group emerged to continue the armed struggle. Meanwhile Christian incursions on Muslim land and culture continued. Because it does not spawn other separatist movements in other parts of the country, Filipinos imagine that they can "afford" to neglect finding a solution to the Moro rebellion. The mirage of normality as viewed from Manila is sustained in part by the fact that election to national offices continues in Muslim areas, confirming Filipino co-optation of a segment of the Moro elite into the majority vision of a democratic nation.

In the Philippines more generally, one could argue that the electoral system based on patronage networks preempted any tendency toward regional linguistic chauvinism. Patronage was indeed a potent characteristic of the system. Even the emergence of the Marcos dictatorship did not eliminate, but only centralized it. In the post-Marcos democratic transition patronage was again decentralized. One small step toward undermining the patrimonial impact—and strengthening the nationalizing one—was taken in the adoption of the 1987 Constitution, which called for 20 percent of the House of Representatives to be elected by the party-list, or proportional representation, system. But Congress, unfamiliar with it and a bit worried that it might actually be able to achieve its intended goal—as members were already immersed in patronage politics—did not pass implementing legislation until ten years later, legislation that has caused as many problems as it solved (Wurfel 1997). So the party-list election in 1998 was poorly carried out. Even so, it brought into the House of Representatives some new blood with a national perspective, more attentive to policy issues and the interests of the ordinary Filipino. After the May 2001 election an even larger number of reformist and, in a few cases, revolutionary faces appeared in the House. They are able to ignore local and emphasize national, supraethnic issues to a degree impossible for those elected from single member districts.

During the martial law period, the Marcos dictatorship sparked a revival of the role the Catholic Church in the formation of national identity that had not been seen for centuries. As in a number of other authoritarian countries—including East Timor under Indonesian occupation—when secular political opposition was crushed, religious institutions took on more political roles. Under the leadership of Cardinal Sin in the mid-1980s the church not only provided crucial direction to the anti-Marcos movement at the elite level, but opportunities for mobilizing mass support. This latter function was much like what was beginning to go on in East Timor at the same time. But within a few years after the return of free elections in the Philippines, the church's leadership had been dissipated by the many pressures of patronage politics, and it resumed the relatively minor role it had had before the 1970s.

East Timor

Though East Timor was liberated from Indonesian colonialism with the arrival of the International Force for East Timor (INTERFET) in September 1999, and the takeover of civil administration by the United Nations Transitional Administration for East Timor (UNTAET) a month later, the UN itself operated a kind of colonialism in the eyes of many East Timorese. UN employees lived apart from the local people, were often haughty in their dealings with them, and enjoyed a life style far above that of the local economy. In the interim, before East Timor gained juridical independence in 2002, political institutions were formed that will largely determine the characteristics of an independent East Timor, often with little consultation with East Timorese. However, one advantage of "UN neocolonialism" is that its negative stimulus may have helped sustain Timorese national consciousness and discourage ethnic distinctions.

Crucial elements of this interim regime were both beneficial and detrimental to stable democracy. The most obvious factor was negative: the UN's very slow pace in reconstructing the devastated economy. With urban unemployment remaining near 80 percent, the potential for social conflict, and its exploitation by every form of chauvinism, continued. In fact, gang fights in Dili and the second largest city, Baucau, multiplied in early 2001.

The second negative factor, which cannot be blamed on the UN, is the psychological letdown after a long struggle, the full consequences of which are not yet known. A whole generation of East Timorese put private gain and family happiness on hold for the sake of national resistance. A revival of personal priorities is almost inevitable. It has, for instance, become a major factor in the national psyche and behavior patterns of the Vietnamese since their series of wars against the French, the Americans, the Chinese, and the Cambodians ended in 1990. One saw the same phenomena in the Philippines among those who emerged from the underground struggle against Marcos in the late 1980s.

Alongside personal priorities it is possible to note a revival of indigenous cultures and the patrimonialism that pervades them (this is not diluted as much by education, urbanization, or NGO activism as in the Philippines). While we have said that patronage networks may cross-cut ethnic identities, it is not yet clear whether a part of the traditionalist revival, which certainly includes a reassertion of the community leadership of the *liurai*, will also strengthen first-language identity. It was overridden by an East Timorese identity for more than two decades of struggle and has even now been given little positive institutional reinforcement.

The positive indicators for East Timor's future as a democracy relatively free of ethnicized conflict are to be found in the institutions and leadership, which are now emerging. Bishop Belo, who recently resigned, was more restricted in his political role by the emergence of competition from civil society and political parties. However, the Church remains the dominant national institution outside government and a major force for integration across ethnolinguistic lines.

Xanana Gusmao, who for a while headed the National Council (an appointive body representing all segments of East Timor's society, which advised UNTAET), remains a strong voice for national as opposed to ethnically particular priorities and against corruption, though not all his friends are above reproach. He helped speed up the planning for independence—though his personal decision-making style is not always democratic. He has championed reconciliation with Indonesia and its East Timorese friends.

Gusmao endorsed what appears to have been the idea of European experts in UNTAET: a constituent assembly/legislature elected primarily from a nation-wide constituency through proportional representation. In fact, seventy-five out of eighty-eight seats were chosen in this way on 30 August 2001, with only thirteen elected from each of the administrative districts. Sixteen political parties presented lists of party candidates for the national constituency.[4] In order to win, parties had to present linguistically balanced tickets. Insofar as the political parties that gradually emerge are differentiated on ideology and policy, this system will weaken patronage politics as well as linguistic identities. The initial winner was clearly FRETILIN, which dominated the re-sistance movement for many years. It won 57 percent of the votes and 62.5 percent of the seats. It also won seats in all but one of the districts, indicat-ing that its support was well distributed geographically, and thus linguisti-cally, and that it would be most unlikely to favor any particular linguistic group.[5] Nowhere else in Southeast Asia has a dominantly proportional rep-resentation electoral system been introduced. Hopefully, it will be hailed as a bold move for national unity. It was particularly appropriate to select in this way the body that drafted the nation's constitution, as it allowed ten smaller parties to be represented alongside the dominant FRETILIN.

Unfortunately, on one dimension Gusmao's leadership has been divi-sive—his backing of Portuguese as the "official language" and the language of education. Given that probably fewer than 5 percent of Timorese have a working knowledge of that language, and that almost all of these are in the older generation, the question has split the people of East Timor on genera-tional lines. High school and university students, who have so far been edu-cated entirely in Indonesian, have been particularly vocal in opposing the in-troduction of Portuguese. Even judges have been resistant to the idea. The vice president of the Dili court has told the press that judges expected to con-tinue to use both Tetun and Indonesian for another fifteen years. He said, "The courts will not risk using a language that is not understood."[6] But a pri-marily generational cleavage that cross-cuts ethnicity is hardly a threat to the most vulnerable dimension of national unity.

There was also a negative side to the rapidity with which independence preparations moved. Administrative institutions after independence were not ready to handle the tasks they faced, made all the worse by the system-atic way in which the Indonesian army destroyed all types of records (the de-struction of land ownership and tax records may have been the most devas-tating). The establishment of a civil service was slow to begin. Departments and bureaus were handed over to the East Timorese, most of whom had no previous administrative experience, when the ink was hardly dry on the rel-evant regulations. To bring massive, but much needed, international funding for rehabilitation into this situation will be a formula tailor-made for wide-spread corruption, undermining the legitimacy of new national institutions.

Following the end of international aid will come a very substantial royalty from the Timor Gap oil field, exploited jointly with Australia, which is estimated at several billion dollars for East Timor over the next two decades.[7] This could soon result in annual revenue more than three or four times the present yearly budget. (The long-term returns would be much greater if Australia would agree to a maritime boundary consistent with precedents in international law.) Some analysts believe that this will be a greater challenge to the growth of stable democracy than will ethnic conflict, because of the widespread corruption that oil royalties may well engender (Ross 2001). East Timorese leaders are aware of the potential dangers and are talking about investing a large portion of oil and gas revenues in something like the Canadian province of Alberta's Heritage Fund. Whether this will really be a solution remains to be seen. Thus, while the prospects for ethnic separatism appearing in the midst of East Timorese democracy are slim, the other problems are sufficiently daunting to make any analyst very cautious about predictions.

CONCLUSION

While this book has recognized that ethnic conflict may emerge in both authoritarian and democratic contexts under certain circumstances, the East Timor/Philippine comparison emphasizes the potential by harmonious compatibility of ethnic diversity and democracy. This is true even when democracy is defined primarily in terms of free and competitive political institutions. When democracy has been "deepened," that is, extended to socioeconomic relationships as suggested by Rankin and Goonewardena, then the prospect of interethnic conflict, intermingled with class warfare, is even less.

The comparison that is our focus recognizes that there are three important conditions that must exist to permit democratic development amidst interethnic harmony: the proper "ethnic arithmetic," that is, "balanced diversity"; a colonial experience that creates a supraethnic national identity; and postindependence institutions, both governmental and nongovernmental, that strengthen that identity, or at least prevent its erosion by ethnic loyalties. Let us recapitulate the importance of those conditions.

Ethnic Balance

The percentage of the population that each ethnic group constitutes in a multiethnic society is a more important factor than much of the literature recognizes. Where one group is large and powerful enough to assume the right to dominate the others, and does so, the outcome is particularly damaging to interethnic harmony, whether under democratic or authoritarian auspices.

In the Philippines and East Timor, there are not only numerous ethnic groups, but also no one that constitutes more than about 25 percent of the population. And in neither country is there a history of a large grouping controlling nearby ethnicities. Thus to reach national decisions, the necessity exists for interethnic bargaining, a process compatible with democracy. In both cases the language of the capital region emerged to "national language" status, but was not imposed on nonnative speakers without a period of commercial and cultural diffusion that expanded the number of "national language" speakers on a largely voluntary basis. In the Philippines, Tagalog did not become the actual lingua franca until about a generation after independence, displacing English, which is still an "official language." According to President Gusmao, Portuguese will remain the "official language" in East Timor for at least another decade, while the use of Tetun expands—but what this means in practice remains to be seen.

Colonial Experience

Colonial rule created, as a reaction, supraethnic national identities within the boundaries of both polities. But the intensity and social levels of that identity varied widely. In the Philippines under Spain, self-identity as "Filipino" was largely limited to the elite, many of whom studied at European universities. During the American period the social basis of nationalism widened due to the rapid expansion of English education, in which there was some coverage of the history of Philippine nationalism, and the rise of specifically nationalist political parties. The brutality of the Japanese occupation spread it still further.

In East Timor under the Portuguese, as under Iberian rule in the Philippines, national identity was limited to a small elite. But the ferocity of Indonesian conquest and occupation, resisted under the leadership of young nationalists, quickly created an awareness of East Timorese identity in the countryside as well as in cities. The best evidence of the width and depth of that identity was in the referendum of 30 August 1999, when nearly all registered voters turned out at the polls and voted for independence, despite considerable coercion by the militias to stay at home and, moreover, even though many feared terrible violence would follow—as it did.

Institutions

Because identities can change over time (see Gorenburg 2000) and are significantly influenced by institutions, the nature of institutions, both governmental and nongovernmental, after independence is crucial. Without appropriate institutions the national identity that emerged from the independence struggle can be eroded. In both East Timor and the Philippines, religious, political, economic, and civil society institutions have served, or may serve, to consolidate a supraethnic national identity. The importance of religion can be seen in Mindanao, where a religious divide helped foster the emergence of a separate identity.

The most influential consolidator among political institutions in the Philippines has been the national constituency to elect the president and Senate, which has spawned national, not regional, political parties. In East Timor the August 2001 elections were dominated by the competition in nationwide constituencies for the Constituent Assembly, making it very difficult for any party with strength only in one linguistic region to win seats. Nor is there yet evidence that cleavages of political ideology reinforce those of ethnicity. In any case, an electoral system that requires parties to make interethnic alliances is likely to overcome any tendencies of this sort.

The significance of economic institutions (i.e., the accepted process for accumulating and distributing wealth) has long been recognized in the building of secessionist movements. For instance, if the territory of an ethnic minority is endowed with mineral wealth over which that minority has no control, a powerful motive for separation is apparent. But even before a secessionist movement has been formed, national/regional disputes over resources may be very contentious, as between Canada and Alberta. In the Philippines, oil is not a factor and mineral wealth is, fortunately, rather evenly distributed throughout the country. Even then, the centralization of revenue collection from mineral development causes center/periphery friction. But such friction is, except in Mindanao, not peculiar to an ethnically defined region. Land is also a basic resource, and particular peoples are tied by tradition to particular lands. The inability of the Moros to prevent Christian encroachment on their land is the root of the Moro rebellion. In matters of wealth distribution, the effectiveness of public administration in implementing the law honestly and fairly is crucial. The Philippine government in Mindanao failed particularly in regards to land law.

Economic institutions in East Timor are just now being formed, and those for controlling oil revenue are by far the most important. Fortunately the Timor Gap oil field, being undersea, is not located in any particular district, though related onshore facilities will be. Yet royalties will apparently accrue to the national government. Thus on these grounds there could be some friction. As noted, oil wealth may also breed corruption and, thus, undermine the legitimacy of the national government, as in Nigeria. Again the effectiveness of public institutions in responding to popular demands for fairness and proper legal procedures will be crucial.

Strong bureaucratic institutions, the legacy of British colonialism, have been said to constitute a potent constraint on ethnic conflict in India and

Malaysia. This is undoubtedly true. But neither East Timor nor the Philippines entered independence so blessed. In Dili it is only in the last two years that Timorese have begun to get experience in the higher civil service. Furthermore, civil service rules are still incomplete, and there is almost no experience in applying them. If strong bureaucratic capacity were an essential prerequisite for ethnic harmony and democratic development, then East Timor is a born loser. Of course, the Philippines was better off at independence. Yet the Philippine bureaucracy is itself much more corrupt and less effective than that in Malaysia. By 1946, in the former polity, there had already been a generation of patronage politics during which elected legislators brought civil servants under their control. Despite several waves of reformist verbiage since, no major change has taken place. An honest, independent bureaucracy may not be essential for a modicum of democratic development, but more and more Filipinos are now recognizing what an advantage it would be.

Civic associations in the Philippines—where the number per capita is the highest in Southeast Asia—are more important than bureaucracy in weaving a network of national identity. Despite the fact that many work at the local level, there are also many national federations. However, again, the Christian/Muslim divide in Mindanao prevented civil society from playing an integrating role there; in Moro society there are very few civic activities not linked to Muslim institutions. In East Timor, on the other hand, secular civic associations, suppressed in the Indonesian period, have emerged since 1998. Now mostly interethnic in character, they have become quite numerous, but may still be dwarfed by the extent and influence of traditional networks based on patrimonialism. As noted above, those networks, usually village-based, do not constitute a nationalizing force, but are more likely to fragment than consolidate ethnic groups, which extend over many villages.

Religious institutions do not contribute as much today in either country to the formation of national identity as they did earlier. However, since the dominant institution in each country is the Catholic Church, with highly centralized and well-articulated communication patterns, the contribution to national unity is still great. Furthermore, since in both countries the church has demonstrated that it is willing to become a channel of citizen protest if the regime becomes authoritarian, this religious institution is also beneficial to the preservation—or, if necessary, restoration—of democracy. In both countries, identity as a Catholic and even, simply, as a Christian is closely associated with national identity. Whereas among Moros religious identity is broader than ethnic, among Christians ethnic identity is a much weaker, subnational phenomenon.

In addition to the demographic, historical, social, institutional, and economic factors we have entered into the explanatory equation, one more cannot be ignored—leadership. This is hardly quantifiable, and thus unpopular in some circles. To be sure, it is a factor that has often been overemphasized, without sufficient analytical rigor, by traditional scholars. Nevertheless, it cannot be disregarded. The role of nationalist leadership in winning and/or consolidating independence has been especially prominent in the literature on Burma, Indonesia, Vietnam, and India. That it was much less important in the twentieth-century Philippines is also deserving of note. The Philippines reaches back to the 1890s for its most celebrated national heroes, who were nevertheless unsuccessful in their struggle against Spain and the United States. Potential national heroes just before and just after independence in 1946 were often tainted by their performance in government. Marcos was certainly a very strong leader, but hardly a "hero." The partial success of national unity and democratic development has not depended significantly on Filipino leadership rising above contextual factors.

It is yet too early to give an unequivocal assessment in East Timor. President Gusmao is undoubtedly a charismatic figure, a quality derived in large part from his skillful and heroic leadership of the resistance against Indonesia even while seeking a negotiated settlement. Given his lack of peacetime experience when he was released from prison in 1999, he has played an especially constructive role in the preparation for independence. Though his record is not spotless, the presidency was his for the asking. After showing considerable reluctance to do so, he finally agreed to run and was elected overwhelmingly. Without him, without his inclusive vision and healing touch, East Timor would be in even worse difficulties than it is. Meanwhile, the Constitution has set up the office of Prime Minister as a formidable competitor to the role of the president. It remains to be seen whether the initial rancor of this competition will abate.

Though Philippine stability has been threatened in recent years by increasing economic inequality, corruption, and military and revolutionary adventurism—all compounding a process of institutional decay—within Christian areas at least ethnic conflict has not contributed to instability, making the Philippines more fortunate in this regard than several other Asian countries. East Timor has some of the same factors impinging on the prospects for democracy there. Interethnic conflict is not likely to be a serious threat, but corruption and economic inequity, not to mention Indonesian machinations, could become serious problems (though Indonesia as a continuing external threat will serve to strengthen national unity). In both countries, history, demography, institutions, and socioeconomic structures will have a profound impact on political developments. However, in both, as well, there is likely still to be a crucial role for the exercise of leadership committed to democracy, good governance, social equity, and harmony between ethnolinguistic groups.

NOTES

1. Despite armed conflict between some of the peoples of the Cordilleras and the Philippine government in the 1980s, the struggle was not for secession. Even though as late as 1943 Carlos Romulo could write "the Igorot [one of the Cordillera ethnic groups] is not Filipino and we are not related" (quoted in Abueva 1998: 211), in the 1980s a highly regarded anthropologist commented, more accurately, "because these highland Filipinos are nationalists, . . . they hope that within an autonomous region, they will no longer be second class citizens" (quoted in Abueva 1998: 199).

2. This recognition of the importance of ethnicity is, quite surprisingly, found only in the Tim Maung Maung Than (1997) chapter on Burma of the Laothamatas book on democratization in East and Southeast Asia. Ethnicity receives no mention at all in other chapters.

3. But to be sure, there were also tensions between different ethnic elites in the course of the Revolution (see May 1987: 163).

4. *AP*, 2 July 2001.

5. For unofficial final results, see *LUSA*, 5 September 2001 and the listserv www.tapol-etimor-1@gn.apc.org, accessed on 8 September 2001.

6. *LUSA*, 6 September 2001.

7. *Christian Science Monitor*, 21 May 2001; *Sydney Morning Herald*, 4 July 2001.

REFERENCES

Abueva, Jose V., ed. 1998. *The Making of the Filipino Nation and Republic: From Barangays, Tribes, Sultanates, and Colony*. Quezon City: University of the Philippines Press.

Anderson, Benedict. 1991. *Imagined Communities: Reflections on the Origin and Spread of Nationalism*. London: Verso.

———. 1993. "Imagining East Timor." *Arena Magazine* 4 (April–May).

Constantino, Renato. 1975. *The Philippines: A Past Revisited*. Quezon City: Tala Publishing Services.

Gorenburg, Dmitry. 2000. "Not with One Voice: An Explanation of Intragroup Variation in Nationalist Sentiment." *World Politics* 53 (October): 115–42.

Gowing, Peter G. 1980. *Muslim Filipinos: Heritage and Horizon*. Quezon City: New Day.

Gusmao, Xanana. 2000. *To Resist is to Win!* Richmond, Victoria: Aurora Books.

Hicks, David. 1976. *Tetum Ghosts and Kin*. Palo Alto, Calif.: Mayfield.

Hill, Hal, and Joao Saldanha, eds. 2001. *East Timor: Development Challenges for the World's Newest Nation*. Singapore: ISEAS.

Horowitz, Donald. 1997. "Self-Determination: Politics, Philosophy, and Law." In *Ethnicity and Groups Rights*, eds. Ian Shapiro and Will Kymlicka. New York: New York University Press.

Jolliffe, Jill. 1978. *East Timor: Nationalism and Colonialism*. St. Lucia: University of Queensland Press.

McKenna, Thomas. 1998. *Muslim Rulers and Rebels*. Berkeley: University of California Press.

May, Glenn A. 1987. *A Past Recovered*. Quezon City: New Day Publishing.

Mojares, Resil B. 1999. *The War against the Americans: Resistance and Collaboration in Cebu*. Quezon City: Ateneo de Manila University Press.

Lennox, Rowena. 2000. *Fighting Spirit of East Timor: The Life of Martinho da Costa Lopes*. Annandale, Australia: Pluto Press.

Ross, Michael L. 2001. "Does Oil Hinder Democracy?" *World Politics* 53 (April): 325–61.

Steinberg, David Joel, ed. 1971. *In Search of Southeast Asia: A Modern History*. New York: Praeger.

Taylor, John G. 1999. *East Timor: The Price of Freedom*. London: Zed Books.

Tin Maung Maung Than. 1997. "Myanmar Democratization: Punctuated Equilibrium or Retrograde Motion." In *Democratization in Southeast and East Asia*, ed. A. Laothamatas. Singapore: Institute of Southeast Asian Studies.

Varshney, Ashutosh. 2001. "Ethnic Conflict and Civil Society." *World Politics* 53 (April): 362–95.

World Bank. 1998. *World Development Indicators, 1998*. Washington, D.C.

Wurfel, David. 1985. "Government Responses to Armed Communism and Secessionist Rebellion in the Philippines." In *Governments and Rebellions in Southeast Asia*, ed. Chandran Jeshurun. Singapore: Institute of Southeast Asian Studies.

———. 1988. *Filipino Politics: Development and Decay*. Ithaca, N.Y.: Cornell University Press.

———. 1997. "The Party-List Elections: Sectoral or National? Success or Failure?" *Kasarinlan* 13, no. 2: 19–30.

Wurm, Stephen, and Shiro Hattori, 1981. *Language Atlas of the Pacific Area*. Canberra: Australian Academy of the Humanities in collaboration with the Japan Academy.

11

Elusive Democracy: Appropriation of "Rights" Ideologies in Malaysian Ethnic and Religious Political Discourse

Judith Nagata

The quest for democracy is elusive. Identifying democracy in different political cultures and regimes raises as many questions as it resolves. Such is the case with postcolonial Malaysia, a country with diverse ethnic and religious populations united in the legal fiction of a unitary state. Its constitution simultaneously guarantees fundamental human rights and unitary citizenship, even as it circumscribes these on grounds of ethnicity, religion, and security, measures that legitimate authoritarian government and Malay dominance. The institutional trappings of a democratic state were put in place after independence, in the form of a constitutional, multiparty, parliamentary system offering regular elections. However, the constitution itself sets the limits of human rights expression. In fact, as this chapter shows, the discourses and institutions of democracy and human rights are polysemic. They are used to claim ethnic and religious as well as elite privileges, even while the same concepts are mobilized to counter such claims. However, most serious challenges to the inequalities created by ethnic and religious quotas have either been deflected by economic opportunism, or by the pressures of the system. This requires contextualization if we are to understand why Malaysians have yet to escape their iron cage of exclusive ethnic and religious identities, and the role played by democratic norms and institutions in their perpetuation.

TOWARD A PLURALIST APPROACH TO DEMOCRATIZATION

Over the past decade, some promising new approaches and insights into older issues in political philosophy have begun to take shape. In the quest for understanding and common meanings within the multiplicity of today's political cultures, scholars are formulating ancient and perennial questions in a more pluralist perspective. Such pillars of Western political philosophy as liberal democracy, civil society, equality under the rule of law, and individual rights and freedoms, widely assumed to be universal ideals, are now facing the test of ethical, moral, and political diversity, both within particular states and globally. Thus, older debates over universalism and relativism are resurrected (Taylor 1994; Kymlicka 1995; Tully 1995; Hefner 1998; Kymlicka and Norman 2000).

Similarly, less self-evident than United Nations covenants and many globally active NGOs concerned with human rights might claim, is the existence of a universal normative set of ethical principles as the foundation for a global code of human rights or social justice. Ethical and moral diversity is a challenge in many human rights and activist circles, for whom this is not a negotiable issue and who are among the last to yield to postmodern relativisms. By contrast, it is the premise of this chapter that now is the time to bring the human rights discourse into line with the emerging pluralist approaches to processes of democratization, minority/majority relations, citizenship rights, and even constitutionalism (Tully 1995). It is also time to recognize the linkages between them (Kymlicka and Norman 2000). From this perspective, human rights may be as much a political as a moral agenda.

The Discourse of Democracy and Democracy as Discourse

If democratization is to be understood as a process of continual adjustments over rights and relationships in a political system, rather than an essentialized state of being (a "democracy"), set of institutions, or ballot box rituals, it must inevitably reflect the above concerns as part of the internal dynamics of state nations. A processual approach allows for the fact that, while many of the ideas and institutions widely associated with democracy appear to be accepted and in place in countries across the world (including the People's Democratic Republic of North Korea), the diversity of meanings and practice operating under its banner is remarkable. Globalization of terminology and discourse is, in part, the name of the game (or a prerequisite for playing the game). While it might suggest the end of history (Fukuyama 1993) the polysemic nature of such ideas means history is still unfolding, even if the widespread use of European-origin terms in local vernaculars creates a false impression of convergence. Democratization is a metanarrative, by which political actors at all levels assess the merits of friends, allies, and enemies in terms of democratic correctness. This allows for some otherwise democratically dubious allies, such as Indonesia's Suharto regime, to be included (for reasons of security or trade), while political enemies can be vilified as less than democratic. The hermeneutic confusions of terms like democracy in several Asian countries is compounded as their leaders persist in using and appealing to the icon of democracy, even as they vigorously deny the possibility of a single universal form and criticize its Western provenance and hegemonic imperative, in a kind of reverse orientalism.

A growing awareness among scholars of several disciplines of democratic diversity and of the problems of governance in multicultural states is leading to a revision of some central ideas from Western political philosophy in favor of more culturally sensitive measures. Open to cross-cultural contestation are some of the normative hallmarks of Western democracies, particularly in what might be considered "fundamental" matters of individual versus group rights and freedoms; the primacy of secular over religious values in public and political life; and the preoccupation with equity/equal opportunity and mobility over hierarchy. The claim that any rights are fundamental, self-evident, supracultural, or universal may be historically embedded (Hall 1995; Keane 1988). It is the task of the observer to seek out both commonalities and differences, to engage in what Hefner (1998) calls a "pluralist dialogue." This applies equally to many multicultural societies, where deep ethnic, religious, and other cultural cleavages complicate the expression of civil democracy or common civic virtues in most standard Western senses.

Democracy and Citizenship Status

As noted by Kymlicka and Norman (2000), scholarly discourses on civil society, rights, and democracy have rarely been systematically linked with issues of citizenship. Citizenship, as a bundle of rights and obligations in relation to the state, may be constitutionally and legally enshrined, but modified through policies and practices that create de facto majorities and minorities (e.g., Gladney 1998), or first- and second-class citizens. Minority group claims or rights may simultaneously reflect or create ethnic, religious, or other cultural identity conflicts (e.g., Bertrand and Brown in this book) and compromise the unifying or leveling process of democratic citizenship understood in liberal terms (e.g., Taylor 1994; Kymlicka 1995). Or they may find a modus vivendi in some form of "differentiated citizenship" (Kymlicka and Norman 2000), affirmative action, or quota arrangements. Whether minority identity necessarily conflicts with civil or national loyalties, or group identity with the civic virtues of the citizen, is open to empirical investigation. Moreover, the very contested nature of these identities reminds us that democratization is a balancing process and cannot be captured by institutional analysis alone.

Democratization is commonly linked to market liberalization and development on the assumption that equality of economic opportunity and merit should override inequalities of status in other domains. However, not only does the market process lead to inequalities of wealth or class, but sometimes ethnic or religious groups have preferred access to some re-sources, which reduces efficiency and optimum development, as Jesudason (1989, 1995) has argued for Malaysia. Such situations also give rise to accu-sations of corruption, cronyism, and nepotism. This raises the question of whether class inequities are more or less acceptable than those created by ethnic or religious identity, and what role interethnic cronyism has in reduc-ing group conflict.

Rule of or by Law

Democracies are commonly linked with the functioning of lively and open legal institutions, a judiciary free from political or ideological interference, respect for some kind of constitution, as well as what is usually termed the "rule of law." An open legal system is a leveling mechanism that affords all citizens equal access to courts and justice and common protections in mat-ters of civil and political rights, freedoms of expression, assembly, and so on. However, the existence of universally recognizable legal institutions and dis-course alone is not a guarantee of predictable and equal legal process for all citizens. In praxis, the rule *of* law may become a rule *by* law, or even the tyranny of law, where certain segments of society can co-opt and utilize le-gal processes to their own ends. Restrictions on public freedoms and demo-cratic rights to assembly in official secrets or internal security acts (detention without trial or justification) may be deployed indiscriminately against a po-litical opposition, affectively legalizing injustice. Libel laws can also be used creatively to forestall the exposure that an open democratic or functioning civil society expects, making litigation a weapon of the strong, rather than a protector of the weak.

Human Rights as Secular Religion

Historically, morally universalistic and ethically inclusive values have been offered by the world religions, which sometimes strive to override merely mortal social status differences. Religions purvey their own versions of justice, compassion, rights, and mutual obligations, which, like democratic citizen-ship, level social playing fields, regardless of ethnicity. However, in practice, the playing field may be restricted to followers of the faith in question, who may then become an exclusive moral community. In states claiming to be democratic, some religious customs may conflict with rights of citizenship (e.g., Kymlicka and Norman 2000), for example in matters of women's status. Religion, however, may also provide a base for forms of civil society action and resistance to the state. Or, as in the case of Indonesia's *Muhammadiyah*, religious groups may organize in the breach some of the central functions the state is unable to provide, such as welfare and family planning services.

International covenants on human rights and justice also purvey forms of inclusive morality, as secular parallels to those of world religions. Like religious codes, interpretations of human rights charters may undergo mutation as they to travel between political cultures and engender resistance, giving a false sense of orthodoxy to signatories of the International Covenant on Civil and Political Rights and other agreements.

THE LANGUAGE OF MALAYSIAN
POLITICAL CULTURE: ETHNIC VERSUS HUMAN RIGHTS

The Early Postcolonial State: Ethnicity and Citizenship

The political antecedents of modern Malaysia include an assorted mix of indigenous Malay sultanates, with their blend of Indianized kingship, feudalism, and Islamic authority, and a multiparty parliamentary democracy bequeathed by British colonialism. This was complicated by the presence of substantial ethnic Chinese, Indian, Arab, Thai, and other immigrant communities who retained a distinct cultural, institutional, and political identity at every level of society. The prelude to independence, during the late 1940s and early 1950s, was marked by a series of acrimonious debates as to the future citizenship status and rights of all of these communities. Initial Malay reluctance for a universal citizenship was animated by fears that ethnic (then "communal") identities would be incompatible with national loyalty. It was publicly rationalized in terms of the historic rights of the Malay peoples, as the original inhabitants vis-à-vis the "immigrants," a position endorsed by colonial British policies. Given the demographic realities at the time of independence (1957), when the non-Malay "immigrant" populations collectively made up almost 50 percent of the total, the question of majority/minority status, whether defined politically or numerically, was sensitive. It has remained so to the present.

In the first national Constitution following independence, the defining features, rights, and obligations of each of what came to be recognized as the three principal ethnic communities, were laid down, thus entrenching and essentializing Malay, Chinese, and Indian identities. These have remained the basis of most social and political institutions. This fundamental plural society classification became something of an iron cage that imprisoned people's minds and imagination as to possible alternative ways of perceiving and organizing activities and relationships (e.g., Ratnam 1965; Nagata 1979; Boulanger 1996). It also provided few opportunities for, or encouragement of, assimilation toward a common (Malayan/Malaysian) nationality. Although each (ethnic) community has been able to retain its own language, primary school system, and religious institutions intact, these concessions also deepen divisions, assuaging the sense of cultural deprivation that has afflicted, for example, the Indonesian Chinese.

The Constitution also affirmed rights of equal citizenship for all communities, although subsequent policies have skewed this balance somewhat in favor of the Malays. The new Constitution enshrined a secular state and legal system, with Islam as the official or ceremonial religion, under the titular leadership of the Malay sultans. Article 153, concerning the "special position" of the Malays, guaranteed the preservation of certain historic (including urban) Malay lands as "reservations." Article 153 also referred to the sultans' responsibility for ensuring "reasonable" Malay presence in (state) public services and access to educational and other facilities, subject to the rulers' discretion (Ratnam 1965). This became a keystone of Malay claims to special rights and dominance, stretching its original legal intent and undermining ethnic harmony.

The Constitution accorded the sultans the important symbolic, although politically weak, titles of heads of Malay Religion and Custom, with the ceremonial post of King of Malaysia rotating every five years among the nine royal families. These arrangements reinforce the Malay claim to be the founding nation, and the only one retaining its indigenous rulers. The last perceived obstacle to the Malay myth of indigenousness, in the persons of the Aboriginal, forest dwelling, and hunter-gatherer *orang asli*, was put to rest by a new census classification uniting both Malays and *orang asli* as *Bumiputra* ("sons of the soil"). This also gave "indigenes" a small numerical edge over the "immigrants," a 53 percent majority in 1980. The *orang asli*, however, have remained largely economically and politically marginalized, an internal *Bumiputra* minority (e.g., Dentan, Endicott, Gomes, and Hooker 1997).[1] The non-*Bumiputra* are still frequently referred to publicly as "immigrants" (*kaum pendatang*), even after many generations' residence on the peninsula.

While freedom of religious affiliation and worship is guaranteed for all Malaysian citizens, ironically, the ethnic status and privileges of Malays are contingent upon their practice of Islam. In matters of personal, family, and ritual observance, Malay Muslims are subject to Islamic (*shari'ah*) law, whereas non-Malays are governed by British-derived civil law and are free to convert between faiths at will. However, the benefits available to Malay Muslims in many domains of Malaysian life have made (at least any public record of) conversion out of Islam so unlikely as to be almost impossible to imagine. Islamic culture too is one of the most distinctive attributes of Malay identity and serves as a social boundary with the other communities.

Most political parties are structured along ethnic and religious lines, helping to entrench these identities in many public activities. Three parties representing the principal constitutionally defined ethnic communities—the Malay United Malays National Organization (UMNO), the Malaysian Chinese

Association (MCA), and the Malaysian Indian Congress (MIC)—collectively dominate a National Front coalition (*Barisan Nasional* or BN). In coalition with a number of minor ethnic parties, some combination of these have governed Malaysia since 1957. Alternative ethnic parties have largely remained in opposition, including the Chinese Democratic Action Party (DAP) and the Malay Islamic party (PAS) except between 1973 and 1978. A number of smaller parties based on ethnic communities in Sarawak and Sabah oscillate between the BN and the opposition. Other parties purporting to be more multiethnic tend in practice to be identified with specific ethnic groups, such as the Malay-led socialist-oriented People's Party (*Parti Rakyat Malaysia* or PRM) and the Chinese-dominated *Gerakan*.

The Making of a Political Majority

Perennially sensitive to their fragility as a numerical and political majority, and to their economic disadvantages vis-à-vis the Chinese, the Malays have over time launched various initiatives to reaffirm their majority status. Gradually, formal equality of citizenship has succumbed to a series of affirmative action policies favoring the Malays. The most egregious and enduring has been the New Economic Policy (NEP).[2] Following the 1969 national elections, when unanticipated Malay electoral losses to Chinese led to the most vicious ethnic confrontation since independence, a state of emergency was declared, which served as a cover for some political reengineering. This was when a certain small-town doctor, Mahathir Mohamad, began to make his mark on the national political scene. Mahathir was already notorious for the publication, in the previous year (1970), of his controversial *The Malay Dilemma*. The book chastised the Malays for their lack of initiative and ambition, while declaring the need for special provisions to help level the playing field between the Malay and non-Malay (but principally Chinese) communities. The culmination of his efforts was the ending of the career of the ethnically tolerant first prime minister, Tunku Abdul Rahman, and the launching of the NEP. Malays (*Bumiputras*) were afforded privileged access to senior civil service and other jobs, scholarships, education and training schemes, loans, licenses, and business contracts. With increasing prosperity and the stunning economic growth of the 1980s and 1990s, the magnitude of these opportunities escalated, creating the foundation of the Malay "crony" class.

One irony was the continuing unpreparedness of the Malay community for open competition with the Chinese. Even with the NEP, the Malays found it productive to form alliances with Chinese partners (known locally as "Ali-Baba partnerships"). These combined Malay (the Ali partner) political license-granting privileges with Chinese (Baba) capital and business expertise, which became an essential underpinning of the burgeoning Malay crony elite class. This arrangement also confirmed Mahathir's reluctant conclusion that the Malay community should emulate Chinese attitudes and learn their "secrets," which has complicated ethnic tensions until the present.

As the NEP took hold, not just as an economic policy, but as a style of interethnic relations, its ethos became so pervasive as to instill a myth of "Malay special rights" (*hak istimewa Melayu*) and, subsequently, of Malay dominance (*ketuanan Melayu*) as part of the received wisdom of all Malaysians. This special status, in company with the special rights of the Malay religion (Islam) and their rulers, was also declared legally nonnegotiable. They were even forbidden topics for public discussion or debate. It has remained a source of perennial tension with the other ethnic communities.

Consequently, after more than forty years of independence, Malaysia's nation-building remains unfinished. In the absence of overriding principles transcending segmentary ethnic and religious ideologies, conflicts tend to be self-perpetuating. The Malaysian state commonly retreats from the awesome challenge of seeking common civil or ethical values by invoking the ultimate force of a draconian Internal Security Act (ISA),[3] another residue of colonial rule. The ISA allows for obsessive secrecy, detention without trial, and penalties without accountability. Or, as we shall see, the state plays the ethnic or religious card.

Further, since 1988, the autonomy of Malaysia's Supreme Court, together with its judiciary, has been gradually eroded by creeping political interference from the center, threatening its credibility and effectiveness as a court of appeal.[4] Until as late as July 1999, Malaysia had stubbornly resisted signing the International Covenant on Civil and Political Rights and had even tried to remove diplomatic immunity from Param Cumaraswamy, the country's own Rapporteur to the United Nations, in order to indict him for public statements allegedly critical of Malaysia. The eventual appointment of a Human Rights Commission (*Suhakam*) had to wait until April 2000, and until 2001 for ratification. Critics noted that most of its commissioners are drawn from the ranks of conservative and government-approved retired professionals, businessmen, and politicians, and the fact that it is located in the Ministry of Foreign Affairs. Also criticized is the fact that the purview of the commission is restricted to liberties permitted in the Malaysian Constitution, which, as noted above, has been severely emasculated over the years. These developments have been accompanied by a parallel reduction in the independence of all the media, including strict controls over publication licenses,[5] resulting in a prolonged and severe media chill. Under these conditions, few opportunities were available for open and free expression, criticism, or political action beyond the approved limits. The few exceptions emerged in English-educated, cosmopolitan-oriented circles of mixed ethnic and religious origins, in the form of such NGOs as the Consumers' Association of Penang (CAP) and the critical intellectual forum, *Aliran*, founded in

1977. One of the early protagonists, who served a term under the ISA, was the internationally recognized scholar, Dr. Chandra Muzaffar, founder of *Aliran* and Just Society Trust, and one of the first serious advocates of ethnic-blind human rights in Malaysia.

From Interethnic Partnerships to Cronyism

Malaysians' tardiness in paying attention to their country's human and civil rights record was partly due to the numbing effect of the economic "miracle" during the 1980s and early 1990s. During this period, Malaysia's enthusiastic embrace of the global market, aggressive development, and investment and technology transfer from both East and West, led to an unprecedented prosperity. Although unevenly distributed, the new wealth raised the standard of living and prospects for many Malaysians. However, this very prosperity was implicated in the growing conflicts of interest due to the revolving door of political and economic elites, the ambiguous boundaries between public and private resources,[6] and political and personal patronage (Sloane 1999), later labeled nepotism and corruption. The scale of economic enterprise and the intricacy of the partnerships involved helped to entrench a class of super-elites dependent on the BN for contracts and self-preservation. Some became economic virtuosos, featured in glossy local magazines as role models for the new Malay bourgeoisie. Economic advancement required political support, which in turn pressed into service these same economic resources as the infrastructure of power. During this period, economic success did not build civil society, nor promote democratization, but rather enhanced the patronal state and its personal clientships. The minority of politically connected and influential Malays who benefited most transformed UMNO into a closed-circuit business establishment. Top party positions rotated in an ever-narrower bandwidth of a few incumbents wearing several hats simultaneously. In the 2000 UMNO leadership convention, none of the top posts were even open for election.

Such are the realities of Malaysian business capital and expertise in an era of globalization that, even on the uneven playing field of affirmative action and state capitalism, the Chinese commercial community cannot be marginalized. Similarly, the success and support of the MCA is essential to the BN's stability and dominance. Throughout his political career, Mahathir has kept the Chinese politically on side, even as they are often marginalized as immigrants and as allegedly chauvinistic. Mahathir makes political mileage out of his own ambivalence and plays the field according to the situation.[7] In practice, therefore, the composition of Malaysia's business and political elites today is ethnically mixed, whereas the public rhetoric and official paradigm remain ethnic. Although, it appears that ethnic divisions are being replaced by pan-ethnic elite self-interest, as we shall see, a cynic might ask whether this kind of interethnic cooperation is the most effective means of reducing ethnic tensions.

Crony capitalism has not escaped the attention of other Malaysians, although tangible public reactions were slow in coming. The inertia of the "Asian miracle" kept at bay awareness of the constant erosion of personal freedoms described above. Grievances were muted by the "performance legitimacy" of the governing class, who merely delivered the goods. However, in the popular mind over the past decade, these elites have been transformed from fairly benign "Ali-Baba partners" to "cronies" engaged in "collusion," "corruption," and "nepotism." Increasingly, local terms for graft are being replaced by alien labels (with local spelling) to convey a taint of corruption of global provenance and proportions. External standards are being applied to local arrangements. It should be noted that indigenous Malay terms for corruption already exist (*makan rahsua*, or *makan suap*, with their metaphors of illicit eating and consumption). However, they seem to be perceived as inadequate for the scale and scope of today's activities. It took the Indonesian events accompanying the overthrow of Suharto, in a context of Byzantine global business connections, to embed these foreign concepts in Malaysian minds at the end of the 1990s. Along with the Indonesian terms for cronyism, and for collusion and nepotism (*kronisme, kolusi dan nepotisme*, or its punchy acronym, KKN), Malaysians also picked up the associated sense of social outrage and injustice, for which they readily found examples at home.

While it might appear that such language and judgments are ethnic-free, they actually carry their own ethnic cultural baggage. Conversations with Malay and Indian civil servants reveal that there is a strong sense that the escalated corruption now current is the result of Chinese influence: that the *guanxi* practices acceptable within Chinese clan and community circles have spilled over and "contaminated" the other communities and, further, have moved from the private to the public sector. Non-Chinese complain that this is the source of the irritating realities of contemporary business, where nothing can be accomplished or even contemplated without the requisite "appreciation" (*penhargaan*), paybacks (*tarik duit*), or "coffee money" (*duit kopi*) at every level.[8] Meanwhile, Chinese point to the inbuilt patronage of Malay quotas, which allow favored Malays to dispense further favors down the line for a consideration (*suap; rahsua*), in a process they call "eating money" (*makan duit*). Among the Malays, those less favored by the NEP voice resentment that fellow Malays with big government contracts often fail to spread the largesse, for example in subcontracts to smaller Malay entrepreneurs. There is a sense of betrayal of ethnic loyalty or obligation (which is felt by some to be implicit in the original NEP). In reverse, Malay UMNO or government elites fault those Malays who fail to vote for them, or scholarship-funded Malay students involved in antigovernment demonstrations, for lack of "gratitude." To critics such as Chandra Muzaffar and the new Human Rights Commissioner, Musa Hitam, this represents a residual "feudal" mentality on the part of the elites, who construe citizenship in terms of personal obligations, loyalties, and patronage, rather than rights. Locating the fault outside the formal economic or political sphere also conveniently shifts the onus to the individual rather than the system itself. To observers with an eye on global trends and values, these cultural interpretations of reciprocity are examples of cronyism and corruption.[9]

Thirty years after the initiation of the NEP, a new generation of Malays has grown up seemingly under the impression that "special rights" are their birthright as *Bumiputra*. Almost imperceptibly, without any legal adjustments, the original constitutional protections of the Malay "special position" (*kedudukan Melayu*) has been transmuted into the "special rights" (*hak istimewa*) claimed today. This *mitos hak istimewa* (myth of special rights), according to Abu Bakar Hamzah, an opposition PAS Member of Parliament (MP), was never intended by the original NEP. In his view, "if one (ethnic) group enjoys special rights, that means there must be second class citizens— it goes against the principle of equality." Further, he adds, distinctions between citizens based on ethnicity, religion, ancestry, or birthplace contradict fundamental freedoms (*kebebasan asasi*). Among non-Malays, affirmative action is seen as just a prop for the weak and has ultimately led to Malay dominance (*ketuanan*) by a small minority of top Malays, trading on their *Bumi* (*putra*) name.[10]

Rule by Law

In the present "rule *by* law" system, notions of "rights" have, in a small but significant number of cases, been appropriated by sensitive crony-politicians fearing loss of reputation from investigative journalists (usually from the alternative press). The latter spring preemptive libel suits of their own, forestalling any further investigation, so the real (corruption) cases rarely reach court. Prominent academics have also been threatened by the legal process for articles in professional journals and sued for impossibly large sums. The law is thus being used to silence, bankrupt, or financially destroy any potential threat, as well as to tie up their time in lawsuits, at the expense of their careers. A few Malay politicians and leaders have become so accustomed to the easy winning ways of using the courts to their own advantage that they have tried to sue overseas journals, as did the son of Mahathir (unsuccessfully) for an *Asian Wall Street Journal* article he found uncomplimentary to himself.

After the 1986 sacking of the Lord President of the High Court, Tun Salleh Abbas, for refusing to comply with the Prime Minister's attempts to use the courts to silence his own political rivals, Mahathir steadily increased his control of the justice system through appointments at the supreme court and of judges.[11] This trend in controlling the judiciary was most blatantly apparent during the trials of the ousted Deputy Prime Minister, Anwar Ibrahim (discussed below). In the eyes of most international observers and many Malaysians, the entire legal process was compromised by the political management of witnesses and evidence during the proceedings, public comments on the case before the courts, and the control of media coverage at every stage. In 2000, concerned rank and file members of the Bar Association initiated attempts to restore the integrity of the legal system. These were preempted by technicalities introduced by a lawyer acting for the prime minister.

Anwar Ibrahim: Muslim Hero or Political Villain?

The trial and its aftermath and the career of Anwar Ibrahim itself illustrate the intractability of the ethnic and religious iron cage and its undermining of democracy and human rights. Between 1984 and 1998, Anwar was one of the most visible and influential figures in Mahathir's cabinet, starting as minister of education and ending as deputy prime minister. Throughout his public career, Anwar has either inspired or reflected many of the significant shifts in Malaysian religious, ethical, and political culture, alternately as hero and villain. Beginning in the late 1960s, Anwar was central in turning the hearts and minds of young Malays toward the ideas of the new Islamic globalism then gathering momentum across the world. In his capacity as a student leader at the University of Malaya, well connected to the transnational networks of the Muslim resurgence, Anwar drew some of his inspiration from the emergent revolution in Iran as the foundation for his Malaysian Youth Muslim League (whose Malay acronym is ABIM). This was one of several Islamic movements known as *dakwah* in Malaysia (e.g., Nagata 1980, 1984, 1994, 1999; Hussin 1990; Zainah 1987). Although sometimes locally perceived as religious affirmations of Malay identity and cultural-linguistic hegemony, the *dakwah* followers were simultaneously pursuing a more radical and less chauvinistic agenda.

It was under their influence that some young Malay intellectuals and professionals first began to see their own country in terms of global issues of social justice, ethics, and morality, and, simultaneously, to spearhead a resistance to what they perceived as Western decadence and dominance. Moral critiques of the Malaysian government's aggressive development policies, and especially their impact on internal inequalities, were articulated through the voice of ABIM, the utopian *Al Arqam dakwah* group, and other organizations.[12] They set the tone for an entire generation of Malays being educated and groomed as the first generation of UMNO and national leaders since independence.[13] One of the lasting contributions of the *dakwah* movements was a shift in orientation from a narrowly ethnic and nationalistic worldview to a more universalistic one that dared even to criticize the NEP foundation of UMNO's hegemony. This was the point of tension at which Anwar entered the main stage of Malaysian politics. Launching himself as an antipoverty activist on a platform of rural economic reform to benefit the poor of all "races" and religions, in 1974 Anwar and his powerful ABIM following led a highly publicized march to Baling, Kedah, notable as the national slough of rural poverty. Anwar was briefly jailed. For the next few years, he continued to build a reputation as a subversive Islamist, antigovernment critic, and powerful influence on Malay youth—and a thorn in the side of the UMNO establishment.

In 1984, following his installation as prime minister, Dr. Mahathir decided that, if Anwar could not be morally beaten, he should be joined. This led to the dramatic and, at the time, controversial *coup de theatre*, by which Anwar was co-opted into the UMNO, largely as a form of religious window-dressing to counter its secular image and enhance the party's credibility to its Malay Muslim electorate. Anwar's principal job was to stall the flow of Malay votes to the Islamic party, PAS, and to preempt any moves toward an Islamic state or the rule of *shari'ah* law.[14] Moreover, his departure from the *dakwah* scene substantially slowed the momentum of that movement.

In his other role as a religious leader, Anwar publicly cultivated a universalistic, nonethnic version of Islam and sought common ground between the philosophies of leaders of the major world religious traditions, such as Gandhi, Jose Rizal, the Buddha, Ibn Khaldun, Confucius, and even Thoreau, expounded in his volume, *The Asian Renaissance* (1996). Anwar made conspicuous efforts to promote a more ethnically and linguistically inclusive political discourse,[15] stressing ideas of a "Malaysian race or nationality" (*bangsa Malaysia*) and the growth of a "civil society" (*masyarakat madani*). Debates have swirled among Malaysian intellectuals as to the appropriate translation (and meaning) of this Western term. To both Muslim and non-Muslim critics, the *madani* epithet, derived from seventh-century Madinah, claimed by some Muslims as the original prototype of a just, multicultural/multireligious society,[16] gives this inclusive ideal a Muslim tinge. For such critics, *masyarakat sivil/sipil*, the religiously neutral term used by Indonesians, is more suitable. Ultimately, the meaning of civil society is unraveled more through experience and action than by labels, as the events following Anwar's ouster demonstrated.

The Legacy of Anwar: Local Morality Play on a Global Stage

The trauma of events surrounding the sacking and public humiliation, imprisonment, and trial of Anwar from 1998 to the present[17] was for many Malaysians regardless of ethnicity or religion the magnet for a crystallizing of consciousness about injustice and absence of human rights and due legal process. At the same time, the fallout from the Asian economic crisis removed the prosperity cushion that until then had desensitized the Malaysian conscience from such issues. Meanwhile, the impact of events in neighboring Indonesia and from other global sources further raised an awareness (in the breach) of such ideas as reform (*reformasi*), human rights, justice, and democracy, and of the creeping presence of corruption.

Following his ouster, a kind of morality play over the virtues of Anwar, either as a model of economic and religious rectitude or just another crony, was mounted by spin doctors on both sides. Both dipped into a repertoire of ideologies and epithets to score points, and both used more transcendent or universalistic values to support their own position. From prison, Anwar continued to release a stream of "Prison Notebooks"–style letters, full of revelations about nepotistic practices among his former government colleagues, including Mahathir's sons, while presenting himself as "clean" (*berseh*) and a defender of justice (*keadilan*). This was the time for a flowering of new alternative media forms, including the Internet, while sales of such publications as could slip through the draconian licensing net multiplied at the expense of the self-censored mainstream media. Prominent among the new additions was the Malay-language organ of the Islamic party PAS, *Harakah*, whose sales rose in a few months from 70,000 to over 300,000 copies, twice weekly, and attracted many non-Muslim, including Chinese readers.

Following Anwar's arrest in September 1998, a series of new multiethnic, multireligious opposition movements emerged,[18] culminating in April 1999 in the forming of "National Justice" (*Parti Keadilan Nasional*) political party. Members of Keadilan were drawn from the entire spectrum of Malaysian ethnic and religious constituencies and included university students, notwithstanding the severe official Universities Act banning student politics on campus, in force since the days of Anwar's own student activism. Keadilan's strange bedfellows brought together members of Islamic party PAS, the Chinese DAP, and the socialist-inclined PRM, as well as ex-UMNO followers of Anwar, including members of ABIM, and an assortment of otherwise unaffiliated intellectuals, lawyers, writers, NGOs, and thoughtful Malaysians of all backgrounds. In Anwar's unavoidable absence, his wife, Dr. Wan Azizah, was made Keadilan vice president, while the activist intellectual, Dr. Chandra Muzaffar, became a deputy vice president and ghostwriter for many of her speeches.

Idealistic Birds of a Feather: Out of the Iron Cage?

The prospects of an imminent federal election (called in November 1999) precipitated the transformation of the motley alliance into a political formation capable of contesting the incumbent BN coalition, the *Barisan Alternatif* (BA). Also affiliated to the BA were a host of other smaller constituencies, in-

cluding independent Muslim scholars (*ulama*); a professional Muslim organization, JIM (*Jema'at Islam Malaysia*); a number of students' and
women's groups; independent lawyers and writers; and others representing
such special interests as Aboriginals (*orang asli*), as well as consumer, human rights, and other NGOs. At this point, the new coalition showed a profile more diverse and crossing more traditional boundaries than any previous
formation in Malaysia. The promise of doors opening from the ethnic and religious iron cages was enhanced by calls for justice and legal reform, for a
cleansing of the "democratic" process from money politics and corruption.
At the time, university professor and Keadilan supporter, Mohd Agus Yusoff,
could assert with some confidence that "ethnicity will not be the only factor
in the elections, but more profound issues like justice, good governance and
economic management."

As a participant in this discourse, PAS raised anew issues first promoted by
the *dakwah* movements of the 1970s. It highlighted Islamic justice as a basis
for attacking political corruption and exposed UMNO's proclivity to gild as
"acts of compassion" (*belas ihsan kerajaan*) or "donations" (*sumbangan*)
what should be citizens' rights (*hak*) (Ibnu Daulah 2000: 82). This redefined
the democratic process as patronage.

For a few months in the second half of 1999, an unprecedented, frenetic,
and improbable succession of political partnerships and alliances raised
hopes of a new style of Malaysian politics and ethics. Probably the most dramatic courtship within the BA was the dance between (Chinese) DAP and
PAS, the oddest partners on the floor. Their leaders, Nik Aziz Nik Mat, the
conservative Muslim chief minister of the PAS-run state of Kelantan, and Lim
Kit Siang of the Chinese DAP, cordially shared platforms and food at joint rallies. There were proposals to open up PAS party membership to non-
Muslims.[19] Chinese were avidly buying the PAS party newspaper, seen as
more credible than the government media. DAP leaders were prominently
featured in the PAS press. Later, Lim Kit Siang made heroic efforts to expand
the DAP base in the rural east coast Malay Muslim heartland and PAS territory, even as he tried to rally west coast urban Chinese to visit the PAS areas
to "see for themselves" how benign, uncorrupt, and nonthreatening a Mus-
lim-run state could be. Lim even proposed "politico-tourism," in the form of
interstate visits to enable conservative Malay Muslims to meet their Chinese
compatriots on their own turf, as a means of removing prejudice. Recipro-
cally, Kelantan's chief minister, and the PAS president, made guest appearances at Chinese New Year celebrations.

Limits to Universalizing Moralities

Surface events and appearances, however, were not necessarily reflec-
tive of the popular mood on the ground. The parties soon developed a

split personality. While participating in national-level activities within the BA, the language and style of PAS leaders harmonized well with the more inclusive discourse of its non-Islamic partners. Here, the stress was on Islam's "tolerance of other tribes and communities," while Qur'anic precedents for such core values as justice, compassion, equality, and distaste for "feudalism" and corruption, resonated well with the language of their more secular allies. A consensus from various ideological quarters on Kelantan's record after ten years of PAS rule recognizes that its democracy has progressed further than its economy.[20] Some powerful statements from Chief Minister Nik Aziz declared that "Islam has no place for special rights. . . . [I]t looks at people according to their economic status, not race. A poor Chinese is the same as a poor Malay. . . ."[21]; or "bumiputraism breeds" "umno-putraism."[22] On the ground, however, it emerged that PAS's commitment to social justice is directed almost exclusively to Malay Muslim communities, as part of the party's populist welfare program in its own religious and ethnic base. In home territory, PAS routinely channels aid and comfort to the rural poor and distressed, as long as they are potential voters—a qualified universalism at best, or even a return to moral relativism. Away from the political center too, PAS's restrictions on women's dress and public employment are more limiting than the ideals of equality of citizenship and civil rights to which they subscribe with their BA partners. In Kelantan and Trengganu, *shari'ah* law increasingly prevails over secular democratic freedoms.[23] PAS was thus caught between its traditional electoral constituency and a more national or global vision where it cooperates with other parties.

In turn, DAP leaders too seemed to be ahead of their memberships in their rush toward interethnic camaraderie. Most urban Chinese of the west coast were convinced that more power for PAS generally would threaten Chinese economic, cultural, and religious freedoms; churches and schools; and access to pork and alcohol. For many Chinese, the specter of an Islamic state lurks behind all PAS agendas, and DAP's overtures were seen as a betrayal of its Chinese constituents. These sentiments were evident in the results of the 1999 elections, when the DAP lost most of its parliamentary seats and its official opposition status.

Meanwhile, within Party Keadilan itself unity also proved fragile. A substantial proportion of Keadilan's initial membership were exiles from UMNO[24] and, before that, original ABIM supporters of Anwar who retained some of the ethos of their Malay Muslim *dakwah* background. The party's deputy vice president, Chandra Muzaffar, notwithstanding his role as human rights advocate, has long been an ideological defender of the Malay special position, enjoying (between 1997 and 1999) a patronage position at the University of Malaya created for him by Anwar in his last years of power. Whereas other Keadilan members were expecting that the party, in keeping with its name ("justice"), would renounce the implicit inequality of citizenship rights of the NEP-inspired policies and "Malay dominance" (*ketuanan Melayu*), the deputy vice president did not wish to create disunity amongst Muslims. In the event, in the *Keadilan Reformasi* manifesto of July 1999, the "special position of the *Bumiputra*" was reaffirmed.

Finally, some Keadilan supporters noted that the content of public speeches varied according to language of delivery. In addresses to largely Malay audiences, defense of the Malay special position is never questioned. To Chinese audiences, one bilingual speaker was free with criticisms of a recent government decision to merge primary schools of nonnative languages as a perceived attack on Chinese-medium education intact since independence. However, on switching to English for a multiethnic audience, no mention was made of the issue.[25]

Caught in the crossed ethnic wires and volatile realignment of views and loyalties prior to the 1999 elections, which came to a head in August 2000, were UMNO's Chinese partners in the BN, the MCA and *Gerakan*. Among the parties' powerful political supporters and contributors are the Associated Chinese Chambers of Commerce and Industry (ACCCIM), the Federation of Chinese Associations of Malaysia (FECAM), as well as several thousand other Chinese organizations, who collectively aggregate the views and interests of business and middle class members in particular. In September 1999, a major statement, known as the "Seventeen-Point Election Appeal" (popularly known since by its Chinese title, *Suqiu*, or "appeal"), was issued by over 2,000 associations,[26] including *Gerakan*, a member of the incumbent BN. The seventeen major "points" covered domains of Malaysian political culture, which by any measure transcended merely Chinese particularistic interests, including: the need to curb corruption; review uncontrolled privatization; advance democracy (including the restoration of local government accountability and transparency); uphold human rights and justice (including excessive use of the ISA); protect the environment; upgrade social services; provide housing for all; protect women's rights; allow for a free media; restore confidence in the police force; make provision for Aboriginal peoples; promote enlightened education policies; and cultivate the country's multiethnic cultures. One of the petitions, in favor of "promoting national unity" sparked reactions out of proportion to its disarmingly civic-minded goal. Its recommendations included a race relations enactment to combat racism and discrimination and, in the same spirit, suggested that affirmative action likewise should be detached from racial and religious status and reserved instead for the economically disadvantaged of all communities. Most contentious of all was the "national unity" final clause, recommending abolition of the *bumiputra/non-bumiputra* status. These two clauses alone thus had the potential to challenge two of the pillars of Malay privilege, namely, the NEP and the "special position." In self-defense, the authors of *Suqiu* reminded critics that these were merely recommendations, not demands, and that it was not their intent to "tear up the social contract" (*mencabar kontrak sosial*). Further, one petition originally made by FECAM for the appointment of a Chinese second deputy prime minister was internally rejected as contradictory to the intended spirit of interethnic reconciliation and *reformasi*.

At the time, the Malay electorate was deeply divided between UMNO, PAS, and Keadilan, and, in his bid for reelection, the prime minister acknowledged his dependence on the Chinese vote. Initially, therefore, he made some conciliatory noises over *Suqiu*'s recommendations, while the president of Chinese MCA BN, Dr. Ling Liong Sik, vacillated strategically. As part of a campaign for electoral support, Mahathir even made a point of praising the discipline and achievements of Chinese-medium schools, lauding their "pragmatism" and "rationality" over Malay "emotionalism" and lack of scientific ambition. In the event, these moves tided him over the election brink: the BN's return to a majority, albeit a reduced one, was largely due to MCA and Chinese support.[27]

Once reestablished in power, Mahathir paid little further heed to the *Suqiu*, until it was rediscovered by UMNO Youth in August 2000. Discovering in the appeal a "threat to Malay special privileges," UMNO Youth engaged in a series of verbal and physical demonstrations. They were backed by a defiantly chauvinistic statement from a Malay student association, whose acronym (*Pewaris*) signifies "heirs or inheritors" (of Malay tradition) and who declaimed the need for Malays to "fight for and remake their race (*memperjuang dan memperbaiki kaum Melayu*)" and to reinforce the NEP. These sentiments were compounded by the prime minister's own abrasive comments, in which he called supporters of *Suqiu* "extremists" and like the "communists of the past." In his annual National Day speech (31 August 2000), Mahathir accused Chinese of "sowing misconceptions among moderate Chinese" (Loh 2000: 6), thus playing the "race" card, always in hand at times of perceived political crisis.

Ethnic politics has long been the ultimate weapon in Mahathir's political arsenal, one he uses shamelessly when under siege. His preelection exhortations oscillated wildly between appeals for national unity and a "Malaysian race," failing which he darkly predicted a return to the ethnic riots of Malaysia in 1969 or a replication of Indonesia at the end of the 1990s. In those moments when a Malaysian race (*bangsa Malaysia*) is mentioned, Mahathir distances himself from the "Malaysian Malaysia" long promoted by the DAP. In this particular democracy, opposition parties who offer gratuitous suggestions as to how to achieve a more democratic or ethnically neutral political community are not well received. Moreover, to some Malays, a Malaysia that is too Malaysian might possibly lose sight of the special position. As a last resort, Mahathir freely and randomly accuses "foreigners" of all stripes, but usually Western, of fomenting ethnic discord in Malaysia, which then provides further reason for mandating ethnic cooperation unilaterally (and for chastising such impudent demands as *Suqiu*). When feathers are ruffled, the birds all fly back to their protective cage. The ultimate riposte, from some more irreverent and daring critics of Mahathir, is to turn the tables and remind the prime minister of his "Indian" origins, using offensive ethnic terms, such as *Mamak* or *Keling*.

Concluding that the loss of Malay faith in UMNO represents a crisis of national identity, induced by the political seductions of parties PAS and Keadilan, the prime minister decided early in 2001 that the solution lay in inviting the Malays of both political parties to a cooperative meeting. Significantly, no members of non-Malay parties were invited, underscoring the Malay character of the "national unity" sought. While Mahathir perceived the crisis ethnically, other parties saw the issue as one of social justice, rights, accountability, and transparency, transcending ethnic identity. Both parties refused the "invitation" until the issue was reframed as one of "*Malaysian* unity," with an agenda open to discussion of corruption and reform on behalf of all Malaysians.

Human Rights as Secular Religious Discourse

In a generic way, human rights talk has been central to many recent events in Malaysia. Yet its impact on breaking down the iron cage of ethnicity remains ambiguous. *Suhakam*'s chief commissioner, Musa Hitam, asserted that PAS is a more credible example of clean, transparent, and trustworthy leadership than is UMNO.[28] Yet, in Islamic (PAS) circles, it is axiomatic that justice and rights are fundamentally religious, derived from divine law, even if the ethical principles and consequences resemble secular ones. Muslims, like Westerners, it is claimed, can have their own system of universal values—and universalism lies at the heart of Islam.[29] Opponents of PAS, on the other hand, remind us that its ethical universalism stops at the boundaries of the Muslim community and, moreover, that Muslim Malays do not enjoy the right to choose their own religion. On balance, the evidence suggests a more situational ethics, depending on the audience and whether PAS is acting nationally or locally.

The changing moral climate, initially thrown into relief by the Anwar affair, was first articulated by the imported Indonesian slogan of *reformasi*. *Reformasi* embraces all the breadth and imprecision of its Indonesian source, but has sufficient resonance to rally demonstrations and embellish banners of the opposition. However, like most other terms in the civil and human rights repertoire, "reform" is polysemic: it means something to everyone, but different things to different people. This is its strength and weakness. Understandings of reform range from such specifics as emulating Indonesia (and overthrowing the leader) to changing the entire

Malaysian political system, doing away with preferential policies (such as the NEP), getting rid of cronyism, implementing the *Suqiu* recommendations, and releasing Anwar and other prisoners of conscience. It is also a license to hit back at one's personal enemies. Likewise, the idea of justice (*keadilan*) has different meanings in legal, liberal democratic, and religious contexts. It is invoked by UMNO leaders as central to obligations of reciprocity, loyalty, patronage, and "gratitude" between Malay rulers and their subjects, by Muslims as a scripturally enjoined virtue, and by post-feudal democratic and NGO circles as a universalized measure of individual rights and freedoms.

In the same spirit, most Malaysians endorse "democracy" as a standard of value, although the term evokes different images in various constituencies. While some observers see a trail of eroded democratic rights during Mahathir's tenure, the prime minister himself has persistently redefined, but not rejected, the democratic model. In rejecting the selfishly individualistic, liberal democratic ideals of the West in favor of community-based ethics, Mahathir's view is in keeping with the Malaysian constitutional and political worldview and founding myths, in which group identities and rights are pervasive and "ethnic unity" is equated with national unity. When the notion of democracy is linked to freedoms, the Malaysian leadership further distances its own political philosophy and culture from the Western prototype. The Malaysian official view is that freedom from hunger and economic deprivations should take precedence over "political or civil" liberties, perceived as a Western bias. Sharing this view, to a point, is one of the government's perennial human rights critics, Chandra Muzaffar (1993: 4), who advocates a more "holistic" vision of democratic rights, both economic and political. Politically, the growing appeal to Malaysians of cosmopolitan or alien ideas and agencies is regarded by apprehensive government and UMNO officials as a threat to state integrity and sovereignty.

CONCLUSIONS

In global perspective it has to be recognized that interpretations of key concepts emanating from Western political philosophy discourse commonly assume new meanings and have a different resonance in other political cultures. While terminologies may remain constant and appear self-evident or universal, especially when purveyed through a *langue maîtrise*, they may be opportunistically or strategically adapted to local needs and agendas, hence lose some of their transcendence. With these caveats in mind, by what measures can the process of democratization in ethnically and religiously diverse Malaysia be assessed?

Ethnic divisions, as the foundation for most state policies, have kept the goal of national unity and a Malaysian nation ever on the horizon, yet never quite achieved. Religious cultural and legal differences have divided Malaysian citizens into Muslims and non-Muslims. They make it difficult for spontaneous horizontal ties to be created as part of civil society or other secular contexts. Meanwhile, any moves toward cross-ethnic activities along lines of the more inclusive goals and values of justice or human rights, as in the *dakwah* movements or in the dissidence of 1987, have not been long sustained. For the two decades preceding 1997, this seeming inertia may be attributable in large part to the prosperity that benefited and numbed many Malaysians. This was abruptly interrupted by the Asian economic and Anwar crises of 1997 and 1998. However, the ensuing challenges to the constitutional and political worldview were largely a casualty of party and personal politics and the preemption of legal and human rights.

Government policy, and the self-preservation impulse of the UMNO in particular, has propelled policies that have incrementally enhanced the political and economic edge of the Malays, gradually shifting the balance from a special "position" to special "rights" in public discourse, with the specter of a two-tiered citizenship. Reactively, the non-Malays too tend to view their (civil) rights as ethnic endowments. One consequence is a pervasive zero-sum mentality in intergroup relations, a symptom of what Chirot (1997) calls "this kind of communal democracy." The effects of the NEP and of political patronage have created a class of Malay super-rich in crony collaboration with similarly connected Chinese business partners, but has not succeeded in breaking down society-wide boundaries between ethnic communities more generally. Predictions of economic development and a growing bourgeoisie encouraging democratization do not seem vindicated in the Malaysian experience.

Meanwhile, for BN and especially UMNO, the rhetoric of "race" is always close to the surface, as a disciplinary tactic at times of popular discontent, especially during elections. When necessary, discipline is reinforced by government control of the judiciary (rule by law), and of the media and police, resulting in severe limitations of civic freedoms. As a result of the Anwar affair, however, a higher level of public cynicism generated the most significant cross-ethnic alliances in Malaysia's history, matched by equally high-pitched warnings of ethnic disunity and conflict on the part of UMNO. While still not totally free of their iron cages, many Malaysians are now prepared more openly to think and act along less ethnically exclusive lines and to participate in emergent civil society activities, such as *Suqiu*, in NGOs, in alternate political parties, and in human rights and reform movements. Today this process benefits from the proliferation of transnational ideas about justice and human rights, bringing opportunities for longer-term change.

NOTES

1. A 1954 act imposing extensive government control over the *orang asli* stems from the period of the "emergency," when they were allegedly vulnerable to co-optation by Communist guerillas based in the forests. A federal Department of Aboriginal Affairs continues to exert tight control over mundane religious, educational, and economic activities. It has also used the legal provision of Crown land to justify the takeover of Aboriginal lands, which are subject only to "customary rights" (Dentan, Endicott, Gomes, and Hooker 1997: 73ff).

2. The original NEP was designed to address issues of Malay equity and ownership in the national economy, aiming for a 30 percent share to be achieved within thirty years and terminating by 1990. After 1991, it was replaced by the slightly amended National Democratic Policy (NDP), allowing a greater economic role for non-Malays.

3. The ISA has been used on numerous occasions to remove from public view and influence opposition leaders and groups of all ethnic and religious backgrounds, including many Malay Muslims. The ISA played a prominent disciplinary role during the events surrounding the overthrow and imprisonment of Anwar Ibrahim, beginning in September 1998. In its 2000–2001 edition, the international Freedom House publication, *Freedom in the World*, gives Malaysia a mere five out of ten for its record of "democratic freedoms" and political and civil rights, lower than in the early 1990s.

4. Since the late 1980s, the separation of powers has been steadily reduced, culminating with the political management of the legal process and the selection of judges and even witnesses in the trials of Anwar Ibrahim in 1999 and 2000.

5. The Home Ministry (*Kementerian Dalam Negeri*) has sometimes permitted publications in English, while simultaneously prohibiting their Malay-language equivalents. The majority of the television channels are government controlled, and the private stations are constrained by strict, if "self-managed," restrictions.

6. This blurring was most evident in a rash of privatizations of once-public resources and institutions, the government "borrowing" of the monies of the Employees' Provident (Pension) Fund following the economic crisis, and the activities of the financial holding companies of the major BN political parties, of which UMNO's Renong Holdings is the most extensive.

7. As discussed later, during the federal election campaign of 1999, the prime minister praised the superior quality of Chinese education and private schools, while excoriating Malay scholastic performance. Mahathir concluded that Malays still needed "propping up" by NEP-style quotas in order to compete in an open market (*Utusan Malaysia*, 4 July 1999).

8. It invites comparisons with systems such as the old KMT machine in Taiwan, described by Stainton (2000) as a form of "kleptodemocracy."

9. For example, see *Aliran Monthly* 20, no. 2 (2000): 19–22.

10. Quoted in *Malaysiakini*, 24 December 2000.

11. In 1987 Mahathir was subjected to a major political challenge, when he either lost, or very narrowly won (depending on whose figures are accepted), the federal election. He persuaded the courts to recognize his own UMNO faction as the "New UMNO" (UMNO *Baru*) and to declare the opposition illegal.

12. *Al Arqam* (known originally as *Darul Arqam*) was founded in the late 1960s and, along with ABIM, provided the strongest moral critique of modern secular cap-

italism in Malaysia. *Al Arqam* was distinctive for its communal living arrangements, its emulation of seventh-century Arabian community and family values, and its cultivation of an alternate "petty commodity" economy, all managed by a highly educated, computer literate corps of young Islamists. As it later moved into a more "messianic" phase under its ambitious leader, Ustaz Asha'ari, its potential as a political force caused the government to ban it in 1994.

13. Many of these Malay youth, both men and women, were sent on government scholarships to overseas universities where, ironically, they were even further exposed to the new global religious ideas circulating among international Muslim students.

14. PAS has ruled the largely Malay state of Kelantan since 1990, during which it has several times announced a plan to create an Islamic state in its domain. The party faces constitutional obstacles to any such move in the short term, but its appeal to some rural Malay constituencies keeps UMNO on permanent guard.

15. In the mid-1990s, he challenged the vision of clashes between "Islam and Confucianism."

16. At the time of the Prophet Muhamed, the city of Madinah was home to Jews, Christians, and the emerging Muslims and was allegedly based on freedom of religious practice, equality of citizenship and legal rights, and a just division of political offices among all religious groups.

17. These events came about initially over differences of opinion between Mahathir and Anwar over responses to the economic crisis, which masked a much more convoluted subtext of political rivalry and succession.

18. Among these new formations in Penang, Anwar's home state, were *Gerak* (*Majlis Keadilan Gerakan Raky'at* or People's Movement for Justice), *Gagasan Raky'at* (Idea of the People), and the *Pergerakan Keadilan Sosial* (Movement for Social Justice).

19. *Harakah*, 16–30 June 2000.

20. Muhd Syukri Salleh 1999; *Far Eastern Economic Review*, 3 August 2000.

21. *Harakah* quoted in Francis Loh, "A Crisis of Malay Rights or an UMNO Crisis? Who is Playing the Racial Card?," *Aliran Monthly* 20, no. 7 (2000): 1–7.

22. *Malaysiakini*, 27 January 2000.

23. In both Kelantan and now Trengganu states, Muslim women are required to adhere to *shari'ah* law and cover their heads and wear body-shrouding dress in public. They are discouraged from highly visible public employment or political office. There are now separate checkout counters for men and women. By contrast, Chinese and foreign women in the same states are not bound by these rules.

24. During the year 2000, over 100 of these gradually returned to the UMNO fold, allegedly seduced by party inducements and, possibly, through disillusionment with the direction of Keadilan.

25. *Aliran Monthly* 20, no. 9 (2000): 17.

26. Among these were associations of Chinese teachers, university alumni, local town halls, and religious organizations, out of a global total of over 4,000.

27. In the 1999 federal election, UMNO, the senior partner of BN, received only 36 percent of the Malay vote, while BN won with a reduced majority of 56 percent, the balance being made up of Chinese (MCA) votes.

28. *Aliran Monthly* 20, no. 2 (2000): 9.

29. *Just Commentary*, no. 31 (1999).

REFERENCES

Anonymous. 2000. "Dari Suqui ke Intifadah" ("From *Suqiu* to Intifada"). In *Sangkancil* (a listserv edited by M.G. Pillai). <Sankancil@lists.malaysia.net>. Accessed 17 August 2000.

Anwar, Ibrahim. 1996. *The Asian Renaissance*. Kuala Lumpur: Times Press.

Boulanger, Clare. 1996. "Ethnicity and Practice in Malaysian Unions." *Ethnic and Racial Studies* 19, no. 3: 660–79.

Chandra Muzaffar. 1993. *Human Rights and the New World Order*. Kuala Lumpur: Just World Trust.

Chirot, Daniel. 1997. "Conflicting Identities and Dangers of Communalism." In *Essential Outsiders: Chinese and Jews in the Modern Transformations of Southeast Asia and Central Europe*, eds. Daniel Chirot and Anthony Reid. Seattle: University of Washington Press.

Dentan, Robert, Kirk Endicott, Alberto Gomes, and M. B. Hooker. 1997. *Malaysia and the Original People: A Case Study of the Impact of Development on Indigenous Peoples*. Needham Heights, Mass.: Allyn and Bacon.

Eriksen, Thomas Hyland. 1994. "Nationalism, Mauritian Style: Cultural Unity and Ethnic Diversity." *Comparative Studies in Society and History* 36, no. 3: 549–74.

Fukuyama, Francis. 1993. *The End of History and the Last Man*. New York: Avon Press.

Hall, John A. 1995. *Civil Society: Theory, History, and Comparison*. Cambridge, U.K.: Polity Press

Hefner, Robert, ed. 1998. *Democratic Civility: The History and Cross-Cultural Possibility of a Modern Political Idea*. New Brunswick, N.J.: Transaction Publishers.

Hussin, Mutalib. 1990. *Islam and Ethnicity in Malay Politics*. Oxford: Oxford University Press.

Gladney, Dru C., ed. 1998. *Making Majorities: Constituting the Nation in Japan, Korea, China, Malaysia, Fiji, Turkey, and the United States*, Stanford, Calif.: Stanford University Press.

Ibnu, Daulah. 2000. *Islam Optimis Melangkah Ke Alaf Baru: Mengapa Pilih Parti PAS?* (*Optimistic Islam steps into a new century: why choose Party PAS?*). Bandar Baru Bangi: Penerbitan Seribu Dinar.

Ignatieff, Michael. 2000. *The Rights Revolution*. Toronto: House of Anansi Press.

Jesudason, James V. 1989. *Ethnicity and the Economy: The State, Chinese Business, and Multinationals in Malaysia*. Singapore: Oxford University Press.

———. 1995. "Statist Democracy and the Limits to Civil Society in Malaysia." *Journal of Commonwealth and Comparative Politics* 33, no. 3: 335–56.

Keane, John. 1988. *Civil Society and the State: New European Perspectives*. London: Verso.

Kymlicka, Will, ed. 1995. *The Rights of Minority Cultures*. New York: Oxford University Press.

Kymlicka, Will, and Wayne Norman, eds. 2000. *Citizenship in Diverse Societies*. New York: Oxford University Press.

Loh, Francis. 2000. "A Crisis of Malay Rights or an UMNO Crisis? Who's Playing the Racial Card?" *Aliran Monthly* 20, no. 7: 2–7.

Mahathir, Mohammad. 1970. *The Malay Dilemma*. Singapore: Donald Moore Press.

Malkki, Liisa. 1994. "Citizens of Humanity: Internationalism and the Imagined Community of Nations." *Diaspora* 4: 41–68.

Muhd, Syukri Salleh. 1999. "Political Economy of Islamic Development: A Comparative Analysis of Kelantan and Trengganu." In *Political Economy of Development in Malaysia*, eds. B. N. Ghosh and Muhd Syukri Salleh. Kuala Lumpur: Utusan Publications Sdn Bhed.

Nagata, Judith. 1979. *Malaysian Mosaic: Perspectives from a Poly-Ethnic Society*. Vancouver: University of British Columbia Press.

———. 1980. "Religious Ideology and Social Change: The Islamic Revival in Malaysia." *Pacific Affairs* 53, no. 3: 405–39.

———. 1984. *The Reflowering of Malaysian Islam*. Vancouver: University of British Columbia Press.

———. 1994. "How to be Islamic without Being an Islamic State: Contested Models of Development in Malaysia." In *Islam, Globalization, and Postmodernity*, eds. Akhbar S. Ahmed and Hastings Donnan. London: Routledge.

———. 1999. "Who Imagines the State? Contested Visions of Nationalism in Malaysia." In *Identités, Territoire et Environnement en Asie du Sudest (Identities, territory and environment in Southeast Asia)*, eds. Rodolphe De Koninck, Steve Déry, Bruce Matthews, and Judith Nagata. Québec: Université Laval.

———. 2000. "Heritage as a Site of Resistance: From Architecture to Political Activism in Urban Penang." In *Risking Malaysia: Culture, Identity, and Politics*, eds. Maznah Mohamad and Wong Soak Koon. Malaysian Social Science Association.

Ratnam, K. J. 1965. *Communalism and the Political Process in Malaysia*. Kuala Lumpur: University of Malaya Press.

Sloane, Patricia. 1999. *Islam, Modernity, and Entrepreneurship among the Malays*. New York: St. Martin's Press.

Stainton, Michael. 2000. Creeping Corruption and Roads of Desire: The "Dynamic Stability" of the Kuomintang System in Taiwan's Kleptodemocracy. Unpublished manuscript.

Taylor, Charles. 1994. *Multiculturalism: Examining the Politics of Recognition*. Princeton, N.J.: Princeton University Press.

Tully, James. 1995. *Strange Multiplicity: Constitutionalism in an Age of Diversity*. Cambridge: Cambridge University Press.

Weller, Robert. 1998. "Horizontal Ties and Civil Institutions in Chinese Societies." In *Democratic Civility: The History and Cross-Cultural Possibility of a Modern Political Idea*, ed. Robert Hefner. New Brunswick, N.J.: Transaction Publishers.

Wilson, Richard A., ed. 1997. *Human Rights, Culture, and Context: Anthropological Perspectives*. London: Pluto Press.

Zainah, Anwar. 1987. *Islamic Revivalism in Malaysia*. Petaling Jaya: Pelanduk Publications.

Index

About the Contributors

Daniel A. Bell is Associate Professor, Department of Public and Social Administration, City University of Hong Kong and a visiting fellow at the Center for Advanced Study in the Behavioral Sciences, Stanford University, in 2003–2004. His recent publications include *Confucianism for the Modern World* (coeditor, Cambridge University Press 2003).

Jacques Bertrand is Associate Professor, Department of Political Science, University of Toronto and a member of the University of Toronto's Asian Institute. Among his publications are *Nationalism and Ethnic Conflict in Indonesia* (Cambridge University Press 2003) and articles in *Pacific Affairs*, *Asian Survey*, and *Comparative Politics*. His research concerns ethnic conflict, nationalism, democratization, and local politics in Southeast Asia.

David Brown is Associate Professor, School of Politics and International Studies, Murdoch University (Western Australia) and has taught at the National University of Singapore, Birmingham University (U.K.), and Ahmadu Bello University (Nigeria). He was recently awarded a Fulbright New Century Scholarship. Among his publications are *The State and Ethnic Politics in Southeast Asia* (Routledge 1994) and *Contemporary Nationalism* (Routledge 2000).

Chang Maukuei, who earned a Ph.D. in sociology at Purdue University (1984), is now Research Fellow at the Institute of Sociology, Academia Sinica, and Professor at National Tsing-Hua University (Taiwan). He has published works on nationalism, ethnic and race relations, and social movements in Taiwan and other regions.

Dru C. Gladney is Professor of Asian Studies and Anthropology, University of Hawaiʻi at Manoa. His books include *Muslim Chinese* (Harvard University Press 1991); *Ethnic Identity in China* (Wadsworth 1998); *Making Majorities* (editor, Stanford University Press 1998); and *Dislocating China: Muslims, Minorities, and Other Sub-Altern Subjects* (University of Chicago Press, forthcoming).

Kanishka Goonewardena trained as an architect in Moratuwa, Sri Lanka, an urban planner in Los Angeles, and in critical theory and political thought at Cornell University. He teaches urban design and cultural geography at the University of Toronto and writes on urbanism, globalism, and nationalism, including "Aborted Identity: The Commission and Omission of a Monument to the Nation, Sri Lanka, circa 1989," *Radical History Review* 82 (Winter 2002).

Susan J. Henders is Assistant Professor, Department of Political Science, York University (Canada) and a member of the York Centre for Asian Research. Among her publications on the politics of cultural difference are "The Self-Government of Unbounded Communities," in *Representation and its Discontents*, ed. David Laycock (University of British Columbia Press, forthcoming) and articles in *Pacific Affairs* and *Nations and Nationalism*.

André Laliberté, who received his Ph.D. at the University of British Columbia, teaches political science at the Université de Québec à Montréal. He has published on various aspects of democratic consolidation in Taiwan, the role of Buddhist organizations in democratization, and welfare policy restructuring in Taiwan and China. His current research looks at social welfare policies in rural China.

John Lie is Professor of Sociology at the University of California at Berkeley. His recent publications include *Multiethnic Japan* (Harvard University Press 2001) and *Modern Peoplehood* (Harvard University Press 2004).

Judith Nagata is Professor of Anthropology, York University (Canada) and has taught at the Institute of Islamic Studies, McGill University, and the Universiti Sains Malaysia, Penang. She has published widely on the politics of identity in Southeast Asia and on transnational world religions, including on Malaysian Islam and Taiwanese humanistic Buddhism. She is Associate Director, York Centre for Asian Research.

Katharine N. Rankin is Assistant Professor of Geography and Planning, University of Toronto. Her research on gender and development, comparative market regulation, financial restructuring, planning history and theory, and South/Southeast Asia has been published in numerous journals and will appear in the book *The Cultural Politics of Markets: Economic Liberalization and Social Change in Nepal* (Pluto Press, forthcoming).

David Wurfel is Senior Research Associate, York Centre for Asian Research, and Professor Emeritus of Political Science, University of Windsor. He has published widely on Southeast Asian politics, particularly the Philippines. He was a volunteer observer of the 1999 referendum in East Timor.